GO

W.D.J.R

How to Make
A GRAND SUCCESS
Of the Christian Life

How To Make
A GRAND SUCCESS
of the Christian Life

JOHN R. RICE

SWORD OF THE LORD PUBLISHERS
Murfreesboro, Tennessee 37130

ISBN 0-87398-381-5

Printed and bound in the United States of America

CONTENTS

Introduction

1. Assurance of Salvation by the Word 15

2. Happy New Converts at Pentecost:
   Our Example 33

3. Does God Keep His Children? 79

4. Daily Striving to Be Like Jesus 88

5. In Doubt or Failure Christ Jesus
   Still Loves and Keeps 105

6. Abiding in Christ for Fruit-Bearing 123

7. "Honour Thy Father and Thy Mother" 138

8. Five Bible Rules About Fellowship 153

9. "Keep Yourselves From Idols" 162

10. You Are Called to Be a Fisher for Men 182

11. Facts About Personal Soul Winning 201

12. "Power From on High" 205

13. Holy Spirit Enduement Always Available 212

How to Make
A GRAND SUCCESS
Of the Christian Life

*To be a good Christian, to be happy, to grow in grace,
to have good influence, to be a soul winner,
to have Holy Spirit power —*

all this is for you!

INTRODUCTION

What kind of Christian are you going to be? Perhaps you did not even know that there could be more than one kind of Christian, but there certainly can! You may be a happy, joyful Christian, rejoicing in the Lord always, as we are commanded to do (Phil. 4:4); or you can be like so many others, happy only part of the time.

You may be the kind of Christian who *knows* that he is saved, never doubts it because he knows just how he was saved and that God keeps His promises. Or you may be the kind of Christian who frequently doubts his salvation and wonders if God has not forsaken him.

You may be the kind of Christian who has regular daily victory over sin, the kind of Christian who is able to overcome daily temptations and, though he will know that he is naturally weak and frail and sinful, yet has such daily cleansing and daily power to turn away from known sin that on the whole his life is one grand victory! Or you may be the kind of Christian who, though truly converted and truly loving the Lord Jesus in his heart and knowing he has trusted Christ for salvation, is nevertheless constantly defeated, often falling into sin or having habits that he seems unable to break. You see, a Christian may be victorious or defeated.

A Christian may find great joy in the Bible and read it daily with increasing profit and help and enjoyment. Or a Christian may find the Bible dull, may feel himself more or less unable to master the Word of God and to live by its precepts because he is not a mature and a victorious Christian. I know Christians like that, don't you?

A Christian may be a soul winner. Certainly that is the

highest aim of our Saviour for every Christian. He may day by day have the power of the Holy Spirit upon him so that he will know what to say to sinners and may find that the blessed Holy Spirit takes his testimony and warnings and uses them powerfully in turning sinners to Christ. Or a Christian may go along from the day of his salvation and never win a soul, and meet God empty-handed at the judgment seat of Christ! What a sad thing to be one of the branches of Christ, the Vine, but to bear no fruit! What a sad thing to be saved, as Lot was down in Sodom, but to have one's family and kinspeople and neighbors destroyed and sent to Hell because one did not have the power to win them!

THE DEFEATED, CARNAL CHRISTIANS AT CORINTH

The Word of God recognizes that there are these two kinds of Christians—the victorious and the defeated, the happy and the sad, the prosperous and the unprosperous, the soul winners and the unfruitful. In writing to the church at Corinth the Apostle Paul was inspired to say:

"And I, brethren, could not speak unto you as unto spiritual, but as unto carnal, even as unto babes in Christ. I have fed you with milk, and not with meat: for hitherto ye were not able to bear it, neither yet now are ye able. For ye are yet carnal: for whereas there is among you envying, and strife, and divisions, are ye not carnal, and walk as men? For while one saith, I am of Paul; and another, I am of Apollos; are ye not carnal?" —I Cor. 3:1-4.

You see, it was a sad fact that many of these new converts at Corinth were still only babes in Christ, though they had been saved some time before. They were still weak and were not able to eat the strong meat of the Word of God, but had to be fed upon milk. They were "carnal" and not "spiritual." They were only baby Christians. They could not have the regular strong food that Christians ought to be able to enjoy. They had divisions and strifes. They were envious. They had a tendency to follow human leaders without having the spiritual wisdom to follow Christ, through Christ's men. And elsewhere in this epistle we find that many of these Christians lived defeated lives. Some of them even came drunk to the Lord's table. One man was living in shameful sin with his stepmother, and others in the church took his part. So there were quarrels. And though Paul writes to these as really born-again Christians, yet he frankly charges that many of them were carnal, defeated, unspiritual Christians.

But the Bible, thank God, shows us just how to be grown-up Christians instead of babies. The Bible shows us how to be happy Christians instead of sad and despondent ones. The Bible shows us how to be fruitful soul winners so that we will not come empty-handed to meet our Saviour and be ashamed before Him. The Bible shows us how we may *know,* know all the time, that we are saved and kept saved by the power of God. The Bible shows us how we may have our prayers answered regularly, daily. And I will earnestly try to show you God's secrets of a happy, prosperous Christian life.

Would you like to be happy all the time, never defeated, never finding yourself estranged from God? Would you like to know how to have your prayers answered every day? Would you like to know how to have the power of the Holy Spirit upon you so you can win souls regularly right on through your life? Would you like to be close enough to God all the time that you could have the leading of the Holy Spirit to know what to do? Well, that is a wonderful thing and I will show you plainly by the Bible just how you may live in that blessed state of a spiritual Christian, just how you can live a happy, victorious, prosperous Christian life all the time!

CHAPTER I

Assurance of Salvation by the Word

First Secret of Christian
Happiness and Success

The first rule for a happy and successful Christian life is to *know* that you are saved! This is the very foundation of Christian happiness and Christian usefulness and spiritual prosperity.

Jesus said, "Rejoice, because your names are written in heaven" (Luke 10:20). And how can you have that rejoicing if you do not know whether or not your name is written in Heaven?

How can you have confidence when you come to pray if you do not even know that you are God's child? If you do not know that the first prayer that you ever prayed—the prayer for forgiveness and salvation—has been answered, how can you have any confidence to pray for the salvation of others?

If you do not know that you yourself were saved, and if you have not understood the Word of God clearly enough to convince yourself of your salvation, then how could you make the same road to salvation clear to others? D. L. Moody said after many years of experience that he had never seen a single successful soul winner who was not sure about his own salvation.

I. Only Those Who Gladly Received
the Word Were Baptized

One can see how wise were Spirit-filled Peter and the other apostles to demand that those who came for baptism should gladly receive the Word of God and base on that Word their assurance of salvation. After Peter had preached and made clear the plan of salvation, we are told, "Then *they that gladly received his word were baptized*" (Acts 2:41).

Who were baptized? Let us imagine the scene. The power of God has fallen in a wonderful way. Multitudes have turned to Christ, this day of Pentecost when the hundred and twenty who have been waiting in the Upper Room for ten days "were all filled with the Holy Ghost." Sinners, pricked in their hearts by Peter's sermon, had been plainly told that they should repent and then should be baptized as an outward declaration of that repentance, and were promised not only that they should be saved but that they should also have, like these others at Pentecost, "the gift of the Holy Ghost." They had been told clearly how Christ had been crucified for them and, from the text in Joel 2:32, that had had it preached to them that "whosoever shall call on the name of the Lord shall be saved" (Acts 2:21). Their baptism, then, was to be strictly a sign that they believed their sins were remitted when they repented, calling upon Christ for salvation. I can imagine that a man steps up and says, "Peter, I want to be baptized, too, as a Christian."

"But are you saved? Are your sins forgiven? Why do you claim that your sins are forgiven, and on what basis do you call yourself a child of God?" I imagine that Peter asked.

To this I can imagine that the new convert plainly says, "I have just heard that God raised Jesus Christ from the dead, proving that He is the Christ of the Old Testament. I believe, then, that He died for my sins. According to the Word of God, 'whosoever shall call on the name of the Lord shall be saved.' My heart has called upon Him, trusted in Him. My heart has turned from its sin, depending on Jesus. I believe that He has forgiven me and saved me because the Word of God you quoted to us from Joel says that 'whosoever shall call on the name of the Lord shall be saved,' and I have called upon Him. Peter, I believe the Word you have preached and I am claiming to be a child of God and to have a right to be baptized on the basis of the Word of God."

The crowd of Christians smile and thank God for a sinner saved, and the apostles nod their heads in united approval. "Yes! He is ready to be baptized. He has gladly received the Word of God, has trusted Christ for his salvation and is depending upon God's Word that he is saved. His assurance is based on what God has plainly promised." And so the man was approved for baptism.

But I imagine that some other man comes and says, "I, too, want to be baptized. I want to be a Christian. In fact, I call myself a Christian already and I think I ought to be baptized as others are being baptized."

"And on what basis do you claim that your sins are forgiven and that you are a child of God?" I imagine that the Apostle John may have asked him. "I'm so glad that you want to be a child of God and I trust that you are. Now if you have really been saved you ought to be baptized, but how do you know that you are saved?"

Let us imagine that this man says, "I've heard the plain preaching of Peter and I am pricked in my heart. My conscience accuses me of my sins. Therefore, I want to do better. I have resolved never to be drunk any more, never to lie or steal. I want to serve God and win His approval. I feel sure that if I live right and hold out faithful He will receive me. Therefore, I want to be in the church with God's people, to live with them and among them, and I hope to hold out faithful to the end and prove myself a Christian."

Here is a man who wants to do right, wants to be saved. But either he is not saved or he, while trusting in his heart, does not have the assurance of salvation based upon the plain Word of God. His assurance may be a fleeting assurance that will leave at the first temptation or persecution. He may "feel" all right now, but what about when he comes into temptation or neglects to pray, or when he finds it difficult to live as a Christian ought? So I imagine that the Apostle John, the Apostle Peter and others would sadly shake their heads and say, "No, no, my friend! Before you are baptized we feel that you ought to have assurance based upon the Word of God. We are baptizing only those who gladly receive God's Word on this matter and base their hope upon God's Word." So the man would either be instructed further and taught to base his assurance upon the Word of God, or he would be denied baptism until that matter was made clear. The man might be an unsaved man depending on his works. Or he might be a really born-again Christian but poorly instructed and with a cloudy understanding of the way of salvation. But at Pentecost, we are told, only those were baptized who gladly received the Word as it was preached by the other Christians, particularly by Peter in the public message.

II. Can One Absolutely Know
He Is Saved?

Years ago I heard a good woman say to her pastor in a public prayer meeting: "But, Brother Pastor, it seems to me it would be very presumptuous for me to say that I *know* I am saved. I can say that I have a hope of salvation but I know that I am unworthy. I could say that I intend to do my part and trust that the Lord will forgive me and take me to Heaven. But would it not be presumptuous for me to say that I *know I* am good enough to go to Heaven?"

To this the pastor very wisely replied, "None of us is good enough for Heaven in our own works. Every one of us is a poor Hell-deserving sinner. The only ones who can ever go to Heaven are sinners who are saved by God's undeserved mercy and grace, sinners cleansed by the blood of Christ. So," he said, "nobody in the world has any right to count on his goodness, on his character, on his righteousness to get him to Heaven.

"But, on the other hand," the pastor continued, "if I have come to Christ and trusted in His atoning blood, and if the Word of God gives me clear assurance that 'he that believeth on the Son hath everlasting life' (John 3:36), and 'he that believeth on him is not condemned' (John 3:18), and that 'whosoever shall call on the name of the Lord shall be saved' (Acts 2:21), then I would not be presumptuous to claim what God has said is true. I would be making Him a liar and doubting Him if I did not claim what He said was true. So when I know I have trusted in Jesus Christ and not in myself; when I know that I have depended on what Jesus has done for me and what He has promised that He would do for me, then it is not presumption but is an honest faith that can say, 'I know I am saved!' "

But does the Bible clearly say, in so many words, that we can *know* we are saved? Yes, thank God, it does! In I John 5:13 are these blessed words: "These things have I written unto you that believe on the name of the Son of God; that ye may know that ye have eternal life, and that ye may believe on the name of the Son of God." A part of the Bible is written, we are told, for the express purpose "that ye may know that ye have eternal life. . . ."

Years ago I was preaching in a tent revival campaign in San Antonio, Texas. Two lovely girls sixteen and eighteen years of age came under the tent one night just before the song service began. I gave each of them a songbook and then said to the older girl, "Are you a Christian? Have you been saved?"

She looked at me with an innocent face and said respectfully, "Yes, I think I am a Christian. Of course, I do not know. I don't think you *can* know. But I do the best I know how and I think I can say that I am a Christian. Of course, nobody can know for sure whether or not he is saved."

"Oh, yes, you *can* know," I said. "And you ought to make sure and know that you are saved."

"But I do not think that you *can* know," she said.

"Well," I said, "let us not argue about it. Suppose I find it in the Bible that you can know that you are saved. Would you believe it then?" I asked.

"Yes, of course I will believe it if it is in the Bible. But I do not believe it is there. I do not believe that one can know that he is saved."

I got my Bible and turned to this wonderful passage in I John 5:13, and holding the Bible before her we read it together: "These things have I written unto you that believe on the name of the Son of God; that ye may know that ye have eternal life, and that ye may believe on the name of the Son of God."

"You see," I said, "you *can* know that you are saved. Here

in the Bible is a portion of Scripture that was written expressly so you can know that you are saved."

I saw the tears start up in her eyes, and then she looked at me and said very softly and with deep emotion, "Yes! One can know!"

"Now read the rest of the verse carefully," I said. "How does one get to be a child of God so he can know it?"

She read the verse again: "These things have I written unto you *that believe* on the name of the Son of God; that ye may know that ye have eternal life, AND THAT YE MAY BE-LIEVE ON THE NAME OF THE SON OF GOD."

"I see it now! One who believes in Christ and depends on Christ has a right to know that he has eternal life!" she said. And then we bowed our heads and asked the Lord Jesus to help her trust Him right there. And she did trust Him. She took my hand earnestly as a sign that there and then she would claim Him as Saviour and went away *knowing* that she had ever-lasting life. And her sixteen-year-old sister likewise trusted Christ and on the basis of this plain Word of God knew that she had everlasting life.

Oh, yes, then, one can *know* that he is saved.

There are a number of similar passages in the Bible which clearly say that one can know he is saved. For example, in I John 5:19 we are told: "And we *know* that we are of God, and the whole world lieth in wickedness."

Again I John 3:14 says, "We *know* that we have passed from death unto life, because we love the brethren. . . ."

Again in I John 2:3 we are told, "And hereby we do know that we know him, if we keep his commandments."

III. But This Perfect Assurance of Salvation Is Not Automatic; One Can Be Truly Converted and Yet Have Doubts, Not Perfect Assurance

Some people think that if anything so wonderful as forgive-ness of sins and the salvation of the soul has happened to a person, that he could never doubt it. Some people believe that when one is saved he automatically knows and can never doubt his salvation. But that position is not supported by the Word of God. Actually, a Christian can know beyond any doubt that he is saved; but many people, in fact, do not know it. That assurance has to come by an understanding of the Word of God.

It is true that many people have such a sweet assurance and peace and joy at the time of their turning to Christ that they are happy and have a sweet assurance, for the time being, based upon the "experience." They say, "I was there when it happened and I ought to know!" Some tell how they felt as light as a feather. Others tell how they saw a bright light shining from Heaven. Others tell how they praised God aloud and felt the glory of the Lord in their souls. Some tell how they were instantly changed and how old habits dropped away and that things they once hated they now loved and what they once loved they now hated. Some people, after they trusted in Christ, have an assurance that is based upon their feelings, their emotions, upon their experiences. But, alas, that kind of assurance does not always last! They feel wonderful for the present, but the time comes when they lose their sense of God's nearness. Perhaps through lack of prayer, or lack of meditation upon the Word of God, or through some sin or some neglect, they lose the sense of God's constant presence and lose the sense of His forgiveness. Immediately such people are prone to believe that they have lost their salvation. Or, when the feelings of joy and happiness disappear, then one who depends upon his feelings may think, "I suppose I was mistaken. Probably I was never saved or I would not feel like this and I would not fall into the sins that trap me now." Or one who depends on his feelings may, after a great struggle with conscience and trying again and again to feel as he once felt, decide that he has committed the unpardonable sin, that the Spirit of God has left him forever because of some real or fancied sin. Oh, I tell you it is an uncomfortable business trying to depend upon one's feelings for the assurance of salvation!

How well I know about this! When I was nine years old I trusted Christ as my Saviour. It was after a good sermon by a godly pastor in Gainesville, Texas. He preached upon the par-

able of the prodigal son and told us how any poor sinner who
would turn to the Lord would receive a glad welcome and forgiveness and peace, and that, like the prodigal son, we would
receive all these blessings without money and without price,
wholly undeserving. Then he asked those who would take Christ
as Saviour and trust Him, turning in their hearts to the Father's
house for mercy and forgiveness, to come forward. I slid off the
pew, walked down the aisle and took the pastor's hand to claim
Christ as my Saviour. They did not take time to teach me any
of the Word of God. Perhaps they thought I was too young. I
went home so happy that day and asked my father if it would
be all right for me to join the church and be baptized since I
was now a Christian. He said, "Well, Son, when you are old
enough to know you are a sinner and honestly repent of your
sins and be regenerated, then it will be time enough to join the
church."

I sat stricken and silent before my father. I did not know
what all those big words meant; *repentance* and *regeneration*
and more. I simply knew my father did not think I was saved!
Well, I thought, my father was the wisest man in the world and
a preacher, besides; and if he thought I was not saved, I supposed I was not. Sadly I gave up the idea of joining the church
and hoped the time would soon come when I would be old
enough to be saved so my father would know that I was saved.

The next morning on the way to school I stopped under a
willow tree down on Pecan Creek and prayed. I asked God to
help me to be a good boy and asked Him to save other people,
since my father thought I was too young to be saved.

I wish I could tell you all the sadness and disappointment of
the next three years. I often prayed. We moved out to a ranch
in West Texas and then to a little cow town. The company
was not always the best. My mother had gone to Heaven, and
I was a motherless boy. I did not get much instruction in the
Word of God. I got no assurance about salvation. Again and
again I prayed for God to save me. Once I asked a godly
preacher to pray for me and he asked me to pray for myself.
So that night when I went home from the little church I went

out into the horses' stall and knelt down and asked God to save me. Then I prepared for bed and knelt by the bed as I usually did for a good-night prayer and asked God to forgive my sins and save me. I felt no change. I did not have any glorious experience. I did not see any light shining around me. I did not hear the flutter of angel wings. No electricity came in at my head or went out at my fingers and toes! So I sadly went to bed without any assurance of salvation. Then I thought, "Well, I had better settle this thing for good someway or other"; so I got out of bed and prayed again. There on my knees I thought how strange it was that when I realized I was a sinner and that there was nothing I could do to earn salvation and when God had promised so plainly that He would save people and that Jesus had died to pay for our sins—how strange, I thought, that God would not save me! I decided I would leave the matter in the hands of God the best I knew how and go to bed.

I offered myself for membership in the church. I could not feel any great conviction for sin, and yet I did not know that I was saved. When, in that little West Texas church, they asked me to stand and give my "experience," give my testimony before being received into the church, I simply said that I had thought about the matter a great deal, that I did not want to be a Methodist so I had decided to be a Baptist! I was a trembling, inexperienced boy, twelve years old. I was frightened at speaking before the people. And they someway had more confidence in my salvation than my testimony would have warranted, and received me in the church as a candidate for baptism!

When I was baptized I was strangely happy. Even yet I could give no clear testimony as to when I was saved or how. Oh, I wished that I knew just how and when I was saved and could know for sure that it was settled for good! But when others gave the very date and place when they were saved and told how happy they had been, I could not give any such experience.

Then one glad day I began reading the New Testament and came upon those wonderful promises in the Gospel of John, like clusters of ripe fruit on a beautiful tree!

"As many as received him, to them gave he power to become the sons of God, EVEN TO THEM THAT BELIEVE ON HIS NAME."—John 1:12.

"He that believeth on the Son hath everlasting life."—John 3:36.

"Verily, verily, I say unto you, He that heareth my word, and believeth on him that sent me, hath everlasting life, and shall not come into condemnation; but is passed from death unto life."—John 5:24.

Oh, that last wonderful promise! I found that when I heard the Word of God and put my trust in the God who had sent His Son to save me, I then and there received everlasting life. I had often tried to remember that incident or that experience when I was nine years old and came to claim the Saviour publicly. I could not remember how I felt. I wondered if I had been as deeply moved as one must be to be saved. I recalled that a twelve-year-old boy who came the same day had been weeping and I had shed not a tear! I had thought many a time, if I were really saved I would not do some of the things I do. But now I saw, praise the Lord, that when I had put my trust in Jesus Christ, then and there I received everlasting life! My doubts and fears were gone; gone, thank God, forever! From that day to this I have never doubted for a moment that I am God's child. I know one thing beyond any doubt: when I trusted Jesus, depended on Him to forgive me, He did! The Word of God says so and that makes it so. On those promises I have hung the eternal welfare of my soul, and how sure, how unchanging is that blessed foundation for my faith!

IV. How Foolish to Base One's Happiness and Assurance on Feelings!

Do you have doubts about your salvation? Do you sometimes wonder if you are truly a child of God? Then, dear friend, let me tell you something I have learned. It may comfort you to know that a great majority of the saints of God, before they became established in this sweet assurance based on the Word of God, have doubted and feared and trembled about their salvation. When they lived victoriously, then they felt sure of their salvation. When they fell into temptation or trouble, then they doubted whether they had ever been saved. Oh, feelings! Oh, emotions and experiences and ecstasies! What a foundation of shifting sand! How unreliable, how untrustworthy, how fleeting is all the assurance which one may have based upon one's feelings!

One may for long years have had sweet confidence that he was saved, until he grew ill. His blood pressure was low and this brought about a natural depression and melancholy. Suddenly he began to have all kinds of doubts about his salvation. Satan, that old accuser of God's children, that enemy of a Christian's peace, takes advantage of every physical ailment, of every temptation to cause doubt and fear in the heart of a Christian who depends upon feelings.

A woman came to me who had been a happy Christian for many years. But when the change of life came on and her health was unstable, her mind became a victim of all kinds of fears, as is frequently the case at such a time. She had come now to believe that she must have committed the unpardonable sin! All her joys were gone. She still loved the Lord, still wanted to serve Him. She had no pleasure in the things of the world. But because now her physical condition led to a natural depression and because she was emotionally upset, as is very customary with many women at such a time, she feared that God had forsaken her. Oh, people who look within themselves and examine their feelings and emotions and try by these feelings and emotions to prove that they are born again, that they are children of God, will have many doubts and fears.

V. Knowing by the Dependable Record; Not by Feeling or Memory of a Feeling

But some preacher may boldly say that if you do not know for sure that you are saved, that if you do not have "an experience" that always satisfies you, then you are not saved. "If you can have it and not know it, then you could lose it without missing it," wisecracks some preacher. And he may say, "I know I was saved because I was there when it happened." Now that is really a very witty saying. It sounds so smart that one may not instantly recognize that such a man is depending not on the Word of God but upon his own changeable emotions and feelings and memories. Actually, the fact that you were there when it happened does not automatically guarantee that you will understand fully what happened and that you will always have perfect assurance of salvation.

Let me illustrate. "I was there when it happened," when I was born into the world the first time. Remember that salvation is simply a new birth. If one can know all about his second birth by the simple fact that he was there, then he ought to be able to know about his first birth for the same reason! Now I was born on December 11, 1895, in Cooke County, Texas. How do I know? Do you suppose that on that eventful day I sat up and looked about me and said, "Well! I see by the calendar that it is December 11, just two weeks before Christmas Eve! I'll put this down in my notebook so I will always remember I was born on December 11!"? Do you suppose that I looked at my mother and said, "Your name, please, lady? I want to put it down in my notebook so I will always know who was my mother, who was my father, and the other conditions surrounding my birth"? I did nothing of the kind! When I was born I did not know much of anything except when I got hungry. I learned gradually to know my mother's voice and to know when I was uncomfortable with dirty clothes or with the pricking of an unfastened safety pin. I later learned to focus both eyes and look at one object! Then I learned, I suppose, to smile when people tickled me under the chin. There were long months before I grew a single tooth, and other months before I learned to walk and talk. It is true that "I was there when it happened" at my first birth. But I was very young at the time, I took no note of my surroundings, and I cannot trust my memory about the matter at all!

And yet I know; in fact, it is beyond any doubt at all in my mind, that I was really born on December 11, 1895, that

William R. Rice was my father, that Sallie LaPrade Rice was my mother, and that Gertrude was my sister, eighteen months older. How do I know? That is easy! I have it on the authority of my mother. It was written down in the family Bible. And recently I saw it written down on a separate piece of paper in my mother's own handwriting. There it was listed by her sweet fingers, "Gertrude Frances, born July 24, 1894. John R., born December 11, 1895 . . ." and so on with Ruth and George and baby Porter! I have the written record of one I absolutely trust. And so I know when I was born and who were my mother and my father.

And, thank God, I have even better assurance than that about my second birth! I have the written record of God's own Word saying that when I put my trust in Jesus Christ I passed from death to life! I have the written record that "he that believeth on the Son hath everlasting life" (John 3:36). I believed in Him, trusted in Him, depended on Him to forgive me. Now I know He has done it because He never failed to keep His word, and He never will!

I know that Jesus said, "All that the Father giveth me shall come to me; and him that cometh to me I will in no wise cast out" (John 6:37). When I came to Christ it was because God the Father had given me to Jesus and put it in my heart to come! And then when I came He did not reject me, did not send me away, did not cast me out. He promised that He did not and would not. When I came to Jesus, He received me. I *know,* because I have the plain Word of God that cannot lie, that "him that cometh to me I will in no wise cast out."

When I say I came to Christ I do not mean when I joined the church or when I was baptized or when I walked down an aisle or when I took the preacher's hand. I mean that in my heart I wanted Christ, I wanted forgiveness, and I decided to trust Him and chose to come to Him. In my mind and heart, when I decided to come to Jesus, I had already come, then, in His sight. And when I came He received me, He forgave me. That is far better assurance than my feelings and my emotions.

"Whosoever shall call upon the name of the Lord shall be

saved" (Rom. 10:13). I know that I called on the Lord. And I know God is not trying to trip me up, not trying to take advantage of my ignorance. I know that He sees the heart and He knows I wanted salvation, that I offered myself to Him and depended on Him to save me. An honest God knows that this poor sinner called on Him for salvation and turned the matter over to Him. Therefore, I have perfect assurance that I have the salvation which He promised. God cannot lie! And on His written record I claim that I have a contract with Him that He cannot and will not break. Oh, God *wants* to save sinners. He gave His Son to die on the cross to save sinners. And one who honestly, in his heart, calls on God for mercy and forgiveness and salvation, is assured of salvation by this clear promise of the Bible.

"Then they that gladly received his word were baptized," we are told of the new converts at Pentecost (Acts 2:41).

If the promise, "Whosoever shall call upon the name of the Lord shall be saved," seems too good to be true, too easy a plan of salvation, let us remember that the next verse, Romans 10:14, says, "How then shall they call on him in whom they have not believed?" Actually, one who calls upon Christ for mercy and forgiveness has trusted Christ in the heart, and the prayer of the heart is simply the manifestation of faith. How would one call on God for mercy and forgiveness if he did not believe there is a God who hears and that God has provided a way of salvation? You see, saving faith is in the heart of one who honestly, penitently calls upon Christ for salvation.

Have you the assurance of salvation based upon the plain Word of God? How precious is this assurance!

Here is another promise to hang the destiny of your soul upon with sweet assurance. Romans 10:8, 9 says: "But what saith it? The word is nigh thee, even in thy mouth, and in thy heart: that is, the word of faith, which we preach; That if thou shalt confess with thy mouth the Lord Jesus, and shalt believe in thine heart that God hath raised him from the dead, thou shalt be saved."

It is so near, so easy! Any penitent heart wanting to be forgiven, wanting to be made new, wanting to be cleansed, can turn and have it settled in a moment, because the word is near, this word of faith, that is, even in your mouth and your heart. What is it? Can you honestly confess with your mouth the Lord Jesus, believing in your heart that God raised Him up from the dead? Then that, this Scripture says, is saving faith!

There are two simple parts to this promise. Take the last part first. Do you believe that God raised Jesus from the dead? That proves His deity. Do you believe that Jesus really paid for our sins and rose for our justification, and that therefore He is God's own Lamb given to save us? Now if you believe that this resurrected Son is God come in the flesh (as His resurrection proves), are you ready to claim Him as your own Saviour? That is what God here requires. And He says simply that anybody who claims Christ, believing that He is God's own resurrected Son, is saved!

It is so simple as this: every one who is willing to take Christ, God's own resurrected Son, as his Saviour, can have Him. And one who, thus believing in Christ, claims Him is instantly saved!

The very minimum is required. If you know that God raised up Jesus from the dead, then you know that He is not an ordinary man. He is God's Son, our Saviour. Now if you trust in that kind of a Saviour enough to claim Him, that is enough to insure your salvation! So says the Word of God. And you who have so trusted Christ and claimed Him have an argument that you have a right to bring before God or anybody else that you are saved! According to the Word of God you can *know* that you have passed from death to life, on the authority of God.

VI. Do You Make God a Liar, Doubting His Word?

Let us go back to the passage in I John, chapter 5. We noticed it above, and found that it plainly promised that one may know that he has eternal life. But now consider the whole passage, I John 5:9-13.

"If we receive the witness of men, the witness of God is greater: for this is the witness of God which he hath testified of his Son. He that believeth on the Son of God hath the witness in himself: he that believeth not God hath made him a liar; because he believeth not the record that God gave of his Son. And this is the record, that God hath given to us eternal life, and this life is in his Son. He that hath the Son hath life; and he that hath not the Son of God hath not life. These things have I written unto you that believe on the name of the Son of God; that ye may know that ye have eternal life, and that ye may believe on the name of the Son of God."

How strange that anyone would receive the witness of men instead of the witness of God! Now God has given a certain witness concerning His Son. "He that believeth on the Son of God hath the witness in himself." That is, Christ Himself comes into the heart and saves the soul through the regenerating work of the Holy Spirit. Thus one has within himself the new nature and indwelling Spirit of God, as witness that he is saved. And one who does not believe what God has written on this matter makes God a liar "because he believeth not the record that God gave of his Son."

And then God gives us plainly again the written record, which we are to believe; and thus to know that we are saved.

"And this is the record, that God hath given to us eternal life, and this life is in his Son. He that hath the Son hath life; and he that hath not the Son of God hath not life."

Then comes this blessed promise: "These things have I written unto you that believe on the name of the Son of God; that ye may know that ye have eternal life, and that ye may believe on the name of the Son of God."

Will you believe this record, put down in the Bible so you might know for sure that you are saved? Are you ready to believe God on the matter and risk Christ on this naked word of Scripture? If you have trusted Christ, He says you are saved. If you have opened the door and received Christ, then you have everlasting life. Oh, today put your trust in Jesus and then know by the Scriptures that you have eternal life!

If one reads this who has not trusted in Christ alone for salvation, I beg you in Jesus' name to trust Him today and take the salvation so freely offered.

Now, dear doubting friend who may read this, will you throw away your doubts and risk the plain Word of God? Or will you make God a liar by doubting His Word?

Now one who bases his assurance on the plain Word of God may have other assurances also. He may love other Christians in a way that a lost man cannot love them. And thus he may know that he is saved, according to I John 3:14 which says, "We know that we have passed from death unto life, because we love the brethren. He that loveth not his brother abideth in death." The Christian graces will develop in a good Christian so that he can have an added assurance of his salvation in the fact that he has a love for Christians in his heart. But I remind you that this is not the main assurance. The main assurance is the record God has written which, He said, is written "unto you that believe on the name of the Son of God; that ye may know that ye have eternal life. . . ." But there is a sweet added assurance when we discover that we love Christian people as an unsaved person cannot love Christians.

Again, a Christian will find as he grows in grace that he keeps God's commandments. Not perfectly, of course. All of us are sinful and weak. "If we say that we have no sin, we deceive ourselves, and the truth is not in us," says I John 1:8. Yet a Christian does love the Word of God and does want to please God. There is something in every born-again Christian that hates sin and wants to keep God's commandments. If a Christian lives near the Lord and grows in grace, he will find that sweet added assurance of his salvation. "And hereby we do know that we know him, if we keep his commandments" (I John 2:3).

Should a Christian have joy? Yes, and thank God I have much of it. How many, many times the Lord has been so near to me! Sometimes I have rejoiced in His presence so that I have laughed aloud for joy. Sometimes I have said over and over again, "Praise the Lord! Praise the Lord!" It is very sweet and precious to be conscious of the Lord's presence and to know that He hears our prayers and answers them and to know that He has His power upon us and will use us. I have such feelings and joys, praise His name! But when feelings fade or change or disappear, thank God, I have the solid rock of God's Word that never changes! God still loves the world! It is still true that God gave His Son, Jesus, to die for sinners; it is still true that the Scripture says, "Whosoever believeth in him should not perish, but have everlasting life." Bless God, when I change, the Bible does not change! When my feelings change, my emotions, God's blessed truth does not change. And I know that I am God's child, that He still has not cast me out, because He said He would not. I know that I have everlasting life and shall not come into condemnation, but am passed from death unto life, because Jesus in John 5:24 plainly says so. Oh, praise the Lord for the solid assurance of the Word of God that one who comes to Jesus Christ and trusts Him for forgiveness is saved! Salvation is by faith in Christ, not faith in one's emotions. So the strongest assurance is by the Word.

I urge everyone who reads this, then, to throw away all your doubts and depend from this time forth on what God has promised in the Word and what Jesus has done on the cross and is doing now as our High Priest at the right hand of God. Our sins are paid for! And if we have trusted Him for salvation we are saved. We know so because He said so! How blessed are those who know they are saved and who have this assurance based on the Word of God.

So we are told about the converts at Pentecost that "they that gladly received his word were baptized."

CHAPTER II

Happy New Converts at Pentecost: Our Example

In the book of Acts we have a marvelous example of New Testament Christians who lived happy and prosperous and victorious lives; who got their prayers answered, who won their loved ones to Christ, who knew they were saved, who continued on the high plane of daily revival blessing all the time! I refer to the Christians at Jerusalem who were converted at the revival of Pentecost. Since this book will fall into the hands of many new converts, I want to use these Pentecostal converts as an example for you. These converts of the greatest revival in the history of Christianity went on to live for God so boldly and happily that we will do well to study from the Word of God just they did it. What were the secrets of their wonderfully prosperous and happy Christian lives?

That question is answered in Acts 2:41-47. Let us read this Scripture telling of those who were saved at Pentecost and of what followed in their lives, and learn their secrets of a happy, prosperous Christian life.

"Then they that gladly received his word were baptized: and the same day there were added unto them about three thousand souls. And they continued stedfastly in the apostles' doctrine and fellowship, and in breaking of bread, and in prayers. And fear came upon every soul: and many wonders and signs were done by the apostles. And all that believed were together, and had all things common; And sold their possessions and goods, and parted them to all men, as every man had need. And they, continuing daily with one accord in the temple, and breaking bread from house to house, did eat their meat with gladness and singleness of heart, praising God, and having favour with all the people. And the Lord added to the church daily such as should be saved."—Acts 2:41-47.

How my heart is thrilled as I read this passage and see how happy were these new converts, how joyful was their fellowship! They ate their meat "with gladness and singleness of heart, praising God." And the Lord kept on saving souls through their earnest, Spirit-empowered pleading and their glad testimony!

But as we read the passage we note that there did not come a great crisis by which they were instantly made holy, sinless, with all the natural temptations and weaknesses of the human flesh taken away. No, if we study the Scripture here carefully we will find instead that there were certain rules these new converts followed and by so doing they continued in the joy and power of the blessed revival in which they were converted. Here we find some secrets of a happy Christian life.

You will be surprised, perhaps, when I say that all these secrets are shown in this passage. But when I call them to your attention, you will recognize them, I am sure.

FIRST SECRET: These converts had the assurance of salvation based upon the plain Word of God. *"Then they that gladly received his word were baptized . . ."* (vs. 41).

The new converts were baptized, thus publicly confessing Christ, each one thus publicly renouncing and counting dead and burying the old sinner that each had been; and publicly rising from the waters of baptism to live a resurrected life, in the power of Christ. "Then they . . . were baptized" (vs. 41).

SECOND SECRET: The new converts were added to the local assembly of Christians; they joined the church. "And the same day there were added unto them about three thousand souls" (vs. 41). "And they continued stedfastly in . . . fellowship, and in breaking of bread . . ." (vs. 42).

THIRD SECRET: They continued stedfastly in the apostles' doctrine, that is, in the Word of God, learning and following and meditating in the teachings of the Bible, which is the apostles' doctrine written down. "And they continued stedfastly in the apostles' doctrine . . ." (vs. 42).

FOURTH SECRET: They continued constantly in prayer. "And they continued stedfastly . . . in prayers" (vs. 42).

FIFTH SECRET: They put God first in their possessions, counted all they had as belonging to God and used possessions to please Him. "And all that believed were together, and had all things common; and sold their possessions and goods, and parted them to all men, as every man had need" (vss. 44,45).

SIXTH SECRET: They were so joyful, so filled with the Spirit, so constant in their pleading and their testimony for God that they won souls daily. And the church, instead of receiving converts once a year, at Easter, or once a month, received the new converts daily! "And the Lord added to the church daily such as should be saved" (vs. 47).

Here we have the principles by which these new converts lived. We have their secrets of a happy, prosperous Christian life. Oh, if the converts in every revival would set out to live after these same principles, live so joyfully and victoriously and fruitfully, how soon we would see multiplied thousands of souls saved! Well, dear reader, you yourself may learn here and now to live such a happy, victorious and prosperous Christian life by following the example of the Christians at Jerusalem who were converted in the revival at Pentecost. I know these principles work because God has graciously worked them in my own life. And I have seem them demonstrated in the lives of thousands of others. So take most seriously these lessons, and I can assure you that you will be a joyful, victorious Christian, having your prayers answered, winning souls to the Lord and being wonderfully prospered in all good things.

I. Christians Should Be
Baptized

In the great revival at Pentecost the converts were baptized. "They that gladly received his word were baptized: and the same day there were added unto them about three thousand souls." Those who want to be happy, successful and prosperous, like the converts were at Pentecost, should follow the same plan. Those who know they have trusted Christ for salvation should then be baptized to show their faith in Christ.

1. How Important Jesus Made Baptism!

It is rather surprising how much importance is given to baptism in the New Testament. Jesus Himself was baptized in the River Jordan before the multitude, by John the Baptist (Luke 3:21, 22). There the Holy Spirit came visibly upon Him in form like a dove. John the Baptist had baptized multitudes of repentant, believing people. Now Jesus, through His disciples, baptized more than John (John 4:1, 2).

In the Great Commission Jesus gave strict orders about baptism. As it is given in Matthew 28:19, 20, Jesus said: "Go ye therefore, and teach all nations, baptizing them in the name of the Father, and of the Son, and of the Holy Ghost: Teaching them to observe all things whatsoever I have commanded you: and, lo, I am with you alway, even unto the end of the world." All the new converts were to be baptized on profession of their faith in Christ.

In Mark 16:15, 16 the command is given again: "Go ye into all the world, and preach the gospel to every creature. He that believeth and is baptized shall be saved; but he that believeth not shall be damned." Note that baptism was such a natural and customary accompaniment to a profession of faith in Christ that "he that believeth and is baptized" is the form in which Jesus said it. And you will see that Jesus did not mean that baptism was essential to salvation, because the same verse plainly says, "But he that believeth not shall be damned." Not to trust Jesus Christ personally is the cause of damnation. But those who trust Christ and are saved would naturally then follow His command to be baptized. In John 3:36 we are plainly told, "He that believeth on the Son hath everlasting life." This one who believed in Christ was saved before he was baptized, but was expected to be baptized, and of course when he was baptized he was still saved. But one who did not trust in Christ would be damned. Salvation was settled by personal faith in Christ, but it was naturally taken for granted that those who trusted Christ would be baptized.

And that is the way it happened in the New Testament, just as Jesus intimated that it should be. At Pentecost the believers were baptized at once. The Ethiopian eunuch, when Philip taught him the way of salvation, understood that after trusting Christ he should be baptized. And he was baptized there in a wayside stream or pond (Acts 8:38). Lydia and her household, when they trusted in Christ, were baptized (Acts 16:15). The jailer and his household were baptized the same hour of the night after they had heard the Gospel and after they had obeyed the plain command and promise, "Believe on the Lord Jesus Christ, and thou shalt be saved, and thy house" (Acts 16:31-33).

In Acts 2:38, 39 we are taught that the attitude of mind that is properly exhibited in baptism is required for the fullness of the Holy Spirit. It is not that the outward rite of baptism will guarantee that one is filled with the Holy Spirit, but that one who honestly gives himself up to God in the meaning which baptism normally teaches is therefore prepared for the fullness of the Spirit for God's work.

Thus any Christian who cares about the words of Jesus and the practice of the New Testament Christians must seriously face the duty of being baptized. Baptism never saves a sinner. Salvation takes more than water, whether a spoonful or a tankful. Yet one who has been saved ought to be baptized because Jesus plainly commanded it, and because it is a public declaration of his faith in Christ, a public confession. And the meaning of baptism is so rich that many a Christian misses the fullest blessing and fullest prosperity by disobeying Christ in this matter.

2. The Meaning of Baptism

I do not mean here to go into the form of baptism. I have done that elsewhere in my book, *Bible Baptism*. I should rather leave that aside for the moment. The meaning and spirit of baptism are far more important than the form. I do not want to bring in any unnecessary controversy. I want this message to be a help to every new convert who will read it, of every denomination. By the study of the Word of God and the counsel and help of Bible-believing pastors the reader will be enabled to study further the matter of the mode of baptism. So we will not discuss it here. We are concerned here about the spiritual meaning which God intended baptism to have and why baptism is a step in happiness and prosperity and spiritual success for every Christian.

That meaning of baptism is made clear, I think, in Romans 6:1-8 as follows:

"What shall we say then? Shall we continue in sin, that grace may abound? God forbid. How shall we that are dead to sin, live any longer therein? Know ye not, that so many of us as were baptized into Jesus Christ were baptized into his death? Therefore we are buried with him by baptism into death: that like as Christ was raised up from the dead by the glory of the Father, even so we also should walk in newness of life. For if we have been planted together in the likeness of his death, we shall be also in the likeness of his resurrection: Knowing this, that our old man is crucified with him, that the body of sin might be destroyed, that henceforth we should not serve sin. For he that is dead is freed from sin. Now if we be dead with Christ, we believe that we shall also live with him."

Everyone who was baptized was baptized with reference to Christ and with reference to His death. Baptism pictured the burial and resurrection of Christ, so we are told that everyone who was baptized in Bible times thus pointed to the death and burial and resurrection of Jesus Christ. Christ died for us; so the new convert is counted dead to sin, dead to the old life. And when the new convert is baptized and comes out of the water in the likeness of Christ's resurrection, he means that now he counts himself dead to the old life and not to be controlled by it any more. He is dead in Christ and risen with Christ. His sins have been paid for by the Saviour's death, and he is free. But now he is raised up to live a new life for God. He is not to count himself the same man at all. He is no longer supposed to be under the dominion of sin and death. Although he is yet in a natural body, subject to some of the weakness and the coming death that sin brings, yet the Christian is to reckon himself a new creature, and so to live out and out for God.

Every new convert, then, when he is baptized, says to himself, to the world and to God, "I'm not my own any more! The old sinner that I was is now dead. Now I am a new creature. I will live a new life. I am raised up to live for Jesus Christ alone."

I maintain that every person who was ever baptized and did not mean to count the old sinful self dead and to overrule it and override it and keep it down, and thus to live a life surrendered to God and pleasing to God in the power of the Holy Spirit, falsified his testimony when he was baptized. It was a lie, a wicked lie, a hypocritical profession, if one was baptized and did not mean to lay self on the altar, unreservedly, to live for Jesus Christ.

When Jesus was baptized He had in mind His own coming crucifixion, His burial and resurrection. He did not shrink from it but gave Himself openly to the plan of the Father for Himself. And Jesus said, "Thus it becometh us to fulfill all righteousness" (Matt. 3:15). If it were suitable for Jesus to be baptized, picturing His own coming death, burial and resurrection, then it is suitable for a Christian to follow the example of His Saviour and to be baptized picturing the same thing—the Saviour's death for us, our death to sin in His death, and our glorious future resurrection pictured in His resurrection.

Can you see, then, how important it is for a Christian to be baptized? To be baptized means to put on the uniform of your King, to take the oath of allegiance, to publicly claim your Saviour. To be baptized means a conscious giving up of one's own way and a full surrender to the will of God. To be baptized means giving self up to crucifixion, to live a resurrected life for God. Every Christian ought to have that time of surrender, that time of holy dedication, that time of reckoning himself dead. In fact, it ought to be the first great decision that every Christian makes after he has taken Christ as his Saviour. And that decision ought to be confirmed by the outward rite of baptism.

The world, it is true, often does not understand the meaning of baptism. And yet this much at least is true—everyone who sees a new convert baptized understands that the new convert means now to live for Christ.

I remember the joy that welled up in my heart on that cold November day when, at a little artificial lake or "tank" in West Texas, I followed my Saviour in baptism. How my heart warmed! I did not know all the doctrine involved, and I was not even as thoroughly sure of my salvation as I afterward became. But, thank God, I felt in my heart the approval of the Saviour because I had publicly taken my stand for Him and had publicly announced my intention to serve Him at any cost for the rest of my days. How many, many times I have seen joy unspeakable fill the faces of new converts as they followed the Saviour in baptism!

So, young Christian, if you would be happy, make that great decision and consecration that is properly involved in baptism and obey the Saviour in this blessed pictorial ceremony. Use for Christ this object lesson that pictures the death of Christ and His resurrection and our faith in this crucified, risen Saviour, and our surrender with all our souls to serve Him and live His life.

A great southern preacher has called our attention to the fact that Jesus left two object lessons, "the Gospel for the eye," that ought to keep straight forever the great doctrine of salvation by the atoning blood of Christ. When one makes profession of his faith in Christ and is publicly baptized, it pictures that Jesus died and rose again, died for our sins and rose for our justification. And every time one takes the Lord's Supper he reminds himself and others that only by the death of Christ, only by His body broken on the tree and His blood poured out on the cross are we saved and made fit for Heaven.

How important it is, then, that everybody should be reminded that we believe in the death of Christ, that we count ourselves crucified with Him and raised to live for Him. And this holy resolution of the heart is publicly announced in baptism. Every new convert, then, should follow the example of those at Pentecost. "They that gladly received his word were baptized" (Acts 2:41). Thus one will be obeying also the plain command of Jesus Christ in the Great Commission.

II. Church Membership

So many churches (we here mean local congregations) have failed God, have turned away from loyalty to the Word of God and Christ's soul-winning program as given in the Great Commission, that it has become customary among many Bible-believing people to make light of local church membership. Now I would not encourage anybody to join with unbelievers in Christ and the Bible, in churches or anywhere else. I would not encourage any Christian ever to give a dime to a modernist who denies the deity of Christ, the inspiration of the Bible and Christ's atoning death on the cross. I am not saying that it is all right to join any church, whether it is true to Christ or not. But I do say as plainly as I know how that every Christian ought to join in with some local congregation of born-again Christians. He ought to do this for his own good and for the good of other Christians, and to help carry on the work of Jesus Christ.

1. Local Churches in New Testament Times

Were there churches, local congregations of Christians, banded together in New Testament times? There certainly were such churches. Of about 110 times that the word *church* or *churches* appears in our English Bible, at least ninety of these times the word refers to a local congregation of Christians or to more than one local congregation of Christians. The Bible speaks continually of "the church of God at Corinth" or "the church at Rome" or "the church that is in thy house" or "the churches of Galatia" or "the seven churches of Asia." The regular language of the New Testament refers continually to local congregations of Christians, as separate, complete churches.

These churches had simple but definite organization. They had deacons (Acts 6:1-6) to help wait on the poor of the congregation. In Jerusalem these deacons were appointed by the apostles and ordained, after they had been selected by the people (Acts 6:3). Elders, or pastors, were appointed or elected in the churches, also. Paul admonished the church in Corinth to come together and officially withdraw fellowship from a certain man living in sin, "to deliver such an one unto Satan for the destruction of the flesh, that the spirit may be saved in the day of the Lord Jesus." They were to do this "in the name of our Lord Jesus Christ, when ye are gathered together . . ." (I Cor. 5:4, 5). Saul (later called Paul the apostle), was converted, and returned to Jerusalem where "he assayed to join himself to the disciples: but they were all afraid of him, and believed not that he was a disciple" (Acts 9:26). But good Barnabas took Saul's part, convinced the apostles that Saul had been converted, and thereafter he was received among the people as a Christian. We would say that Paul "joined the church," that is, that he joined the assembly of Christians at Jerusalem and became known as one of them. But he was rejected until it was proved that he had truly been converted.

After that wonderful revival at Pentecost, the new converts joined in the assembly, the church at Jerusalem. "Then they that gladly received his word were baptized: AND THE SAME DAY THERE WERE ADDED UNTO THEM ABOUT THREE THOUSAND SOULS" (Acts 2:41). It is clear that these three thousand were carefully questioned, were baptized and enrolled in the local assembly. Thereafter "they continued stedfastly in the apostles' doctrine [teaching] and fellowship, and in breaking of bread . . ." (vs. 42). Continually, "The Lord added to the church daily such as should be saved" (vs. 47). And throughout the account of the New Testament Christians at Jerusalem much is made of their sweet fellowship, their sacrificial serving of one another, their hospitality one to another, eating from house to house.

2. The Benefits of Church Membership

There are many, many reasons why every new convert should join in with other Christians in a local church and there serve God.

First, a Christian needs Christian fellowship and Christian company. Nobody in the world can live a good Christian life without keeping good company. Bad company ruined Samson, the Spirit-filled judge of Israel, and led him to commit terrible sins so that the Spirit of the Lord departed from him. Bad company ruined Solomon. In his old age he married heathen wives and they led him into idolatry. Bad company caused Simon Peter to lose his courage, to deny the Lord and to curse and swear! Oh, young Christian, you cannot possibly live at your best as a Christian unless you seek the company of other Christians.

Someone says, "I can live as well outside the church as in the church." No you cannot! How could anyone live as well running with the Devil's crowd as he could running with the Lord's crowd? How could anyone live as well with the bad influence of the Christ-rejectors and the God-haters as he could live with the prayers and counsel and encouragement of Christians? It is better for a Christian to work with other Christians in a job. He is more likely to find a good job with Christians in the church than out of it. It is right for a Christian to marry only a Christian. He is more likely to marry a Christian if he attends the church with other Christians.

Second, one needs the public services of the church. He needs to sing, and people sing better in groups. He needs to hear Christian testimony. He needs to join others in earnest prayer and have others pray with him and for him.

Third, the Christian needs a pastor. One needs to hear preaching, but one needs also to be under the spiritual supervision of some pastor who holds himself accountable to God for his soul. One needs to have a pastor as a spiritual father, or as a spiritual overseer. In fact, the word *pastor* means overseer or superintendent, and Christians need their Christian lives superintended by godly, Spirit-filled men. God knew what He was doing when He gave orders for local New Testament congregations, called churches, and planned for them to have pastors and teachers and to meet in public assembly.

Fourth, a Christian ought to have some place where he can go regularly to be taught the Word of God. Whether it is in

Sunday school or in the preaching service, the church owes a duty to its members and every member ought to take advantage of the privilege that is afforded to learn the Word of God.

Fifth, every Christian ought to have some place where it would be convenient to do much of his Christian giving. Every Christian ought to support the preaching of the Gospel by supporting his pastor. Every Christian ought to support mission work, and usually that is most easily done and most properly done through a church. Every Christian ought to have some part in the relief of the Christian poor, and often that is done better through the church than by individual charity, or by the lodges, or by government relief agencies. Christians ought to do the work of Christians, and most of these things they do better in churches than they can do outside of churches.

I have found that many love the Lord who do not join churches. But they are irresponsible Christians. They do not have anybody in authority over them whose word they eminently respect and follow. They do not hold themselves to some strict schedule of serving God, or of worship, or of giving. They feel no responsibility for getting the Gospel out to others about them. It is important that every Christian should get in with other Christians, have fellowship with other Christians, feel a responsibility to a local church and be ministered to by a local church.

Therefore, I urge every convert, for your own happiness and for the good of the cause of Christ, to find a church that believes the Bible; a church where the Gospel is preached and souls are saved; and help to make that church stronger by your membership and by your prayers and your example and testimony and gifts. So they did in the revival at Pentecost.

III. The Bible

We are told about the new converts at Pentecost that ". . . they continued stedfastly in the apostles' doctrine . . ." (Acts 2:42). Well, we have no apostles alive now, and yet the apostles' doctrine is with us. The Apostle John wrote some of it in the Gospel of John, in the First, Second, and Third Epistles of John, and in the book of Revelation. Matthew wrote part of it in the Gospel According to Matthew. Peter wrote part of it in the First and Second Epistles of Peter. Paul the apostle wrote some of it in the thirteen books of the New Testament (fourteen if we count Hebrews from Paul, as I think we should). The Bible we now have is the same apostles' doctrine that New Testament Christians followed. The apostles and other preachers preached the Old Testament and they had divinely revealed to them the doctrine, the teaching which is now in our New Testament, and they passed this on to the people. So if we set out to continue steadfastly in the Word of God we will be doing the same thing as these converts of the revival at Pentecost did.

1. Wonderful Promises to Those Who Read, Memorize, Meditate Upon and Follow the Word of God

I think we may safely say that the Christian's use of the Bible is the most important factor of all in securing Christian happiness and success and every blessing of God upon His child. You see, if a Christian knows the Bible, loves the Bible, follows the Bible, and spiritually understands the Bible, he will already have all the other of the secrets we are naming in this book. The Christian who has the Bible has the road map for the Christian pilgrim, the orders for the Christian soldier. The Bible maps out the way to find all the hidden treasures a Christian needs, all that is necessary to make him happy, useful and successful.

With this in mind we should not be surprised to find many wonderful promises about what the Bible will do for the Christian.

The *reading* of the Bible is blessed of God. And if one cannot read, it is equally blessed to hear, just so the Christian keeps the things that are written in the Book. For Revelation 1:3 says, "Blessed is he that readeth, and they that hear the words of this prophecy, and keep those things which are written therein: for the time is at hand." *Knowing* and *loving* the Bible will help a Christian to have his prayers answered. For John

15:7 says, "If ye abide in me, and my words abide in you, ye shall ask what ye will, and it shall be done unto you." Christ says that the Christian who is wrapped up in Christ, absorbed in Christ, wholly surrendered to and occupied with Christ, and provided His Word abides in the Christian, may ask anything he wishes! One thoroughly committed to Christ can be trusted in his will, when he knows enough of the Bible, to know the will of God and to know what will please and honor God. A proper understanding of and devotion to the Bible is so closely connected with having our prayers answered!

The blessed Word of God, as we read it regularly and absorb it and love it, will help us conquer the sins in our own lives. "Wherewithal shall a young man cleanse his way? by taking heed thereto according to thy word," says Psalm 119:9. This means that it is an impossibility for a Christian to live an overcoming life without taking heed to his life according to the Word of God. That is the reason David said, by divine inspiration, "Thy word have I hid in mine heart, that I might not sin against thee" (Ps. 119:11).

A knowledge of the Word of God will guide us in the way we should go, guide us in our decisions of right and wrong, and in our choices. For Psalm 119:24 says, "Thy testimonies also are my delight and my counsellors." In that same great chapter on the Word of God, Psalm 119:105 says, "Thy word is a lamp unto my feet, and a light unto my path." Since we know that the Bible is the very Word of God, doesn't it seem silly that any Christian should presume to know how to live and have wisdom to meet life's daily problems without being familiar with this rich and miraculous letter from God, the Bible?

Now let me give one of the strongest promises in the whole Bible. How wonderfully reassuring is this promise to the young Christian! It is given in Psalm 1:1-3.

"Blessed is the man that walketh not in the counsel of the ungodly, nor standeth in the way of sinners, nor sitteth in the seat of the scornful. But his delight is in the law of the Lord; and in his law doth he meditate day and night. And he shall be

like a tree planted by the rivers of water, that bringeth forth his fruit in his season; his leaf also shall not wither; and whatsoever he doeth shall prosper."

The blessed or fortunate or happy man described in this Psalm is one that does not walk in the counsel of the ungodly, does not stand in the way of sinners and never sits in the seat of the scornful. The young Christian should be careful, of course, to keep good company, to walk with Christian people and never to be influenced by bad companions.

But the positive condition here mentioned which is to bring immeasurable blessing is that the blessed man has his delight in the Bible and meditates in it day and night. "His delight is in the law of the Lord; and in his law doth he meditate day and night."

Now what shall be the daily and continuing results? This Christian, meditating day and night in the Bible, ". . . shall be like a tree planted by the rivers of water, that bringeth forth his fruit in his season; his leaf also shall not wither; and whatsoever he doeth shall prosper." In West Texas where there is not much moisture one does not find great forests of trees extending over the countryside. There may be small, brushy mesquite and other shrubs, but when one sees tall cottonwoods and other large trees growing in a thin line in some valley, he may know that that marks a creek, a watercourse. There great trees may rise tall and strong because their roots are down in the moist earth about a stream of water or a watercourse where at least in rainy times the water runs. So is the Bible-believing, Bible-reading and Bible-meditating Christian in this spiritually drought-stricken world! The leaf of his Christian joy and testimony never withers! He always brings forth fruit in his season. And everything he puts his hand to prospers! What a wonderful promise for a Christian!

And what is the river of water into which the Christian tree may push his roots and so always be sure of green leaves and of heavy fruitage? It is the Bible, the Word of God! And how does a Christian draw from this inexhaustible source of help and strength and happiness and fruit? He meditates on the Word of God day and night; he delights in the Word of God, absorbs it and lives by it!

A similar promise was given to Joshua when he succeeded Moses as commander of the Israelites and led them into the land of Canaan. The Lord promised to be with Joshua as He had been with Moses, never to forsake him nor fail him. Here are the words of encouragement and of command and promise given to Joshua:

"Only be thou strong and very courageous, that thou mayest observe to do according to all the law, which Moses my servant commanded thee: turn not from it to the right hand or to the left, that thou mayest prosper whithersoever thou goest. This book of the law shall not depart out of thy mouth; but thou shalt meditate therein day and night, that thou mayest observe to do according to all that is written therein: for then thou shalt make thy way prosperous, and then thou shalt have good success."—Josh. 1:7, 8.

Joshua was to be very careful to observe all of the law (the part of the Bible they then had). He was to turn not from it to the right or to the left in order "that thou mayest prosper whithersoever thou goest." The Book of the Law was not to depart out of Joshua's mouth. He was to read it, think of it, talk about it all the time, day and night. "But thou shalt meditate therein day and night, that thou mayest observe to do according to all that is written therein." And then comes the wonderful promise, just like that in Psalm 1:3, "For then thou shalt make thy way prosperous, and then thou shalt have good success."

You see, then, that a Christian does have a definite promise that if he fulfills certain conditions he shall have good success, he shall make his way prosperous. Or in the words of Psalm 1:3, the man who meditates day and night in the Word of God to follow it—"whatsoever he doeth shall prosper." Let me insist, then, that the young Christian start out from the very first to love the Bible, read the Bible, meditate over it, study it, and learn it and live by it! This is the greatest single secret of success that I can give, for it will lead the honest heart aright about all the other duties and privileges of a Christian.

2. Suggestions to the Young Christian About the Use of the Bible

I once helped a young man to find peace and joy again after he had backslidden and lost his joy and assurance. Then I said to him, "You must set out now to read the Word of God and use it."

He answered hastily: "But I do! I read a verse of the Bible almost every day!" A *verse* of the Bible! Do you think that young fellow really strained himself in reading the Bible, a whole verse of it nearly every day? That kind of reading of the Bible will not do. That is childishly inadequate. It is foolish to suppose that anyone who treats the Bible like that, reading only a verse a day, can have its full strength and blessing.

Let me make some simple suggestions that will, if followed, certainly lead to happiness, prosperity and success for every Christian.

First of all, set out to read the Bible. I mean read all of it. I mean read it like you read other books, to enjoy it, to learn it, to absorb it, to be educated by it. I do not mean just a careless and piecemeal reading, but a thorough reading of the Bible. I suggest that every Christian set out to read the Bible through at least within a year. And that is a very simple and easy thing to do if you mean business. It will only require that you read one chapter a day in the New Testament or the Psalms, and three chapters every day from the Old Testament, and you will read the entire Bible through in a little less than eleven months. It will require only a few minutes a day, it will help to develop a lifelong habit of orderliness and self-discipline. But best of all, it will acknowledge that God's Word is for you to know and it will certainly make it so God can help you to learn the Bible. You may have two bookmarks in your Bible, or three, and keep one in the Old Testament and one in the New (perhaps a third in the Psalms). Then every day read one full chapter in the New Testament or the Psalms and three chapters in the rest of the Old Testament besides the Psalms. Any Christian who has not read the whole Bible through, including all the genealogies, all the historical narratives, every line of it, ought to be ashamed of himself. He has never taken the Bible seriously. It is all God's Word and it ought to be read through, every line of it, frequently.

Let me urge, too, that one read through chapter after chapter in consecutive order, in any given book. The Psalms were divided up into separate chapters originally. They are not connected. It is about the same with the book of Proverbs. But in the rest of the Bible each book is a consecutive whole, and each ought to be read chapter after chapter through the whole book. When you start on Genesis, then keep going right on through Genesis until you finish it.

And let me suggest, too, that many times a whole book of the Bible ought to be read at one sitting. You might read the whole book of Genesis in one long evening or a Sunday afternoon and be wonderfully blessed by it, or likewise the books of Matthew or Luke or Acts. There are many shorter books of the Bible that can be read in fifteen or twenty minutes. You will gain much to take frequently a whole book at a time and read it through earnestly and carefully.

Then a Christian should set out to memorize a lot of the Bible. Mark the verses that are specially sweet and good which you plan to memorize. Some Christians try to do a little memory work every day, either to memorize one verse that is in the daily reading they have selected, or to refresh one's mind on an entire Psalm, for example. You will remember that David said, "Thy word have I hid in mine heart, that I might not sin against thee." A verse in the Bible that one has only read may not come up to warn him and reprove him and keep him from sin, but a verse that one has memorized and hid in the heart will surely do so. So be sure to memorize a lot of Scripture. I suggest that Christians should get my little booklet, *"What Must I Do to Be Saved?"* and memorize a lot of the verses used there in order to use them in personal soul winning. The Gospel of John has many verses on the plan of salvation, like John 1:12; John 3:14-18; John 3:36; John 5:24; John 6:37; John 6:40; John 6:47. But throughout the Bible there are many verses that one ought to know by heart to use in dealing with others.

Then every Christian ought to memorize some of the Psalms —Psalm 1, Psalm 23, Psalm 34, Psalm 103, Psalm 126, and many others. As you read over the Psalms, pick out some favorite Psalm which is not too long, learn it, say it over frequently and enjoy it. It will help to mold your life and make you happy and keep you near to God.

In the New Testament one certainly ought to memorize a good many Scriptures. Perhaps you should memorize John, chapter 14; or John, chapter 3; or Romans, chapter 8; or Romans, chapter 12; or I Corinthians, chapter 13. God will help you. But hide the Word of God in your heart, some of it every day if possible. How sweet it will be in the years to come and how blessed when it keeps you from sin and encourages you in prayer and gives you faith to call on God for greater things!

Reading the Bible is not enough, and even memorizing much of the Bible is not enough. The Christian is commanded to "meditate therein day and night." Have the Bible often in your mind. Ask God to help you think about it and enjoy it and delight in it. For it is in meditating on the Word of God that the Holy Spirit does His blessed work of developing the Christian graces in your heart and in giving you faith and in showing you what is wrong with your life, or how to have your prayers answered, or which course you should pursue. So take time to think about the Bible and meditate upon its teachings, its promises and its blessings.

And I need not say that any honest dealing with the Word of God will mean that the Christian is to live by what he finds therein. To read the Bible and not follow it would be hypocrisy. The new converts after the revival at Pentecost "continued stedfastly in the apostles' doctrine." And so you should make a holy vow, "By God's grace I will do what God makes clear in the Word of God. I will follow the Word of God in my life, as the Holy Spirit helps me to understand it and gives me grace to follow it." How precious is the life that is built upon the solid Word of God! How sure and believing will be your prayers, how confident your joy as you set out to follow the Word of God everywhere it leads! Oh, just to know and do the sweet will of God as revealed in the Bible! That surely is the highest way of life for a child of God and is the sure road to happiness, prosperity and success. Then the leaf of your Christian joy will not wither, you will bring forth fruit in season, according to the clear promise of God's Word, and whatsoever you do will prosper! What a rule for success is given us in Psalm 1:3!

IV. Prayer

The young converts and the older Christians alike, after Pentecost, "continued stedfastly in the apostles' doctrine and fellowship, and in breaking of bread, AND IN PRAYERS," we are told (Acts 2:42). These Christians had certain plans that they followed regularly. Their lives had a definite pattern. The Word of God was first with them. They kept on following the apostles' doctrine. They kept up Christian fellowship and love and unity. They regularly broke bread, remembering, in the Lord's Supper, the death of Christ and their salvation by His blood, through faith. And they continually maintained their prayer life.

1. The Importance of the Christian's Prayer Life

In the Bible God talks to the Christian. In prayer the Christian talks to God. And if one really obeys the Bible he will be drawn more and more to prayer about everything. Prayer is the great resource of the Christian.

The young convert had as well remember at the very start that all around him there are evils which he cannot control nor overcome alone. Satan, who has lost the battle about keeping the soul away from God and salvation, still sets out to tempt the Christian, to cause him doubts and fears and troubles and to ruin his happiness and ruin his influence. The Christian who is to overcome Satan and live a victorious, happy life must be not far away from God at any time, but able to go to his Heavenly Father for strength and wisdom.

The work that a Christian is supposed to do will require miracles. For example, to save a soul is beyond any human strength or wisdom. It takes a miracle of God to make a black heart white, to make a child of God out of a child of the Devil. It takes a miracle, the working of the Holy Spirit of God, to save a soul. And any Christian who wants to win souls must, in the nature of the case, be in touch with God so he can call for God's power and God's wisdom and receive them.

A Christian ought to learn to live by prayer every day. The Christian should depend not on his labor for his daily bread, but on God. Perhaps he will labor all the more because he is a Christian, and do better work; yet still the Christian's dependence should be upon his Heavenly Father. He should be able to pray for daily bread and get daily bread. He should be able to pray through any problem of sickness, or problems of a job, or marriage, or friends, or Christian service, or temptation. You see, "Prayer is the Christian's vital breath," and no one can live a good Christian life without being constantly in touch with God and on praying ground.

I am not surprised, therefore, that the new converts at Pentecost continued steadfastly in prayer, as we are told in the Bible that they did. And everywhere you find Christians who continue steadfastly in prayer, along with prayerful meditation and the following of the Word of God, you will have wonderfully victorious and happy Christians.

It is clear, then, that every Christian ought to pray every day. In fact, in the Lord's Prayer, given as our example, the Lord Jesus told us to pray, "Give us this day our daily bread." So we know that one should pray somewhat after that fashion every day.

2. Regular Times for Prayer

And prayer is so important that it should have some regular time, a time that would have priority, a time that would be remembered and honored daily. We think that eating is important enough to set apart regular times each day for eating. Sleeping is regarded as important enough that we set aside certain hours for sleeping. A job is counted important enough that a man is supposed to reserve certain hours, arriving on time and working through the full shift of his day. Then you may be sure, dear Christian, that you would be wise to religiously set aside certain times and seasons to pray and seek God's face every day.

Let me suggest also that the early morning is one of the very best times to pray. "Those that seek me early shall find me," the Lord has said in His Word (Prov. 8:17). Then we have the blessed example of our Saviour who prayed early in the morning. "And in the morning, rising up a great while before day, he went out, and departed into a solitary place, and there prayed" (Mark 1:35). Multitudes of Christians have found that to meet God early in the day and take time for prayer would make the whole day sweeter and would prevent many a heartache and many a careless sin.

3. Praying Without Ceasing

It is true that to have regular times of prayer is good. I hope the new convert will have a "morning watch" with the Lord regularly, before breakfast, if possible, or immediately after breakfast. But that is not enough praying for a Christian. For the Bible has many clear commands, teaching that one should pray continually and that prayer should get to be second nature to the Christian. One should become so conscious of the Lord's presence that he will be crying out to God about certain burdensome matters or about the salvation of souls or be in sweet communion with God about the Lord's work or the Christians' needs, all the time. Notice these clear commands of Scripture:

"And he spake a parable unto them to this end, that men ought always to pray, and not to faint."—Luke 18:1.

". . . continuing instant in prayer."—Rom. 12:12.

"Continue in prayer, and watch in the same with thanksgiving."—Col. 4:2.

"Praying always with all prayer and supplication in the Spirit, and watching thereunto with all perseverance and supplication for all saints."—Eph. 6:18.

"Pray without ceasing."—I Thess. 5:17.

Here we have five clear statements that a Christian ought to pray all the time! So when a Christian comes to prayer and says, "Heavenly Father, we come into Thy presence this morning . . ." it may mean that the Christian is wrong in not having remained in the Lord's presence, consciously, all the time!

Nothing can be sweeter than to pray all the time. A Christian ought to get to be conscious of the dear Lord's presence so that everything that is done is done as in the presence of God, and thus one can pour out his burdened heart to God about everything, and may do it continuously.

Let me earnestly urge, then, upon the Christian who wants to be happy, who wants to be blessed, who wants to be prospered, that he pray all the time and make prayer the biggest thing in his life.

4. Some Suggestions About How to Pray

Let me suggest some very simple rules that may be helpful to those who want to learn to pray as they ought.

First, remember that you are coming to your loving Heavenly Father. I would try to learn never to speak *about* God in the third Person while in prayer. Talk *to* God, not *about* God. You do not need to say, "We want God to be with us." You should be able to say, "Dear Heavenly Father, please be with me!" As that truth becomes real to you, that God is now your Father and that you are now His child, that you are His heir, that God who has given His Son for you will give anything else that is good for you, then surely it will be easier and sweeter to pray. Oh, come boldly! You are speaking to your own dear Father in Heaven.

Second, every Christian should remember that Christ, the same dear Lord Jesus who died on the cross to save us, is now at the right hand of the Father in Heaven, and there He intercedes for us. He is our Advocate, our Mediator, our Intercessor. He stands as our High Priest before God so that we know He takes our part, and that ought to give us great comfort as we come to pray.

In Hebrews 4:14-16 the Lord urges us to be bold when we come to pray, since we know that the Lord Jesus is there to take our part and He understands our weaknesses and has made atonement for our sins. Listen to that blessed promise and make it yours, young Christian:

"Seeing then that we have a great high priest, that is passed into the heavens, Jesus the Son of God, let us hold fast our profession. For we have not an high priest which cannot be touched with the feeling of our infirmities; but was in all points tempted like as we are, yet without sin. Let us therefore come boldly unto the throne of grace, that we may obtain mercy, and find grace to help in time of need."—Heb. 4:14-16.

Remember that there is mercy, wonderful mercy for you, to cover all your sins! Remember that the Lord Jesus knows about your infirmities and can be touched in His dear heart with the feeling of your need, your trouble, and your weakness. Though He Himself never sinned, yet He was tempted as much as you are and like you are about anything.

"Let us therefore come boldly to the throne of grace," we are entreated. There you may find mercy and you may find grace to help in any time of need.

Third, remember that a Christian has a right to take every burden he has to the Lord. We have this blessed exhortation, "Casting all your care upon him; for he careth for you" (I Pet. 5:7). We have the blessed invitation, "Cast thy burden upon the Lord, and he shall sustain thee" (Ps. 55:22). Do not think any burden too heavy and do not think any problem too trivial to bring to God. He wants to bear your burden. He wants you to trust Him about all your problems. Come, dear Christian, to your Heavenly Father and so have your burden lifted and be happy.

In Philippians 4:6 we are commanded, "Be careful for nothing; but in every thing by prayer and supplication with thanksgiving let your requests be made known unto God." "In every thing"! You have a right to make your request to God about everything. Ask everything your heart desires; for Mark 11:24 says, "Therefore I say unto you, What things soever ye desire, when ye pray, believe that ye receive them, and ye shall have them." Pray for whatever would delight your heart, for He has said, "Delight thyself also in the Lord; and he shall give thee the desires of thine heart" (Ps. 37:4).

If you learn to take everything to God in prayer and stay there and pray through, then you will find that the blessed promise is true, as Philippians 4:7 says, "And the peace of God, which passeth all understanding, shall keep your hearts and minds through Christ Jesus."

> **What a Friend we have in Jesus,**
> **All our sins and griefs to bear!**
> **What a privilege to carry**
> **EVERYTHING to God in prayer!**
>
> **Oh what peace we often forfeit,**
> **Oh what needless pain we bear,**
> **All because we do not carry**
> **EVERYTHING to God in prayer!**

Fourth, I would encourage you, dear Christian, to claim God's promises when you pray. You should learn them, mark them in your Bible, review them again and again—such promises as Jeremiah 33:3, as John 14:13, 14, as Mark 11:24, as Mark 9:23. Learn the blessed promise of James 4:2, of Matthew 18:19 and Matthew 21:22. God has many, many promises and He wants you to know them, believe them and claim them. And when you go to pray you will be perfectly safe to quote any of these promises to God. For when you meet God's promise you can certainly expect Him to meet His own part as He has said He would. Remember that praying according to the will of God means praying according to the Scriptures. And how successful that praying is, praying according to the Scriptures!

Fifth, be as definite as possible. Why not keep a little record book of specially urgent prayers? Put down the date when you made the request of God, and keep on praying; then put down the date when the answer comes right beside or under the request. Now and then you would do well to weigh the desires of your heart until you can write down on paper briefly a list of the things that you honestly come to God in petition for. That will help to make your prayers definite. Do not keep the same list every day but amend it and change it as your heart's desire grows or is molded by the leading of the Holy Spirit, or as some answers come and other burdens arise which need prayer.

Sixth, let me urge upon you to pray through about your burdens. That means that you are not to quit easily, not to be discouraged, but to keep on praying. That is in the very nature of faith itself, and it is very precious to God. Read what Jesus said about how a poor widow prevailed with an unjust judge (Luke 18:1-8). Read the story of the Syrophenician woman, and how by her persistence she won the answer to her prayer and greatly pleased the dear Lord Jesus (Matt. 15:21-28). Read the story of the importunate friend who came knocking at a neighbor's house for bread and by his importunity won it (Luke 11:5-10). That shows how Christians should beg God and plead with God and wait on God to receive bread for sinners, soul-winning power. So do not give up easily, but keep on praying. If God shows you that your prayer is wrong, then ask Him to help you change it. But as long as you do not have clear evidence from the Word of God or by the Holy Spirit's leading that your prayer is wrong, then keep on praying. Ask God to change your desires if your prayer is wrong, or to give you faith to expect the blessing you seek if your prayer is right. Keep on praying!

Seventh, when you come to pray, be sure to confess your sins. Any honest child of God who stays near the Lord will find his heart grows very sensitive and tender about his sins. Oh, these hateful sins that creep into our lives! They grieve God; they will grieve us, too, if we stay very near Him and His Word. So take time to confess your shortcomings, your failures; take time to confess everything you know grieves God in your life. Do that every day. You will find that as you confess your sins, God forgives them and takes them out of the way and you will have a sweet assurance that He does not hold them against you. And more than that, by confessing your sin, you will find that God will give you more power to overcome sin and to live victoriously.

And, last, let me urge that when you come to pray you must be sure that you forgive others. For Jesus said we are to pray like this: "And forgive us our sins; for we also forgive every one that is indebted to us" (Luke 11:4). Jesus also plainly said, "For if ye forgive men their trespasses, your heavenly Father will also forgive you: but if ye forgive not men their trespasses, neither will your Father forgive your trespasses." Any Christian who does not forgive others finds that day by day differences pile up between him and God. He will find his fellowship with God broken. He will find the sweet Spirit of God is grieved and does not seem to lead as clearly as before. So if a Christian wants the daily cleansing, the daily renewal of fellowship, the daily taking of sin out of the way between him and God, he must forgive others when he comes to pray.

How merciful God has been to forgive us our sins and save us! And if we will but forgive others, how merciful He will be daily to cleanse us anew of our daily sins, though we are already saved. Those who would not grieve the Holy Spirit of God must put away bitterness and wrath and anger and clamor and evil-speaking and all malice, and remember, "Be ye kind one to another, tenderhearted, forgiving one another, even as God for Christ's sake hath forgiven you" (Eph. 4:30-32).

Prayer is one of the greatest steps to a happy, prosperous, successful Christian life. Dear Christian, take time, take time, take time to keep up your prayer life and keep things settled up with God all the time. Confess to Him all your sins, take to Him all your burdens, thank Him for all your blessings!

V. Giving

Of the happy Christians at Jerusalem after Pentecost we are told that ". . . all that believed were together, and had all things common; and sold their possessions and goods, and parted them to all men, as every man had need" (Acts 2:44, 45).

What a remarkable effect it had on these Jewish people when they were converted to Christ, when they were assured of their salvation by the Word of God, when they were baptized, joined the local assembly, set out to follow steadfastly the apostles' doctrine, and continued in prayer! They were happy Christians, victorious Christians. And they seemed to have committed all their possessions to God and stopped worrying about whether they would have food and clothes and housing for the future. What a wonderful example of happy trust, of Christian fellowship and mutual care one for another!

And one of the important principles on which a new convert must live, if he is to be a really happy, prosperous and victorious Christian, is that he must put God first on the money question. He must learn that everything he is and everything he has belongs to God. He must set out to please God by the way he handles all his possessions, and symbolize this by the way he gives to the Lord's cause.

There are a number of lessons that a young Christian can learn from these Christians at Jerusalem who were so wonderfully filled with the Spirit and lived such victorious lives after they were saved.

1. These Christians Were Not Communists; the Bible Does Not Teach Communism

There are many striking differences between these New Testament Christians at Jerusalem, about whom we are told, and communists. These people were devoted Christians, believers in Christ as their own Saviour and committed to follow Him until death. Communists are atheists, Christ-rejectors and Christ-haters. Another difference is that here there was no dictatorship. Here there was no seizing of property, no compulsion whatever. In communism it is just the opposite. Stalin and Lenin were bank robbers. The Russian Soviet "Republics" were founded on murder, assassination, confiscation, blood purges, and everything contrary to law and morality and Christianity. No well-informed person, then, could give this Scripture as a model teaching communism.

As we read the story here and follow on through the book of Acts we find that there was a great emergency at Jerusalem. Thousands were saved. Of course there was great opposition.

Many lost their means of livelihood. And these new Christians, fired with holy zeal for God and with earnest love for each other, gladly gave up their possessions and divided up their means to other Christians who were in need. It was an emergency and not an ordinary occasion. And the choice was entirely voluntary when anyone gave up his property. It must be remembered that the Bible nowhere commands people to give up all their property to the church or to the support of other Christians, and certainly it does not command one to give up property to the state. In fact, in this same church at Jerusalem when Ananias later sold his property and pretended to give all his means to God but withheld some, Peter said to him: "Why hast Satan filled thine heart to lie to the Holy Ghost, and to keep back part of the price of the land: Whiles it remained, was it not thine own? and after it was sold, was it not in thine own power? why hast thou conceived this thing in thine heart? thou hast not lied unto men, but unto God" (Acts 5:3, 4).

Ananias had a right to keep his property. He had not been commanded to sell it. When he sold it he had a right to keep the money. He had not been commanded to give it. His sin was in *pretending* to give everything when he did not; he lied instead of telling the truth. He sought honor and gave to please men and pretended to give what he did not give. His insincerity, his falsehood before God was the terrible sin. But Peter told him plainly that he could have kept the property or could have kept all the money, and it would not have been forbidden.

Later there was such a terrible famine and depression and want in Jerusalem among the Christians that Paul went to many churches collecting money and bringing it back to these saints at Jerusalem for the support of the poor (Acts 11:27-30). The great poverty at Jerusalem following Pentecost required heroic measures, and these earnest Christians gladly gave all for the Lord and for other Christians. However, even then the division of food caused distress and criticism (Acts 6:1), and the plan of everyone giving all of his property was abandoned at Jerusalem later and was never taken up in the other places where Christian churches were formed. But everywhere in the New Testament young Christians were taught to put God first in their money problems, and that was much of the secret of their happiness and prosperity and of God's wonderful care and provision for them. Oh, young Christian, you can learn from these Jerusalem converts!

2. Spirit-Filled Christianity Makes a Revolutionary Change in Attitude About Property!

Jews are thrifty people. Everybody ought to be thrifty. Jews on the average lay up carefully for their old age, they get their children well started in business, they often take care of their own poor. This is an admirable quality. But wonderfully, these Jewish converts at Jerusalem had an entire change of attitude. They did not worry about tomorrow. They simply trusted the Lord about everything. They gave their property into His hands.

And that is exactly what the Lord Jesus, in Matthew 6:25-34, teaches us to do. In that remarkable passage Jesus said:

"Therefore I say unto you, Take no thought for your life, what ye shall eat, or what ye shall drink; nor yet for your body, what ye shall put on. Is not the life more than meat, and the body than raiment? Behold the fowls of the air: for they sow not, neither do they reap, nor gather into barns; yet your heavenly Father feedeth them. Are ye not much better than they? Which of you by taking thought can add one cubit unto his stature? And why take ye thought for raiment? Consider the lilies of the field, how they grow; they toil not, neither do they spin: And yet I say unto you, That even Solomon in all his glory was not arrayed like one of these. Wherefore, if God so clothe the grass of the field, which to day is, and to morrow is cast into the oven, shall he not much more clothe you, O ye of little faith? Therefore take no thought, saying, What shall we eat? or, What shall we drink? or, Wherewithal shall we be clothed? (For after all these things do the Gentiles seek:) for your heavenly Father knoweth that ye have need of all these things. But seek ye first the kingdom of God, and his righteousness; and all these things shall be added unto you. Take therefore no thought for the morrow: for the morrow shall take

thought for the things of itself. Sufficient unto the day is the evil thereof."

A Christian is not to worry about his food. If he puts God first, the Lord will provide. He is not to worry about clothes. God feeds the fowls of the air and God clothes the lilies of the field. The God who takes care of His flowers and birds will take care of a Christian who trusts Him. Those who fret about the future and try to save lots of money and lay by in store for the future are of little faith, Jesus said. The Gentiles, heathen, unconverted people, are burdened about laying up money, having property, saving for the future. But a Christian has a better rule than that. Jesus said, "But seek ye first the kingdom of God, and his righteousness; and all these things shall be added unto you" (vs. 33).

That is the instruction of the Lord Jesus about property. And that is the way these New Testament Christians at Jerusalem felt. What a joy to be done with worry and fret about financial matters, just to labor and give and trust! I am sure they worked as hard as before, or harder. A good Christian makes a better workman than one who is not a good Christian. A good Christian will do more work in a day, will please his master better, will look after the welfare of his employer more than one who is not saved. The right kind of brotherly love will make Christians into good workmen and good businessmen. Thank God for the freedom from care and worry which comes when a Christian turns his financial affairs over to the Lord and depends upon God to provide, depends upon God to give him food and clothes and to care for his family so he is not afraid to give liberally to God's cause.

Is it not a shame that many a Christian is saved but has not had his attitude about money converted?

It is said that a number of new converts were being baptized once in a river, and a friend called to one man, saying, "Hey, Bill! You still have your billfold in your pocket. Do you want me to keep it for you?"

"No!" he replied. "I want that baptized, too!"

Of course it would do no good to baptize a pocketbook,

literally, but certainly when a Christian gives himself to God, lays himself wholly on the altar, sets out to count himself dead to the old life and raised up to live a new life in Christ, it will mean that he will have an entirely different attitude toward money. Every good Christian who sets out to live by the blessed principles of success given here will have a Christian attitude toward his property.

3. Should a Christian Tithe?

Some people say that tithing is an Old Testament law, perhaps that it is ceremonial law, and that it was for Jews only under the ceremonial law. But in that they are mistaken. It is true that it is Leviticus 27:30 that says, "And all the tithe . . . is the Lord's: it is holy unto the Lord." But does it seem likely that a Jew under ceremonial law would need to acknowledge that he belonged to God and the tithe belonged to God, and a Christian, under grace, would feel no obligation to please God about his possessions? How strange that God should not claim the tithe of the Christian's income when He claimed the tithe of the Jews under the Mosaic ceremonial law! Actually, the tithe did not begin with the ceremonial law. Abraham gave tithes to Melchizedek (Gen. 14:17-20) long years before Moses was born and before the law was given at Mount Sinai; before there was a Hebrew nation. So the tithe did not originate with the Mosaic law. Hebrews, chapter 7, in the New Testament, tells us that Abraham in giving tithes to Melchizedek was a type of Christians giving tithes to Christ. Melchizedek was a type of Christ, and so, runs the divinely-given argument, the new covenant with Christ, represented by Abraham giving tithes to Melchizedek, is far superior to the old covenant wherein Jews under the law gave tithes to the Aaronic priesthood. Certainly Christians, then, would do well to follow this divinely-approved pattern.

In fact, the Lord Jesus spoke to the Pharisees in Matthew 23:23 and said, "Woe unto you, scribes and Pharisees, hypocrites! for ye pay tithe of mint and anise and cummin, and have omitted the weightier matters of the law, judgment, mercy, and faith: these ought ye to have done, and not to leave the other undone." The dear Lord Jesus called the Pharisees "hypocrites," not because they paid tithe even of the mint and anise and cummin, the little spices that grew in their gardens. No, He said, "These ought ye to have done"! They ought to have tithed. That was right. But He called them hypocrites because they left undone the weightier matters of the law, judgment, mercy and faith.

When Jesus said, "These ought ye to have done" about tithing, a Christian of course finds it easy to do.

In I Corinthians 16:2 we find proportionate giving taught in the New Testament. There Paul said, "Upon the first day of the week let every one of you lay by him in store, as God hath prospered him, that there be no gatherings when I come." They should lay by in store, each one, in proportion "as God hath prospered him." Now what percentage, what proportion do you think these New Testament Christians were expected to take out and lay by for the Lord? Certainly not less than the tenth. The inference is, it seems to me, that these people already knew what they should do, and they were encouraged to do it weekly. They should take out a proportionate part, and I have no doubt that they all understood it should be not less than a tenth. You see, all the preaching of the apostles and New Testament preachers was done out of the Old Testament. The New Testament was not yet written. People were familiar with the Old Testament before the New Testament was collected, and of course they would know what proportion of giving was customary.

It is an Old Testament Scripture that says, "Bring ye all the tithes into the storehouse . . ." (Mal. 3:10). But do you think God would ask less love, less faith and less cheerful giving from a New Testament Christian than from a Jew under the law? That does not seem reasonable.

If there is any difference in the teaching of the Old Testament and the New Testament on this question, the difference is that the New Testament always stresses that not only one tenth but the other nine-tenths, also, belong to God! I should bring tithes and offerings to the Lord, but I should remember that all the rest I have belongs to God just the same. Not a dime should be spent for anything except as we believe it will please God.

Why do you suppose God set a definite percentage, ten percent, as the minimum of giving? I think that God intended this to be something like rent. If you live in a man's house and pay him rent, that is an acknowledgment of his ownership and that he has a right to demand possession of the house any time he is not pleased with you as a renter. When you borrow a man's money you pay him interest on the money. That is a token that the money belongs to him, must be paid back to him and that he must be given a strict accounting of the money that is borrowed. So when a Christian gives God tithes and offerings he simply means, "Dear Lord, I recognize that all I have belongs to You. When I bring You a part of what You have given me, it simply acknowledges that all belongs to You and I'll try to use it all for Your glory. This is a token of rent, or a token of interest on Your money, or an acknowledgment of Your ownership of me and all that I have!"

Should a Christian be content with giving exactly a tithe? By no means! Remember that in Malachi 3:8, 9 the Lord said to Israel: "Will a man rob God? Yet ye have robbed me. But ye say, Wherein have we robbed thee? In tithes and offerings. Ye are cursed with a curse: for ye have robbed me, even this whole nation." Those who did not bring God the tithe robbed Him; and those who did not bring offerings also robbed God. You see, God has a right to more than the exact one-tenth.

Tithing should not be a matter of bondage. It is a matter of grace and not law. That means that a Christian ought to give cheerfully and lovingly, more and more as God provides and makes it possible and as the urgency of the Lord's business and of getting out the Gospel is felt in his heart.

I remember that I once carefully sought to give God exactly one penny out of every dime, one dime out of every dollar; and I kept books on it. But one day I felt ashamed that I was so strictly watching God as if I feared He would get more than He deserved. I threw away my account book and adopted the simpler plan of taking out the Lord's part once every week, or whenever the money came in. And my dear wife and I set out to give God at that time about twenty percent, or more, and since that time He has helped us to be very, very happy in our giving. It has never been a burden, but a joy, and sometimes we gave literally all that came in beside the barest necessities.

4. Here Is a Christian's Promise of Material Prosperity and Daily Provision

In this chapter I have been trying to lay on your heart ways to be happy Christians, principles upon which you will be soul winners, will have your prayers answered, will have daily victory over sin and will be spiritually prosperous. I know there is great spiritual prosperity, great spiritual growth in grace in the matter of regular, liberal, conscientious and faithful giving to God's cause. But on this matter a Christian has a promise of more than spiritual blessing; he is promised material blessings, too.

Somebody says, "One should not give in order to be prospered." Well, perhaps that is not the highest motive for giving. One should love the Lord and be glad to do whatever He says. But the Bible gives this as a motive for giving. Again and again the Bible makes the plain offer and promise that one who gives according to the plan outlined in the Bible will find his needs met and he will be blessed.

Consider the following great promise:

"Bring ye all the tithes into the storehouse, that there may be meat in mine house, and prove me now herewith, saith the Lord of hosts, if I will not open you the windows of heaven, and pour you out a blessing, that there shall not be room enough to receive it."—Mal. 3:10.

This blessed promise is that material prosperity would come because Jews brought the tithes into the storehouse. It is material prosperity God speaks about here, for the next verse plainly says, "I will rebuke the devourer for your sakes, and he shall not destroy the fruits of your ground; neither shall your vine cast her fruit before the time in the field, saith the Lord of hosts" (Mal. 3:11).

The New Testament equally has explicit promises. In Luke 6:38 Jesus said:

"Give, and it shall be given unto you; good measure, pressed down, and shaken together, and running over, shall men give into your bosom. For with the same measure that ye mete withal it shall be measured to you again."

One cannot avoid the plain meaning here. According to the way a Christian gives, it is given to him. God sees that men will supply his needs as he gives. The way one receives is in proportion to the way one gives. Every Christian can trust the word of the Lord Jesus Christ about that.

Again, in II Corinthians 9:6-8, Paul the apostle by divine inspiration writes to the church at Corinth:

"But this I say, He which soweth sparingly shall reap also sparingly; and he which soweth bountifully shall reap also bountifully. Every man according as he purposeth in his heart, so let him give: not grudgingly, or of necessity: for God loveth a cheerful giver. And God is able to make all grace abound toward you; that ye, always having all sufficiency in all things, may abound to every good work."

Do you see the argument that God gives us here? The chapter starts with an explanation that Paul is talking about the offering for the saints at Jerusalem. And now he is sending others to collect the bounty of these saints at Corinth, and says, "He which soweth sparingly shall reap also sparingly; and he which soweth bountifully shall reap also bountifully." When one gives to God he is sowing. He will reap according to the way he sows! If he gives stingily, or sparingly, he will be prospered less. So is the clear statement of the Word of God.

To be sure, God wants the giving to come from the heart. He says, "Every man according as he purposeth in his heart, so let him give; not grudgingly, or of necessity: for God loveth a cheerful giver."

Oh, I would like to be so cheerful, so trusting, so joyful in my giving that the dear Lord would love me more because of my cheery and happy giving!

And verse 8 tells us frankly that God is able to supply all sufficiency in all things, and we ought to give with that in mind.

Oh, how many times I have proved for myself that when I put God first in money matters He supplies my needs. I wish I could tell you a hundred incidents to prove from my daily experiences that God cares for those who trust Him and put Him first in their giving.

I remember that in 1926 I gave up the pastorate of the First Baptist Church of Shamrock, Texas. I felt clearly led of God to go into the work of an evangelist. We had a new church building, a new pastor's home; the church had doubled in membership in two years. The Lord had wonderfully blessed and the people pleaded with me to remain. But I felt the urge and burning in my soul to go out into wider fields of soul winning in revival campaigns. So Mrs. Rice and I talked and prayed about the matter. We decided to give up our $10,000 life insurance which I had taken out with the government when I was a soldier in World War I. We decided not to have a regular salary from that time forth. I do not think insurance is necessarily wrong. Each one will have to decide that for himself. God simply showed me that if I would trust Him wholly on this matter He would provide. I do not think that for a pastor to have a salary is wrong, although when I was pastor later I did not take a salary. God simply showed me that the more I would trust Him on this matter, the better He would take care of me. So we went out by faith. I had a holy covenant with God. "Lord," I said, "I'll take care of Your business, and You take care of mine!" Oh, how well God has cared for my business! I only wish I had cared for His business one-half as well!

Raising a big family of girls, paying for music lessons, paying college tuition, paying thousands of dollars for radio time, paying for the publication of books and pamphlets by the million, paying the deficit on the weekly paper, THE SWORD OF THE LORD, year after year—how well I had a chance to try God out and to see if He would give as I gave, if when I sowed bountifully I would reap bountifully. And I found it works!

Dear Christian, you cannot beat God at giving! The more you give from an honest, loving, trusting heart, the more God will see that you are prospered even in daily provision and in financial matters. So this is certainly an important principle upon which a Christian should build his life if he hopes to be a happy Christian, a successful Christian; if he hopes to have his prayers answered and to have his daily needs provided. God's people do not need to be helpless nor left orphans and unprovided for. If you seek first the kingdom of God and sow bountifully, you will reap bountifully even in material things. God's promises say so and millions of Christians who have tried it prove the point!

5. Some Suggestions About How to Give

I believe that the following suggestions will help a young Christian to get started giving in a way that will please God.

First, it seems to me wisest for most Christians simply to take out the Lord's part of the income each week. That is the plan given in I Corinthians 16:2, "Upon the first day of the week let every one of you lay by him in store, as God hath prospered. . . ."

For those who get paid by the day or by the week, certainly this is the ideal plan. You may take the tithe and any freewill offerings you feel led to give out of the income and put it in a safe place to be given later, for the Lord. Some people like to give the full tithe every Sunday, and that is all right, though the Scripture does not command that the money all be given at one time. The command is simply to "lay by him in store." One should put the Lord's money in a separate place. It may be put in a separate bank account, or put in a safe place about the home, or it may all be given at once; but the Lord's part should be taken out once a week where the income is daily or weekly.

Let me earnestly suggest that every Christian take the Lord's part out *first*. God should be first in our plans. In the Old Testament ceremonial law God required that "the firstling of the flock" should be given to Him. The Prophet Elijah, in a terrible time of drought, was fed by a widow of Zarephath. She had only a handful of meal in a barrel and a little oil in a cruse, and was gathering two sticks to make a fire and cook her last little pitiful cake before she and her son died. But Elijah said, "Fear not; go and do as thou hast said: but make me thereof a little cake first, and bring it unto me, and after make for thee and for thy son. For thus saith the Lord God of Israel, The barrel of meal shall not waste, neither shall the cruse of oil fail, until the day that the Lord sendeth rain upon the earth" (I Kings 17:13, 14). And as certain as God's promise, so certain was His doing. The widow made first a little cake for the prophet of God and God then increased the meal and oil enough to feed her and her son until the famine was over! Oh, take the Lord's part out first as a token of your full surrender and your faith because you really want to put God first in your heart.

Do you run a business? Do you own a store or laundry or farm or manufacturing plant? If you take for yourself a regular salary, you would simply tithe the salary. Otherwise you would not tithe the total gross income, but only the income after supplies were paid for, after the rent was paid and other expenses necessary in running the business. Of course I do not mean you should deduct your own personal expenses or your family's expenses. One who owns a grocery store, for example, would first pay for the groceries bought and pay rent on the building, taxes and upkeep on the building, and pay his store help, heat, lights and gas; and then out of the money left, net profit, he would give tithes and offerings.

Perhaps one on a farm would wonder whether to tithe all the increase on the farm or to take out the money spent for actual farming operations, the money for seed, the feed bought for cattle, etc. It seems to have been the custom among the Jews to give tithes of all the increase of the land. If one desires to first pay for the seed used, the feed bought, machinery bought, and hired labor, that would be all right; but in that case one would need to charge himself so much rent, charge himself for garden vegetables, eggs, pork and other provisions which were supplied him by the farm. It is much simpler for a farmer living on a home farm to simply give a tenth of all the crops, a tenth of the cattle, a tenth of the chickens, eggs, etc. What he might spend for seed or feed or machinery would thus be overbalanced by his own free rent and for much of the food he would get from the farm on which he would not otherwise pay a tithe.

Shall a Christian give all his tithes through his local church treasury and allow the church board to decide how the money shall be spent? Usually not, I should think. Remember that the Scripture says, "All the tithe . . . is the Lord's." It does not say, "All the tithe is the church's." The tithe does not belong to the pastor, does not belong to the church, does not belong to the denominational headquarters. The tithe belongs to the Lord. And you are the Lord's steward, which means that when God puts money in your hand, you must account to God for the way it is used and where your gifts go.

Usually it is certainly right for a Christian to give money through the local church. Every church member properly feels a burden to help support his own pastor, to help take care of the house of God, to support the missionary program of the church. If one is a member of a church where he cannot honestly put his money, it is doubtful whether he ought to put his influence and his presence there. I think every Christian who is in a Bible-believing church should have a regular, definite part in the church's financial program and should do it cheerfully and, as far as possible, in ways pleasing to the church leaders.

However, it is clearly implied in the Bible that the Christian himself must decide where he gives and how he gives, "every man as he purposeth in his heart." For example, in I Corinthians 16:2 Paul expressly commanded that each Christian should lay aside a proportionate part of his income and keep it until Paul should come to take it with him for the poor saints at Jerusalem. In that case there is no evidence that the money necessarily would go through the church treasury at all. The individual Christian would save up the money and turn it over to Paul. Possibly they all brought it and put it in a common fund, and the church may have turned it all over to Paul together. That we do not know. But the Scripture mentioned certainly does not teach that all the money has to go through the local church treasury.

Malachi 3:10 says, "Bring ye all the tithes into the storehouse, that there may be meat in mine house. . . ." The storehouse there mentioned was the Temple in the Old Testament. The work to be supported for the whole nation was the support of the priests and Levites at the Temple. In that case the tithes were all to be brought to Jerusalem. But the New Testament does not teach that the church treasury takes the place of the Temple treasury.

Many of the finest soul-winning works go on without the official backing of denominations. Great radio preachers carry on their work at tremendous cost, supported by Bible-believing Christians. I believe God has blessed these works and wants them to continue. Very little of the offerings to support these works come in through church treasuries. The great faith missions receive their support largely outside of denominational headquarters and local church treasuries, as I understand it. I believe God wants these works to continue and wants them supported by people who give in Jesus' name.

And that leads me to say that giving without praying and without earnest consideration could not please God. Ask the Lord what He wants you to do with His money! Pray definitely that God will use it to win souls. Pray that He will help you to give more for His glory!

And of course the tithe must be used to honor Jesus Christ. It is His money, not yours. It must be used to His glory. And we know the thing closest to His heart is the saving of sinners. So set out to be a happy, prosperous Christian by putting God first in all your possessions. And how wonderfully He will prove Himself to you!

VI. Soul Winning

We sometimes speak of "the revival at Pentecost." Actually, the revival did not end at Pentecost. We are told, "And they, continuing daily with one accord in the temple, and breaking bread from house to house, did eat their meat with gladness and singleness of heart, Praising God, and having favour with all the people. And the Lord added to the church daily such as should be saved" (Acts 2:46, 47).

People were added to the church daily! And I think this means the local congregation.

1. How New Testament Christians Won Souls

Some churches these days receive new converts into the church once a year, at Easter time. Other churches have a membership committee that meets once a month, and once a month new converts, if any, may be received into the church. When I was a pastor we regularly received members each week and it was a very, very unusual Sunday in which there were not converts coming for baptism on profession of their faith in Christ and for membership in the church. But this wonderful revival church in Jerusalem received members every day! "The Lord added to the church daily such as should be saved."

Ah, there is the purpose of a church! These people knew what God intended churches for! The Lord Jesus left us here to win souls. He has given to us the Great Commission to take the Gospel to every creature. He told the apostles that they should go out and make disciples of all nations and that the new converts, when baptized, should be taught "to observe all things whatsoever I have commanded you" (Matt. 28:20). Every convert at Jerusalem had the instructions to carry out the Great Commission just as Jesus gave it to the apostles. So these wonderfully happy, Spirit-filled Christians kept on winning souls and daily God added to the church the new converts. That is the seventh great principle of happiness and prosperity for a Christian life: soul winning.

And these converts kept it up! In Acts 4:4 we are told, "Howbeit many of them which heard the word believed; and the number of the men was about five thousand." There were five thousand men in that church, besides the women and children! And Acts 4:33 says, "And with great power gave the apostles witness of the resurrection of the Lord Jesus: and great grace was upon them all." Acts 5:14 says, "And believers were the more added to the Lord, multitudes both of men and women." Acts 5:42 tells us, "And daily in the temple, and in every house, they ceased not to teach and preach Jesus Christ."

Oh, for Christians who carry on the work of a revival like that, daily winning souls, carrying on the blessing to everybody about them! That is what new converts, as well as older Christians, are supposed to do.

2. Soul Winning, the Dearest Thing on Earth to Jesus!

I wonder, dear Christian, do you remember the main thing on the heart of Jesus Christ? Do you not know how He gave Himself to leave Heaven, to live among the poorest of people, and then to be abused and hated? Do you remember that Jesus suffered the torments in Gethsemane, sweat the bloody sweat in an agony of soul, and then was kissed with a traitor's kiss and led away to be tried? Do you remember the crown of thorns they put on his Head and how they spit in His face and plucked out His beard? Do you remember how they bound His hands and feet, tore off His garments and beat Him with a Roman scourge, the cat-o'-nine-tails? Do you remember how they laid upon Him the heavy cross, how He stumbled along the road to Calvary with it until He fell; then how He was nailed to that cross and then it was lifted up to hold Him there six hours until He died? Do you remember that even God the Father turned His face away from Jesus and He prayed, "My God, my God, why hast thou forsaken me?" Do you remember the three hours of darkness and then that He gave up the ghost? And, dear friend, remember that all this was to keep souls out of Hell! The third day He arose again from the grave, to be our justification. He ascended up to the Father and there He is today, our High Priest, interceding for us. Oh dear Christian, we know what Jesus wants; He wants souls saved! He Himself told us, "Likewise joy shall be in heaven over one sinner that repenteth, more than over ninety and nine just persons, which need no repentance" (Luke 15:7).

How can God be pleased with any Christian who is baptized and joins the church and reads his Bible and gives his money and prays, but will not do the main thing that Jesus wants people to do? Oh, this is the crowning climax of a happy, prosperous Christian life, to win souls! There is no happiness that I know anything about that can compare with a soul winner's joy. You remember that Psalm 126:5, 6 says, "They that sow in tears shall reap in joy. He that goeth forth and weepeth, bearing precious seed, shall doubtless come again with rejoicing, bringing his sheaves with him." I know what it is to sow in tears; but, thank God, I know what it is to reap in joy, too! I know what it is to go forth weeping; but, oh, praise the Lord, I know what it means to come back rejoicing with sheaves! If you ever really get this blessing of soul winning and get a habit of soul winning you will have the highest kind of joy of which a Christian is capable in this world. And you will know that one day when you meet Jesus, He will be pleased. You will know in Heaven you will have a rich reward, for Daniel 12:3 says, "They that be wise shall shine as the brightness of the firmament; and they that turn many to righteousness as the stars for ever and ever."

Even a new convert can do it. How well I remember when I was fifteen years old and won my first convert, a boy about fourteen. Thank God, he was happy about it, too! I never shall forget how he loved me. One day after both of us were men I went back to that little cow town where I grew up, to preach, and a tall, strong man came to me and said, "John, do you remember me?"

I said, "Albert, is it you?"

What a glad meeting it was! Then he brought in his wife and children to meet me, the man who had won him to Christ when I was fifteen years old and he was about fourteen.

3. Some Suggestions About How to Win Souls

Here are some suggestions about how to do it.

First, use the Word of God. You should set out to memorize some verses of Scripture so that you can tell people how to be saved and why they need to be saved, and settle their doubts. I suggest that you read carefully, over and over, my little pamphlet, *"What Must I Do to Be Saved?"* As you read it, note the Scriptures, then look them up in your Bible, mark them there and memorize them. There you will find many, many Scriptures that show people they are sinners, that show them good works will not save and that show them how to trust in Jesus Christ. Then perhaps you might like to get Dr. R. A. Torrey's *Vest Pocket Companion for Soul Winners*. It has 118 pages with collections of Scriptures for every use of the soul winner. If you will have this at hand for a time until you learn it and grow familiar with it, it will help you to win souls. But remember that it is wiser to read directly out of the Bible itself and show sinners what God's Word really says. After you learn where the soul-winning promises are and what they say, use the Bible itself as far as possible.

Second, make your soul winning a matter of earnest prayer. You know that if you are to be a soul winner the Holy Spirit must come upon you, must fill you, must teach you what to say. The Holy Spirit must convict sinners when you speak to them if they are going to be convicted. So spend much time in prayer for sinners, asking particularly that the Spirit of God will guide you and give you power as you work for Him.

Third, I suggest that, where that is possible, you get sinners out to church to hear some gospel preacher, some soul-winning evangelist or pastor. If you talk to them about Christ ahead of time and sit with them in the service, you may often encourage them by simply offering to walk down to the front with them, or to an inquiry room. Or you may ask such a friend to go with you to meet the pastor after the service, and frankly tell the pastor in his presence, "Here is a friend of mine I want you to meet; I am praying for him that he may be saved." God will help you. Many young and inexperienced Christians have been able to win souls by cooperating with the pastor or the evangelist in the public services.

Fourth, press for real decision. Just talking in general terms is not enough. No salesman is a good salesman who does not get names signed on the dotted line, who does not get actual orders. So urge upon sinners to accept Christ and pray that God will give you definite results day by day.

Last of all, you cannot expect to win many souls unless you go after them wherever they are. Ask God to give you boldness. Ask the Spirit of God to show you where to go and what to say. And if He guides you He will help you to find the key to hungry hearts. He can help you to get in touch with people who need the Gospel. Talk with men where you work. Talk with other students with you in school. When you meet people it is often an easy matter, if you are kindly and if you show yourself to be a genuine friend, to find out whether or not they know the Lord Jesus. It takes an earnest heart and genuine sincerity, and also it takes lots of work. So go after sinners and may God give you wisdom and grace. May God give you a burning heart and a loving heart as you win souls to Jesus Christ.

When you win a soul, then of course you should try to see that that new convert learns the lessons you are learning in this chapter so he, too, can follow the Great Commission and be a successful and happy Christian and be a soul winner. So take time to see that one converted has assurance of salvation by the Word of God, to see that the new converts are enlisted in attending church, in reading the Bible and in regular prayer habits.

A Closing Word

The matters discussed in this chapter are so important that I urge every reader to plan to go through the entire chapter again, reading it carefully and prayerfully, and set out to check your life habits and plans by those followed by the Christians at Jerusalem, about whom we have studied. Then if you really follow these plans I know you will be a happy, prosperous Christian with the blessing of God upon you, with great joy in your heart, and with much fruit to present to the Saviour who died for you. God bless you as you set out to be a prosperous, happy, successful Christian!

Does God Keep His Children?

---

*Answering the Slander That the Bible Doctrine
of Everlasting Life for Believers Gives
Christians a License to Sin*

The natural, human heart wants to have religion of doing, doing. It is natural for the carnal nature to want to earn Heaven by our good works and get the credit for it. So continually the young Christian must remember that it is only by the grace of God that he is forgiven and made a child of God, and accepted in the beloved.

Many Scriptures teach that salvation is wholly of God's grace, and not earned by man's works.

"For by grace are ye saved through faith; and that not of yourselves: it is the gift of God: Not of works, lest any man should boast. For we are his workmanship, created in Christ Jesus unto good works, which God hath before ordained that we should walk in them" (Eph. 2:8-10). Here the Scripture says that people are saved by grace through faith, and that it is not of ourselves, it is the gift of God. God saves people not by their works, lest we should boast about it. And we are not saved by good works—but we are "created in Christ Jesus UNTO good works." Good works are a result of salvation and not a way to get salvation.

Again Titus 3:5 says, "Not by works of righteousness which we have done, but according to his mercy he saved us, by the washing of regeneration, and renewing of the Holy Ghost."

Again and again the Scripture plainly teaches that people are not saved by good works, not kept by good works, but saved by God's grace. People do not deserve salvation when they get it. They do not deserve it after they get it.

The Word also clearly teaches that one who is saved has a new nature. He is "born again," "born of God." The Christian "being born, not of corruptible seed, but of incorruptible, by the word of God, which liveth and abideth for ever" (I Pet. 1:23). Christians are made "partakers of the divine nature" (II Pet. 1:4). The Christian still has the old nature, but now being converted, he has also a new nature, and of this new nature, the newly-created person within, we read, "We know that whosoever is born of God sinneth not; but he that is begotten of God keepeth himself, and that wicked one toucheth him not" (I John 5:18). That does not mean that a Christian never sins—but it means that there is a new nature within the Christian, and this new nature, born of God, does not sin, but hates sin and cannot be content with sin.

In I John 3:9, we are plainly told that this new creature within, this divine nature implanted in the Christian, cannot sin. "Whosoever is born of God doth not commit sin; for his seed remaineth in him: and he cannot sin, because he is born of God." The Christian still has the old nature; and Romans chapter 7 tells of the struggle between the old nature which does sin and the new nature which does not sin. In Romans 7:15-17, Paul writes by divine inspiration: "For that which I do I allow not: for what I would, that do I not; but what I hate, that do I. If then I do that which I would not, I consent unto the law that it is good. Now then it is no more I that do it, but sin that dwelleth in me." Again in verse 25 he says, ". . . So then with the mind I myself serve the law of God; but with the flesh the law of sin."

Every person who has been born again has a new nature, is a partaker of the divine nature, is literally a child of God. But until the resurrection he will be troubled with the old nature, and must constantly fight against it if he would live a happy and victorious Christian life.

Many Scriptures Say That the Christian
Has Everlasting Life

Many Scriptures say that a born-again child of God has

everlasting life, and that the truly born-again Christian will not be lost. John 5:24: "Verily, verily, I say unto you, He that heareth my word, and believeth on him that sent me, hath everlasting life, and shall not come into condemnation, but is passed from death unto life."

John 3:36: "He that believeth on the Son hath everlasting life: and he that believeth not the Son shall not see life; but the wrath of God abideth on him."

One of the clearest statements which Jesus made about everlasting life is the following:

"My sheep hear my voice, and I know them, and they follow me: And I give unto them eternal life; and they shall never perish, neither shall any man pluck them out of my hand. My Father, which gave them me, is greater than all; and no man is able to pluck them out of my Father's hand."—John 10:27-29.

The Bible plainly tells us that Christ gives His sheep eternal life and that they shall never perish, "neither shall any pluck them out of my hand." The King James Version reads, "neither shall any *man* pluck them out of my hand." But the word *man* is not in the Greek text of the Scripture at all. What Jesus really said was "neither shall any pluck them out of my hand." Neither man, nor Devil, nor circumstances, nor self—none can pluck the Christian out of Christ's hand, or out of the Father's hand. Note in your Bible the word *man* in verse 28 and the same word *man* in verse 29 are in italic letters, which means they were not in the Greek at all.

Another great and precious promise of everlasting life is given in II Timothy 1:12, the last part of the verse, "For I know whom I have believed, and am persuaded that he is able to keep that which I have committed unto him against that day." Paul had committed his soul to Christ; and he was persuaded, convinced, that the Lord Jesus was able to keep it. And so every Christian ought to be able to say.

People do not save themselves. They do not keep themselves. People do not partly save themselves by good works, or baptism, or church membership, or giving money, or prayers. They simply trust Jesus Christ and He does all the saving.

Then people do not partly keep themselves. They leave the matter with Christ. That is what they have committed to Him, and He who did the saving by grace does the keeping the same way, by grace. People do not deserve salvation when they get it. People do not deserve salvation after they get it. It is by God's grace, and God's power, and on the merits of Jesus Christ, not our own merits.

A Letter Answered

The author had a good letter from a brother in St. Francisville, Illinois, and we believe my answer to that letter will help many.

"Dear Brother:

"I have your letter in which you say:

" 'We have heard two Free Methodist evangelists and one Mennonite evangelist quote you as saying, "When the Lord comes, He will call His children even out of the brothels, taverns, movies, and dance halls." In other words, you were preaching that our . . . doctrine of eternal security gave the believer a license to sin!'

"I am very happy to answer frankly and fully because a great truth is involved.

"I did not say just what the Free Methodist evangelists and the Mennonite evangelist quoted. They took a statement out of its context, and perverted it to mean exactly opposite of what I expressly said I meant.

"The teaching which they have perverted and misquoted is in a sermon called 'Tears in Heaven' in the book, *And God Remembered*. With six devotional, Bible sermons, it sells for $2.75. Anybody who wants to know what I said can easily find it and verify for themselves the meaning of the whole passage.

"The entire sermon on 'Tears in Heaven' is to show Christians that they had better not sin. The text of the sermon is in Revelation 21:4, where we learn that more than a thousand years after the rapture and the resurrection of Christians, God will wipe away tears in Heaven.

"The outline of that sermon is as follows:

"*1. In Heaven Christians will weep tears of shame because they were not abiding in Christ as they ought, when they were caught away.* And the proof text for that is in I John 2:28: 'And now, little children, abide in him; that, when he shall appear, we may have confidence, and not be ashamed before him at his coming.' Here the Scripture plainly says that God's little children may be ashamed before Jesus when He comes, if they are not abiding in Christ, living out and out for Christ.

"*2. Christians in Heaven will have tears of terror, when they are called before the judgment seat of Christ to give an account and to receive the things done in the body, whether good or bad.*

"The proof text for that as I give in the sermon is in II Corinthians 5:10, 11: 'For we must all appear before the judgment seat of Christ; that every one may receive the things done in his body, according to that he hath done, whether it be good or bad. Knowing therefore the terror of the Lord, we persuade men. . . .' That Scripture says that we all, including Paul the inspired writer, and all the Christians at Corinth to whom he was writing, and Christians everywhere, must appear before the judgment seat of Christ, 'that every one [Christians] may receive the things done in his body, according to that he hath done, whether it be good or bad.' And that at that judgment seat of Christ, terror will take hold of Christians who have not lived right. So the Bible teaches and so my sermon declares.

"*3. There will be tears of loss in Heaven when Christians find that they have let their loved ones go to Hell, and their works are burned up.*

"The proof text for that is in I Corinthians 3:11-15, as follows:

"*'For other foundation can no man lay than that is laid, which is Jesus Christ. Now if any man build upon this foundation gold, silver, precious stones, wood, hay, stubble; Every man's work shall be made manifest; for the day shall declare it, because it shall be revealed by fire; and the fire shall try every man's work of what sort it is. If any man's work abide which he hath built thereupon, he shall receive a reward. If*

*any man's work shall be burned, he shall suffer loss: but he
himself shall be saved; yet so as by fire.'*

"Here we see that Christians in Heaven who have the foundation Jesus Christ, but who build on that foundation worthily,
will receive a reward in Heaven, besides the salvation they already have. And here we see that Christians who have Jesus
Christ but who do not build upon that foundation worthily,
and their works are burned up, will suffer loss. 'If any man's
work shall be burned, he shall suffer loss: but he himself shall
be saved; yet so as by fire.' Here we have a picture in the
Bible of people in Heaven saved but suffering loss because their
works are burned up and loved ones have gone to Hell.

"Now on this basis, in the sermon, 'Tears in Heaven,' I
solemnly warn Christians everywhere that their sins will break
their hearts later on. They will have tears of shame when they
meet Jesus. They will have tears of terror when they stand
at the judgment. They will have tears of loss when they see
their loved ones gone to Hell, and their works burned up,
though they themselves are saved, 'so as by fire.'

"I said that when Jesus comes He will take all His really
born-again Christians. I said that God took Lot, whom the
Bible calls a righteous man, a godly man with a righteous
soul, out of Sodom. And if Jesus should come and some Christian man should be where he ought not be, like Lot was in
Sodom, Jesus would take him if he were a born-again Christian.
I said that David had no business being with Bathsheba, but
David was a saved man. He was greatly shamed and embarrassed when his sin was found out, and that is the way it will
be with Christians when Jesus comes, if they have not lived
right. I said that if there were Christians in movie houses and
other places they ought not to be, they would be taken away,
to suffer loss and shame because of their sins, when they stand
before the judgment seat of Christ.

This Teaching Never Encourages Sin

"Now for anybody to say that the doctrine I preach 'gave
the believer a license to sin' is unfair, is dishonest, and abso-

lutely contrary to the facts. Anyone who reads THE SWORD OF THE LORD, anyone who reads my books, anyone who has heard me preach in a revival campaign knows that I preach hard against sin. My books on movies, lodges, the dance and tobacco certainly prove that. My sermon on the scarlet sin certainly proves that. My preaching against the liquor traffic proves that. Everywhere I go Christian people start family altars, pay up their debts, give up the tobacco habit. Thank God for multiplied thousands who have given up the tobacco habit through my pamphlet on tobacco. Hundreds of thousands of people have been turned from worldliness and the unequal yoke and the blasphemous oaths of the lodges by my book, *Lodges Examined by the Bible.*

"I do not teach that Christians have the carnal nature eradicated and do not sin any more. I do not claim that for myself and I do not believe it when other preachers claim it. But I believe I set as high a standard for holy living as the most radical Arminian. I believe my revival campaigns raise the moral tone among Christian people as much as do the campaigns of any evangelist living. If there is one preacher in America who keeps harping on the truth that sin does not pay, that a man cannot get by with sin, that even Christians suffer for their sins, and the certain punishment of God comes on sin, I am that man. For anybody to take out of its context and twist a statement of mine to make it seem that I endorse sin, or that I preach that being saved gives a person a license to sin, or that it doesn't matter if one sins after you are saved—to so twist and pervert my teaching is dishonest and deceitful.

"I believe that some of those who quote such statements do it ignorantly, because a few untrustworthy men have printed in tract form quotations of mine that perverted what I said. Two or three magazines, anxious to attack and to show how the doctrine that one who believes in Christ has everlasting life, was from the Devil, published perverted and misleading quotations, out of their context, to prove that I preached 'a sinning religion,' and encouraged people to sin. I think that younger and ignorant men have been misled by that. But no man has a right to quote another man without giving the correct meaning and giving the setting from which the quotation is taken and the interpretation which the author himself gives.

Salvation Does Not Make a
Christian Perfect

"And now it is true that I do not believe that salvation makes a person perfect in this life. Would you say that Charles Spurgeon went to Hell because for a good many years he smoked cigars? And that was while he was the greatest preacher in the world, having more people converted than any other living man. Spurgeon came to see that that was wrong and some time before he died, he quit tobacco. But I think in Heaven he has shed many tears over a bad example.

"I gave up movies after I was a preacher of the Gospel and had won many souls. I was in the Southwestern Baptist Theological Seminary, and Dr. Lee Scarborough, the great evangelistic president, urged upon us students to give up the movies. And most of the three hundred ministerial students had attended the movies frequently until that time and most of them quit then, as I did. Now to say that I was not converted before I came to see what was wrong with the movies and before I gave them up would be silly. I was as sincere then as now, but I did not know as much and had not been as well-developed in the Christian life.

"Would you say that old-time Methodist preachers in the South who owned slaves have gone to Hell? Not necessarily! I think slave ownership was wrong, but the question had not been clarified in the minds of many; and we certainly have no right to say that people are not saved unless they are perfect.

"I believe that all these people will have to face Jesus Christ and that they will be sorry for their sins and be greatly embarrassed and shamed before Jesus at His coming, over things that they have done wrong. I believe that the preacher brethren who have slandered me because they hate the doctrine of eternal salvation by grace alone and not of works will have to stand at the judgment seat of Christ, and there confess their sin and suffer shame and terror over it. I believe they are saved but they have sinned certainly worse than the ignorant young Christian who may attend a movie or smoke a cigarette, in my humble judgment.

"I teach now and always have taught that sin does not pay, that nobody gets by with sin. But I do teach that salvation is of God's grace; it is not of works, lest any man should boast. People do not earn salvation before they get it, and they do not earn it after they get it. People are saved by grace and kept by grace. So the Bible clearly teaches.

"I thank you for your letter, and I hope this clears the matter up.

"In the Saviour's name, yours,

"John R. Rice"

Two Pamphlets That Will Help You

Readers who are interested in further study of this question of everlasting life for believers would do well to write for two pamphlets by this editor, *Can a Saved Person Ever Be Lost?* 24 pages, 35¢, and *Eight Gospel Absurdities if a Born-Again Soul Ever Loses Salvation,* 24 pages, price 35¢. Why not order several copies of each to spread among friends who are interested or to use in classes?

CHAPTER IV

Daily Striving to Be Like Jesus

Jesus Is to Be the Pattern, the Example of Every Born-Again Christian

"For even hereunto were ye called: because Christ also suffered for us, leaving us an example, that ye should follow his steps."—I Pet. 2:21.

Years ago a Christian novel was widely circulated called *IN HIS STEPS, or What Would Jesus Do?* It is said that the novel reached the amazing circulation of twenty million copies in many languages. The author, Dr. Charles M. Sheldon, was postmillennial, I suppose, in theology and thought that the world would be won and get better and better, but he did have a great theme. It was simply this: every Christian ought to set out to do what he thinks Jesus would do in his place, in his home, in his job. And that story had a tremendous impact on my life as a lad.

And the novel was written on this text: "For even hereunto were ye called: because Christ also suffered for us, leaving us an example, that ye should follow his steps." We should be like Jesus. We should follow the steps of Jesus! What a blessed theme!

Make sure you do not confuse this Christian duty, this Christian standard, with the plan of salvation. This text clearly states that "Christ also suffered for us." The only hope of anybody for Heaven is in the atoning death of Jesus Christ, and in personally trusting the Lord Jesus and coming to know Him as Saviour, having a new heart, being made a child of God by God's mercy.

No one can honestly set out to follow Jesus as an example

until he has the Lord Jesus as his Saviour and his Christ even in his heart. One must be born of God to be God-like. A wolf might put on sheep's clothing but it is still not a sheep. One may have the outward form of godliness without the power thereof. Oh, I beg you, do not be a Pharisee or hypocrite, pretending to follow Jesus, until you have come honestly as a poor, condemned, lost sinner, trusting Jesus Christ to forgive you and letting the Spirit of God regenerate you and make you a new creature. Jesus is a pattern only for those born in the family, only for those who have Christ in the heart.

But then, a sweet and precious truth is, to be like Jesus is our destiny, it is God's plan for everyone of us who are born-again children of God. Was Jesus miraculously conceived by the Holy Ghost in the womb of the virgin Mary? Oh, yes! And so His conception and His birth were miraculous. Now in my fleshly birth I was not born miraculously. I had a human father and mother and I inherited from them this frail, fallen, tainted, human nature of mine. So, of Jesus Christ it can honestly be said that He was the "only begotten Son" of God, that is, He was the only Son who was physically begotten by God Himself. The translators of the Revised Standard Version and the English Revised Version and some other modern translations deal very foolishly as well as with poor scholarship when they change John 3:16 and instead of saying, "God . . . gave his only begotten Son," they say, "God . . . gave his only Son." In the first place, Jesus is not the only son of God. I, too, am a son of God. But Jesus is the only Son physically begotten of God.

But, praise God, I am in my second birth "born of God," I am "born of the Spirit." In my new birth I am "born from above," as the Greek text in John 3:3 and John 3:7 could properly be translated. And thus God is my Father. I have become literally a "partaker of the divine nature" (II Pet. 1:4). And Hebrews 2:11 tells us, "For both he that sanctifieth and they who are sanctified are all of one: for which cause he is not ashamed to call them brethren." So Jesus is literally my older Brother. And so in Romans 8:16, 17 is this precious promise, "The Spirit itself beareth witness with our spirit, that we are the children of God: And if children, then heirs; heirs of God, and joint-heirs with Christ; if so be that we suffer with him, that we may be also glorified together."

Yes, we are children of God. We are joint-heirs with Christ. What belongs to Christ will belong to us, too.

The Lord Jesus became one of us, became of the seed of Abraham, took on Himself the likeness of sinful flesh, though He knew no sin. He became one of us, was tempted in all points like as we are, yet without sin. He bore all our sorrows and bore all our sins. He became actually, literally, "the Son of man." Oh, He became one of us so we might be "one with him," heirs with Him, reigning with Him.

And it is a sweet and blessed truth in which the psalmist exulted, "I shall be satisfied, when I awake, with thy likeness" (Ps. 17:15). And then some people will come about and say, in the streets of Glory, "I didn't know that John Rice looked so much like Jesus!" for then I will be like Him, not only in looks but far more in character and nature and attitude and personality. Oh, blessed thought!

So then, we who are destined to be perfectly like Christ one day must set out now to follow His steps and to be like Him.

I. The Christian Should Continually Strive to Act Like Jesus

Oh, for characters like Jesus with His humility, His compassion, His holiness, His concern to do only the will of God in everything!

1. The Christian Should Gladly Take the Road of Self-Denial, of Poverty, of Humility to Be Like Jesus

In Philippians 2:5-8 is this exhortation for us to be like Jesus in this matter:

"Let this mind be in you, which was also in Christ Jesus: Who, being in the form of God, thought it not robbery to be equal with God: But made himself of no reputation, and took

upon him the form of a servant, and was made in the likeness of men: And being found in fashion as a man, he humbled himself, and became obedient unto death, even the death of the cross."

To have the mind of Christ, then, is to seek not our own but the welfare of others; to be meek and lowly in heart like Jesus; to be a servant and not a master; to be poor instead of rich!

Sometimes God may lead one of His children in a path of wealth. So it was with Abraham, so it was with David and Solomon. God has been with many other good men. But Jesus Himself was so poor that "the Son of man hath not where to lay his head," although the foxes He made have holes and the birds He created have their nests!

There is an unfortunate break between John chapters 7 and 8 and so many people miss a poignant truth there. After a discussion among the Pharisees and others, John 7:53 says, "And every man went unto his own house." Then comes the unfortunate chapter break and the beginning of a new chapter. But the next verse says, "Jesus went unto the mount of Olives. And early in the morning he came again into the temple. . . ." Other men went to their own houses. Jesus had no house. He slept that night in the Garden of Gethsemane on the slope of Mount Olivet, as, no doubt, He had done many times before. I do not doubt that is one reason Judas knew where to find Him when He must be alone to pray. Christ, who is Creator of all things, became a Man; and He became not only a Man but the poorest among men. He was despised and rejected. He was partly supported by the offerings of good women who followed Him from Galilee. Jesus was poor, and so God's people ought not be ashamed to be poor.

Yes, and if God gives wealth, still we are admonished by the Saviour, "Blessed are the poor *in spirit:* for their's is the kingdom of heaven" (Matt. 5:3). The rich man can only be a good Christian if he is poor in spirit, if he acknowledges that he deserves none of God's blessings, and if he wholly gives himself and all he has to the Lord. Those Christians at Jeru-

salem, after Pentecost—none of them counted ought that they
had as their own. There is a special blessing for those who are
poor for Jesus' sake and those who visit the poor and the sick
and the imprisoned.

Oh, to have a heart and mind like the Lord Jesus! The night
before He was betrayed He washed the disciples' feet but first
He "laid aside his garments; and took a towel, and girded himself." That was not the first time the Lord Jesus had laid aside
His garments. Oh, before He made those stately steppings
down the stairway from eternity to time, down that pathway
from God to man, from Glory, as the fairest of Heaven and
Creator of all things, to be born in a stable, to grow up in
poverty, to die like a criminal—yes, before that Jesus "laid
aside his garments." He laid aside the outward appearance of
deity, laid aside the glory that was His, to be restored after His
resurrection.

And now, dear Christian, are you willing to be a nobody
for Jesus? Are you willing to live in a poor home, to dress in
less expensive clothes, to have the company of the poor and the
unlettered? Jesus sought the company of the Mary Magdalenes
and the Levis and the Zacchaeuses, the poor, the halt, the
maimed, the blind, in His personal ministry.

2. The Christian Is to Have Forgiving Compassion and Charity Like Jesus

It is time now to go back to the context, the scriptural setting of our text today. Back to I Peter, chapter 2, we read verses
18 to 23:

*"Servants, be subject to your masters with all fear; not only
to the good and gentle, but also to the froward. For this is
thankworthy, if a man for conscience toward God endure grief,
suffering wrongfully. For what glory is it, if, when ye be buf-
feted for your faults, ye shall take it patiently? but if, when ye
do well, and suffer for it, ye take it patiently, this is acceptable
with God. For even hereunto were ye called: because Christ
also suffered for us, leaving us an example, that ye should follow his steps: Who did no sin, neither was guile found in his*

mouth: Who, when he was reviled, reviled not again; when he suffered, he threatened not; but committed himself to him that judgeth righteously."

The Christian, then, if he suffers for doing well and takes it patiently, thus pleases God, for so Jesus did. Christ suffered for us and left us an example in that matter. When He was reviled, He reviled not again. When He suffered, He threatened not. Jesus is so quick to forgive and in so suffering wrongdoing, Jesus is our Pattern, our Example. We should follow His steps.

Oh, if we would be like Jesus, then we must remember the instructions, "Be ye kind one to another, tenderhearted, forgiving one another, even as God for Christ's sake hath forgiven you" (Eph. 4:32).

When Jesus washed the disciples' feet the night He was betrayed and before He was crucified, He said to them, "If I then, your Lord and Master, have washed your feet; ye also ought to wash one another's feet." Surely He meant that since all of us walk in this dirty world and all of us need daily cleansing and daily forgiveness, a Christian should help other Christians to do right. That is the command of Galatians 6:1, "Brethren, if a man be overtaken in a fault, ye which are spiritual, restore such an one in the spirit of meekness; considering thyself, lest thou also be tempted." As the Lord invites us to come daily confessing our sins for forgiveness and cleansing, so He wants us to forgive, to love, to think well of others, and to have the charity He has.

And if we would have men to know we are His disciples, trying to be like Him, we must love one another for that is the coin that even an unsaved world takes at face value. The poor, lost world may not have a very clear idea about what it takes to be a Christian and what are Christian duties, but on one matter all the sinners in the world are agreed, along with Christians—one who is a disciple of Jesus should love his brethren, should be slow to anger and quick to forgive. We are to have the Christian charity that "thinketh no evil," and that does not speak evil of others.

II. We Are Called to Suffer
With Jesus

So we are plainly told in the text, "For even hereunto were ye called: because Christ also suffered for us, leaving us an example, that ye should follow his steps." So to be like Jesus is to follow His example in suffering.

1. To Be Like Jesus, We, Too, Must Suffer for This Poor, Lost World, for Sinners About Us

The suffering of Jesus on the cross was neither the beginning nor the end of His sufferings. We remember He said, "I have a baptism to be baptized with; and how am I straitened till it be accomplished" (Luke 12:50). Oh, He was so pressed in His own heart that He must rush on to the cross to pay sin's debt and make sins forgivable. Back in Isaiah 50:6, 7 the Lord Jesus, in prophecy, looking toward His atoning death, said, "I gave my back to the smiters, and my cheeks to them that plucked off the hair: I hid not my face from shame and spitting. For the Lord God will help me; therefore shall I not be confounded: therefore have I set my face like a flint, and I know that I shall not be ashamed." Oh, Jesus set His face like a flint to go on to the cross to pay sin's debt, to redeem sinners He loved so much.

To the ambitious sons of Zebedee, James and John, He said, "Are ye able . . . to be baptized with the baptism that I am baptized with" (Matt. 20:22). And they said, "We are able." And Jesus said that indeed they should enter into that baptism of suffering and compassion and burden for the sins of the world.

It would be a strange thing if the Lord Jesus must weep over Jerusalem and if none of us who love Him would weep. How strange that it was proper for Paul the apostle to go "night and day with tears," warning people, winning people (Acts 20:31), if none of us who now claim the same Saviour should weep nor lose any night's sleep nor sometimes be too burdened to eat or to take ordinary pleasures! A Christian who would be like Jesus must suffer with Him.

*2. Jesus Plainly Said That Every Man Who Would Follow Him
Must Take Up His Cross Daily and Follow Him*

Jesus told the twelve disciples, "The Son of man must suffer many things, and be rejected of the elders and chief priests and scribes, and be slain, and be raised the third day. And he said to them all, If any man will come after me, let him deny himself, and take up his cross daily, and follow me" (Matt. 9:22, 23). Jesus volunteered for the crucifixion. And should I then hold back from giving myself to whatever suffering would be pleasing to God to win souls or to preach the Gospel? And the cross here does not mean a little gold ornament with pleasant associations, but it means that a Christian ought to volunteer to live or die just as pleases the Lord and that a Christian does not count his life as belonging to himself. He ought to give himself as freely to Christ as Christ gave Himself to the crucifixion. So Paul the apostle said, "I die daily" (I Cor. 15:31). And when Paul was in the Mamertine dungeon and wrote II Timothy, he said, "For I am now ready to be offered." Of course, Paul was ready! He had been ready for a long time!

For several years I have taken, each year, a group to the Holy Land, and we always, in Rome, visit the Mamertine prison where we believe Paul was in his second imprisonment and from which he went out to be beheaded. It is a little underground room, with ceiling about seven feet and about seventeen feet across and there is a round hole about two feet in diameter through which they then let down the prisoner and through which they let down his food and such. Now they have a stairway for tourists.

As we met once, a great crowd of us, in that dungeon, I read those farewell words of Paul in II Timothy, how he hoped that Timothy could come soon, that he should try to come before winter and that he should bring the cloak Paul needed. And we read how Paul so gladly faced death and we sang,

> **"Faith of our fathers! living still
> In spite of dungeon, fire, and sword:"**

and then I called on a godly, small-town preacher from Tennessee to lead in prayer. He prayed, with tears, "Lord, don't let us ever complain about anything any more!" Oh, Christians should be glad to suffer for Jesus.

These days are not crowning days; these are cross days. And these are days to go outside the camp to Jesus bearing His reproach. And "if we suffer, we shall also reign with him" (II Tim. 2:12).

3. Christians Are to "Fill Up What Is Behind" in the Sufferings of Christ

Isn't that a strange word Paul gives us in Colossians 1:24?

"Who now rejoice in my sufferings for you, and fill up that which is behind of the afflictions of Christ in my flesh for his body's sake, which is the church."

Is there anything behind in the sufferings of Christ? On the cross did He not cry out with triumph, "It is finished!" (John 19:30)? It seems shocking, at first, that there should be anything "behind," anything lacking, in the sufferings of Christ. Oh, indeed, there is no need for more blood to be shed as an atonement. The perfect Lamb has been slain. Our perfect Substitute has taken our place. Everlasting life is purchased and Heaven and a place in the family of God for everyone who will trust in the atoning blood of Jesus shed for us.

Oh, yes, but the work is not yet done until the Gospel is gotten out "to every creature." So the afflictions that Paul tried to fill up in his body, were those of getting out the Gospel, of being stoned at Lystra and left for dead, shipwrecked, imprisoned two years at Caesarea, beaten again and again, facing the wild beasts at Ephesus, imprisoned at Rome, and finally beheaded! Oh, there is something behind in the afflictions of Christ. That is the part He has given to us to do to be jointly with Him, suffering to get out the Gospel, suffering to save sinners.

So Stephen so ardently witnessed in the power of the Holy Spirit that the Jewish leaders ran upon him and "gnashed upon him with their teeth," and thrust him outside the city to stone him till he died! Thus when he died his face was like the face of an angel, we are told, and he prayed a prayer like the one Jesus prayed on the cross. Jesus had said, "Father, forgive them; for they know not what they do" (Luke 23:34). And Stephen prayed, "Lord, lay not this sin to their charge" (Acts 7:60).

Oh, if we get out the Gospel as we ought, it will not only involve the tears, the burden, for the sinners, but some persecution, some opposition, some poverty, some sleepless nights, loss of dear friends.

When Latimer and Ridley were burned at the stake in England, one could say to the other as the tormenting fire crackled around them, "Cheer up, Master Ridley, for God willing we shall today light a fire that shall light all England."

John and Betty Stam went to China as missionaries but long before had each given themselves unreservedly to please God, to live for Him, to die for Him. And John wrote his vow, his surrender in his diary. John Stam had pledged himself to honor Christ, "Whether it be by life or by death." In China they were captured by communist bandits and beheaded.

I sat one day at the luncheon table at Moody Bible Institute, with Dr. Scott, the father of Betty Scott Stam. He told me that he had just received from China Betty's Bible, found where it had been hidden, and returned to him. And he showed me in the back of that Bible the pledge Betty had made to God to serve Him at any cost.

And we find published a little poem by Betty Stam in which she said:

> **And shall I fear**
> **That there is anything**
> **That men hold dear**
> **Thou wouldst deprive me of,**
> **And nothing give in place?**
> **That is not so.**
> **For I can see Thy face;**
> **I hear Thee now:**

"My child, I died for thee;
And, if the gift
Of love and life you took from Me,
Shall I one precious thing
Withhold to all eternity—
One beautiful and bright,
One pure and precious thing, withhold—
It cannot be."

We must remember, "Christ also suffered for us, leaving us an example, that ye should follow his steps." Suffering is proper for those who would get out the Gospel and thus those who would be like Jesus.

III. Christians Should Do God's Work With the Same Power and Results as Jesus Had

At first glance, this statement may seem ridiculous, may even seem to some blasphemous. But the plain words of the Lord Jesus in John 14:12 are:

"Verily, verily, I say unto you, He that believeth on me, the works that I do shall he do also; and greater works than these shall he do; because I go unto my Father."

Oh, yes, Jesus said, "The works that I do shall he do also." And He said that since He must be cut off and go to the Father early, after only about three and a half years of ministry, others who labor longer and live longer ought to win more souls and do more to get out the Gospel than He had.

1. The Christian Is Sent Exactly as Jesus Was Sent

In His high priestly prayer in John 17:18, Jesus said, "Father, as thou hast sent me into the world, even so have I also sent them into the world." We are sent just as the Father sent Jesus? So He said.

Again, when Jesus arose from the dead and entered that Upper Room among the hushed and frightened disciples that day, He brought them great joy and a grave commitment. In John 20:19-22 we read:

"Then the same day at evening, being the first day of the

week, when the doors were shut where the disciples were as-
sembled for fear of the Jews, came Jesus and stood in the
midst, and saith unto them, Peace be unto you. And when he
had so said, he shewed unto them his hands and his side. Then
were the disciples glad, when they saw the Lord. Then said
Jesus to them again, Peace be unto you: as my Father hath
sent me, even so send I you. And when he had said this, he
breathed on them, and saith unto them, Receive ye the
Holy Ghost."

Yes, Jesus said it again, "As my Father hath sent me, even
so send I you." We are sent exactly as the Father sent Jesus,
so He says.

And we are to remember that this is not just a command to
the eleven, but to all Christians. Every Christian in the world,
since that resurrection day, has the Holy Spirit abiding within
him. Everyone has a Great Commission. The apostles were
commanded by the Saviour, Matthew 28:19, 20, that when
they get someone saved, they should baptize the converts and
then "teaching them to observe all things whatsoever I have
commanded you." And the main thing Jesus had commanded
the apostles was to go and preach the Gospel. So every convert is to be taught that commission and should obey it.

Oh, Christian, you are sent as Jesus was sent.

2. The Christian, Then, Is the Light
of the World

This world is a dark old world. It is so dark that when
Jesus would illustrate the wedding and the ten virgins He said,
"And at midnight there was a cry made, Behold, the bridegroom cometh; go ye out to meet him." So, Spirit-filled
Zacharias could speak of ". . . the dayspring from on high hath
visited us, To give light to them that sit in darkness and in the
shadow of death" (Luke 1:78, 79). And Christ is pictured in
the Tabernacle furniture by the golden lampstand, with the
seven lamps. Oh, when Jesus comes back to reign, we are told,
"But unto you that fear my name shall the Sun of righteousness
arise with healing in his wings" (Mal. 4:2).

So, in John 8:12 Jesus said, "I am the light of the world:

he that followeth me shall not walk in darkness, but shall have the light of life." And in John 9:5 He says, "As long as I am in the world, I am the light of the world."

But Jesus has gone away. The physical Presence of Jesus is in Heaven now, and since He said that as long as He was in the world He would be the light of the world, He indicated then that that light of the world was to come some other way after He had gone away. Oh, we who have Christ in us now, we are the light of the world!

That is what Jesus plainly said in Matthew 5:14, "Ye are the light of the world. A city that is set on an hill cannot be hid." And we are not to hide our light under a bushel or under a bed, but to let it shine.

Dr. A. T. Pierson, perhaps somewhat embarrassed lest we should claim for ourselves something like the arrogant claims of Romanism that the pope is Christ's vicegerent on earth, explained that he thought Christ is the Light of the world as the sun is the real light and that we only reflect the light of Christ, as the moon reflects the sun.

But that likeness is not accurate. I do not simply reflect Christ, I have Christ in me. That simply means that God has planned it that no one will ever be saved except some Christian gets the Gospel to him. God has put upon us the burden, so, if we are honest we must say, as did the inspired apostle:

"For though I preach the gospel, I have nothing to glory of: for necessity is laid upon me; yea, woe is unto me, if I preach not the gospel! For if I do this thing willingly, I have a reward: but if against my will, a dispensation of the gospel is committed unto me."—I Cor. 9:16, 17.

Necessity is laid on us; an awful woe is on all of us Christians who do not get out the Gospel, because "a dispensation of the gospel is committed' to us. And again Paul said, "And all things are of God, who hath reconciled us to himself by Jesus Christ, and hath given to us the ministry of reconciliation; To wit, that God was in Christ, reconciling the world unto himself, not imputing their trespasses unto them; and hath committed unto us the word of reconciliation. Now then we are ambassadors for Christ, as though God did beseech you by us: we pray you in Christ's stead, be ye reconciled to God" (II Cor. 5:18-20).

You can see, then, that we do the work of Christ. And we stand in Christ's stead in this poor, wicked, lost world. Oh, woe are we if we do not preach the Gospel, if we do not shine.

3. We Must Be Endued With the Power of the Holy Spirit Just as Christ Was

It is a strange and wonderful truth that the dear Lord Jesus, entering His public ministry, did not act with His power as Son of God. No, He must be a pattern, a model, to the rest of us. He was born sinless and we are not. He created the worlds and holds the universe together. But He did not presume to use His authority and miraculous power as Son of God in order to preach the Gospel, to witness, to win souls. No, in His atoning death Jesus died as the sinless Son of God but as a perfect Man. As a witness, as a Christian worker, the Lord Jesus waited until He could be endued with the power of the Holy Spirit, then all His ministry was done in the power of the Holy Spirit.

We learn this from Luke 3:21-23a:

"Now when all the people were baptized, it came to pass, that Jesus also being baptized, and praying, the heaven was opened, and the Holy Ghost descended in a bodily shape like a dove upon him, and a voice came from heaven, which said, Thou art my beloved Son; in thee I am well pleased. And Jesus himself began to be about thirty years of age. . . ."

Jesus, about thirty years old, had never preached a sermon, had never worked a miracle, had never won a soul! So He needed to be baptized as our Example, and then He prayed, and as our Example, He was filled with the Holy Spirit.

Then we learn from John 2 that He went to Cana of Galilee and worked His first miracle, turning the water into wine, and began His great ministry.

When Peter preached to Cornelius, he said:

"That word, I say, ye know which was published through-

out all Judaea, and began from Galilee, after the baptism which John preached; How God anointed Jesus of Nazareth with the Holy Ghost and with power: who went about doing good, and healing all that were oppressed of the devil; for God was with him."—Acts 10:37, 38.

Yes, "God anointed Jesus of Nazareth with the Holy Ghost," and He "went about doing good, . . . for God was with him." That is, God the Holy Spirit was with Jesus and doing all His miracles, preaching all His sermons, making every contact. For Jesus, in this matter, was our Example, too.

That is illustrated by the golden candlestick or lampstand in the old Tabernacle. It pictured Jesus as the Light of the world, but burning continually the olive oil which pictured the Holy Spirit.

The anointing of King David as king pictured that Jesus would one day rule also in the power of the Holy Spirit. The anointing of Aaron to be high priest pictured that Jesus, our Great High Priest, would intercede for us as a Spirit-filled Son of man.

Of course it is true as John 3:34 says about Jesus, "For God giveth not the Spirit by measure unto him." Jesus has no frailty, no sin, no lack of prayer, no lack of surrender, no imperfect consecration, and so the power of the Holy Spirit on Him was limitless. But we must have an enduement of power from the same Spirit, if we would win souls and so speak in Christ's stead and be a light of the world.

It is true that when Aaron was anointed to be a high priest, a great abundance of the oil ran down his beard, even to the skirt of his garment (Ps. 133:2). But it is also true according to Exodus 30:30 that Aaron and his sons were alike anointed with the holy oil, picturing the Holy Spirit. We, too, can have, yea, are commanded to have, the fullness of the Spirit! We are to follow the steps of Jesus in power and soul winning and do His work as He did it, in supernatural power.

4. Let Us Be Sure That We Follow Jesus in Putting Soul Winning First

There can be no doubt about the one great intent, the one great burden, of Jesus' heart, the one thing He came for. He said, "For the Son of man is come to seek and to save that which was lost" (Luke 19:10). And in I Timothy 1:15 we are told, "This is a faithful saying, and worthy of all acceptation, that Christ Jesus came into the world to save sinners. . . ." He came to die and the whole purpose of His death was clearly told: "Christ died for our sins according to the scriptures." So the person who is most like Jesus is the one most concerned about soul winning. The one who delights in Bible teaching, in the "deeper life" conferences, but who feels no burden, no call to win souls, is not really following Jesus honestly. Only those who win souls with a holy passion are truly following Jesus. You know Jesus said, "Follow me, and I will make you fishers of men" (Matt. 4:19). And again He said, "Come ye after me, and I will make you to become fishers of men" (Mark 1:17).

Then we should remember that the Lord Jesus was anointed and filled with the Holy Spirit, not as simply a matter of some ecstasy, some holy joy, some private enjoyment! No, He was endued with power from on High. He was "anointed to preach good tidings," as was plainly foretold in Isaiah 61:1, and as He said in Luke 4:18, "The Spirit of the Lord is upon me, it is easy to see what is the real meaning of the fullness of the because he hath anointed me to preach the gospel." Here, then, Spirit, the meaning of Pentecost. The disciples were simply to have the same power Jesus had to do the same work Jesus did! And we should seek and have the same anointing, the same "enduement of power" to do the same work the Lord Jesus had anointing for.

And let us be sure that in this matter we are content to have what Jesus had. The Bible does not tell us of any special ecstasy, any emotional climax that Jesus had when, coming out of the baptismal waters with dripping clothes, Jesus prayed and the Holy Spirit came on Him in form like a dove. He did not "speak in tongues." Everybody present could understand the Aramaic language of His regular speech. So the fullness of the Spirit did not involve any "speaking in tongues." Are you not content to have what Jesus had? to do what Jesus commanded and thus follow His steps?

May the longing of every reader's heart be to be like Jesus, to suffer with Him, to serve with Him and for Him, to be endued with power as He was and to witness with boldness and soul-winning results that He did.

William J. Kirkpatrick said so sweetly long ago in his song, "Oh, to Be Like Thee!"

> **Oh, to be like Thee! blessed Redeemer,**
> **This is my constant longing and prayer;**
> **Gladly I'll forfeit all of earth's treasures,**
> **Jesus, Thy perfect likeness to wear.**
>
> **Oh, to be like Thee! full of compassion,**
> **Loving, forgiving, tender and kind,**
> **Helping the helpless, cheering the fainting,**
> **Seeking the wand'ring sinner to find.**
>
> **Oh, to be like Thee! lowly in spirit,**
> **Holy and harmless, patient and brave;**
> **Meekly enduring cruel reproaches,**
> **Willing to suffer others to save.**
>
> **Oh, to be like Thee! Lord, I am coming.**
> **Now to receive th' anointing divine;**
> **All that I am and have I am bringing.**
> **Lord, from this moment all shall be Thine.**
>
> **Oh, to be like Thee! while I am pleading,**
> **Pour out Thy Spirit, fill with Thy love;**
> **Make me a temple meet for Thy dwelling,**
> **Fit me for life and Heaven above.**
>
> **Oh, to be like Thee! oh, to be like Thee,**
> **Blessed Redeemer, pure as Thou art;**
> **Come in Thy sweetness, come in Thy fullness;**
> **Stamp Thine own image deep on my heart.**

We want to be like Jesus. We feel guilty and sad in proportion as we fail to be like Him. But, oh, the sweet and blessed time is coming, as the psalmist said, "I shall be satisfied, when I awake, with thy likeness" (Ps. 17:15).

CHAPTER V

In Doubt or Failure Christ Jesus Still Loves and Keeps

Will God Show the Doubter the Evidence Again?
Will He Restore the Backslider to Joy and
Fellowship Again?
Will God Call Rejecting Sinners Again and Again?

"Go and shew John AGAIN. . . ."—Matt. 11:3.

Was Jesus really the Son of God, the Messiah, the promised Saviour? Or had John the Baptist been misled in announcing His coming? If Jesus was really the Son of God, why were the prophecies not being fulfilled that he would re-establish David's throne, He would regather all Israel, that the earth should be filled with the knowledge of the Lord?

John the Baptist is in jail. He could hear only rumors about the ministry of Jesus.

That is a strange story about this wonderful preacher as given in Matthew 11:2-6:

"Now when John had heard in the prision the works of Christ, he sent two of his disciples, And said unto him, Art thou he that should come, or do we look for another? Jesus answered and said unto them, Go and shew John again those things which ye do hear and see: The blind receive their sight, and the lame walk, the lepers are cleansed, and the deaf hear, the dead are raised up, and the poor have the gospel preached to them. And blessed is he, whosoever shall not be offended in me."

How much did John the Baptist know and understand about the prophecies concerning Christ's coming?

It is instructive to read again that John the Baptist was preaching in Matthew 3:1-3:

"In those days came John the Baptist, preaching in the wilderness of Judaea, And saying, Repent ye: for the kingdom of heaven is at hand. For this is he that was spoken of by the prophet Esaias, saying, The voice of one crying in the wilderness, Prepare ye the way of the Lord, make his paths straight."

Here John the Baptist is quoting from Isaiah 40 and verse 3. It is true that verse 4 tells of the ministry of John the Baptist as the forerunner of Jesus. But it leaps far ahead also into the future, the return of Christ to reign. Read Isaiah 40:1-5 and you will see:

"Comfort ye, comfort ye my people, saith your God, Speak ye comfortably to Jerusalem, and cry unto her, that her warfare is accomplished, that her iniquity is pardoned: for she hath received of the Lord's hand double for all her sins. The voice of him that crieth in the wilderness, Prepare ye the way of the Lord, make straight in the desert a highway for our God. Every valley shall be exalted, and every mountain and hill shall be made low: and the crooked shall be made straight, and the rough places plain: And the glory of the Lord shall be revealed, and all flesh shall see it together: for the mouth of the Lord hath spoken it."

Doesn't that Scripture say that the warfare of Jerusalem is accomplished, her iniquities pardoned and the long years of trouble for the city over? Doesn't Isaiah 40:5 tell not of the death of Christ so much but of the glory of the Lord when Christ comes to reign?

You see, there are two great lines of prophetic truth in the Old Testament about Christ's coming. First, there is the prospect that God will have a Son of the seed of Abraham to own Palestine. And Abraham's seed as the stars of the sky for multitude and as the sands of the seashore would occupy the land. That promise continues that the throne of David would be established forever and David's descendant would sit thereon. And Isaiah 9:6 and 7 says, "For unto us a child is born, unto us a son is given: and the government shall be upon his shoulder: and his name shall be called Wonderful, Counsellor, The mighty God, The everlasting Father, The Prince of Peace. Of the increase of his government and peace there shall be no end, upon the throne of David, and upon his kingdom, to order it, and to establish it with judgment and with justice from henceforth even for ever. The zeal of the Lord of hosts will perform this."

Deuteronomy 30:1-6 had foretold it and so did Isaiah, Jeremiah and Ezekiel. And John the Baptist had started preaching it, "Repent ye: for the kingdom of heaven is at hand." It is true that the King was offered, but we are not to suppose that John the Baptist fully understood the Saviour would be rejected and the kingdom postponed until this church age was over and Christ should return with saints and angels to reign on David's throne.

That was one great line of truth—the coming Messiah, Son of Abraham, Son of David.

But there is another line of prophetic teaching in the Old Testament about Jesus, too. He was to be the Suffering Servant of Isaiah 53 with whose stripes we are healed and on Him would be laid the iniquity of us all. He is to be the dying One on the cross of Psalm 22 to cry out, "My God, my God, why hast thou forsaken. me?" Is there any wonder that multitudes of people did not fully understand that Christ would first be rejected and crucified and rise again, and then later return to reign on the earth?

So we need not be impatient if when John sent to the Saviour he said, "Art thou he that should come, or do we look for another?"

Perhaps he thought as some others that there would be two messiahs, one who would die for the sins of the people and the other who would reign. We do not know. We know that doubts and trouble were in the mind of John the Baptist. He was behind prison bars. His public ministry was over. He was filled with great concern as to how the ministry of Jesus would go. Was Jesus the Messiah or not?

How tenderly Jesus answered him? "Jesus answered and said unto them, Go and shew John AGAIN those things which ye do hear and see."

John had seen before the marvelous work of Jesus, had heard

Him preach, had announced Him as the Messiah, had rejoiced that multitudes flocked to hear Him and that Jesus baptized more disciples than John. He had been thoroughly convinced one time that Jesus was the Messiah. Now, he feels he must make it certain again and Jesus was glad to have the proof offered again.

I. God Will Show Again His Truth to the Ignorant and the Doubter

I am glad that Jesus had no reproof for John but only the richest of praise. Ah, John was not like many "a reed shaken with the wind." How bold and faithful he was! He was not a man clothed in soft raiment, he was not a weakling, not a child of the age. He was a prophet, the messenger of God, the fore-runner of the Saviour, and never a greater born of women.

1. Our Ignorance Is Such We Must Be Shown the Truth Again and Again

Consider how the faith of the twelve disciples had to be rein-forced again and again. They were astonished when Jesus fed the five thousand with five loaves and two small fishes. They had no faith for that. They were astonished when He came to them on the sea, walking on the water one night. How long did it take to convince them thoroughly, permanently, that He was the mighty God in human form!

And they could not believe that He would die an atoning death. He told them plainly that as Jonah was in the belly of the whale three days and nights so He would be "in the heart of the earth," that is, in the grave three days and three nights (Matt. 12:40). Jesus told the disciples plainly that He would be betrayed into the hands of men and be killed and raised again (Matt. 17:22, 23).

Again in Matthew 20:17-19 He took the disciples apart to tell them, "The Son of man shall be betrayed unto the chief priests and unto the scribes, and they shall condemn him to death, And shall deliver him to the Gentiles to mock, and to scourge, and to crucify him: and the third day he shall rise again." And yet strangely the disciples who loved Him and professed themselves willing to die for Him all forsook Him and fled when the time of His arrest came. Peter cursed and swore and denied Him, the others fled. How much repetition, how much patient teaching it takes, line upon line, precept upon precept, to learn great spiritual truths.

We need not be surprised that John the Baptist wanted to know again. Had he understood it rightly? Was Jesus really the Messiah? Oh, then, let us remember that Jesus has pity on our ignorance, on our weakness. He Himself said to the disciples in John 16:12, "I have yet many things to say unto you, but ye cannot bear them now." A little later He said to them in John 16:25, "These things have I spoken unto you in proverbs: but the time cometh, when I shall no more speak unto you in proverbs, but I shall shew you plainly of the Father." How well it is said, "For he knoweth our frame; he remembereth that we are dust" (Ps. 103:14).

So Paul must write to the Christians at Corinth, "I have fed you with milk, and not with meat: for hitherto ye were not able to bear it, neither yet now are ye able" (I Cor. 3:2).

So John the Baptist inquired and he was right to inquire for proof again that Jesus was really the Saviour. And we are sweetly invited to ask again, to want the facts again, to hear again what we did not fully understand or what we have forgotten.

Many a time I have preached an earnest sermon and people heard me and were blessed. Then in another city, the same people have heard me preach the same sermon again and many times they would come to say, "I heard you preach on that subject before but you preached it better this time." But I know the simple truth is that when I worked for years upon the truth involved and when I may use forty or fifty Scriptures in a sermon and speak for an hour, it is not likely that anybody for the first time over it will understand fully and grasp all the wonderful truth that is taught and implied in the sermon. And the second time they simply understand it better, they have a little foundation to understand it and so it seems to them a better sermon.

So somebody has heard the wonderful gospel message that

all of our sins are laid on Jesus and that one who trusts in Him is given everlasting life, and all of grace and not of works. And he accepts that truth enough to take Christ as Saviour. Yet strangely enough, we may be surprised to find that "everlasting" does not quite mean everlasting to him and he thinks he may lose that which God gave freely. Oh, our ignorance and our poor shallow minds and biased and prejudiced hearts make it so we do not get all the truth at once. How gracious is God to invite us to ask again. He said to the messengers, "Go and shew John AGAIN those things which ye do hear and see."

There were three years after I trusted Christ as Saviour when I had no certainty, no assurance, that my sins were forgiven, that I was saved. Sometimes I felt that they were. Often I felt they were not. I often did not feel like a Christian and sometimes I did not act like a Christian. And when one day I found assurance on the plain statement of the Word of God that "he that believeth on the Son hath everlasting life," and that truth became permanent, explicit, unbreakable and could not any more be clouded by my doubts.

But I have found that in many a congregation at least half of the people have at sometime had doubts about their salvation. That has often been, as in my case, because no one took the Word of God to show them how to base their assurance on the certain promises of God. But sometimes sin in a life brings an accusing conscience, a sense of unworthiness, and so one feels surely he could not claim the forbearance of God and the continued love and mercy. Or sometimes one may be not active in the Lord's work and does not have answers to prayer, does not have the encouragment of Christian fellow-workers, and so has no assurance of salvation. In any case, oh, be sure God is anxious for you to know, and He is glad for you to come to face the promises and the facts again. I am glad Jesus did not rebuke John but offered plainly to prove to him again that his faith was well established, that Jesus was and is the Messiah John had foretold.

2. Our Doubts Do Not Anger the Dear Saviour if We Want to Know the Truth

Did John the Baptist doubt in jail? Well, the days were long.

He could only hear rumors and conflicting accounts about the ministry of Jesus. He was out of the active ministry. He must have brooded sadly that he could do no more for the Lord and there may have been an emotional reaction now that he was put in jail. I am reminded that Elijah, after the marvelous victory on Mount Carmel, ran for his life, frightened of Jezebel and begged God to let him die! At any rate, John the Baptist had some doubts. How deep they went into his soul we do not know. But thank God he sent messengers to ask and to find out.

Let us be sure of this, any honest doubter is invited to come and find out the truth. And, of course, the doubter who does not seek to find the truth, who does not want to know, is not an honest doubter. The scoffer who does not pray, who does not read the Bible, who does not seek the will of God, is not an honest doubter. He is a rebel; he is a deliberate sinner. But the troubled heart that wants to know about Jesus can find out.

Don't you remember His promise, "Draw nigh to God, and he will draw nigh to you" (Jas. 4:8). And Philip was right when he challenged Nathanael, who was doubting if there was any good thing could come out of Nazareth, if Jesus could be the Messiah—and Nathanael said, "Come and see." He did come and one sentence from the dear Lord Jesus and he was convinced. Jesus was glad to tell him that when he was under the fig tree with a heart seeking God's light, Jesus knew about him.

Jesus gave a great promise in John 7:17, "If any man will do his will, he shall know of the doctrine, whether it be of God, or whether I speak of myself."

So no one needs to stay in doubt about the Lord Jesus and who He is and about His truth and the Word of God. And the Old Testament makes the same promise, "Then shall we know, if we follow on to know the Lord" (Hos. 6:3).

Jesus said plainly in John 3:19-21 that those who love darkness because of evil deeds will not come to the light, "But he that doeth truth cometh to the light, that his deeds may be made manifest, that they are wrought in God." The Lord Jesus welcomes the heart that wants to know the truth, that wants forgiveness. That means that one is without excuse who doesn't believe the Bible, who does not believe that Jesus is the Son of God. The only ones who do not believe the Bible are those who do not follow on to know. Those who do not believe that Jesus is all He claimed to be, God in human form, the virgin-born Saviour, are those who have a wicked, sinful heart and stay in the darkness lest their deeds should be reproved. The doubter is not reproved if he honestly seeks to find the light and to know the truth and he will find the truth as certainly as Cornelius, the heathen Italian, sought and found the Saviour in Acts, chapter 10.

II. Jesus Calls the Backslider Back to Fellowship and Joy

I was saved as a nine-year-old boy. Then we moved out to the ranch country in West Texas. There I had no resident pastor. We had preaching only two Sundays a month. My mother was gone, and I lost all my joy, all the sense of God's presence. I remember that one time in a little Presbyterian church a blessed revival was on and many of the young people came back to Christ in renewed joy and surrender and blessing. They sang,

> **Pass me not, O gentle Saviour,**
> **Hear my humble cry;**
> **While on others Thou are calling,**
> **Do not pass me by.**

And I prayed with a broken heart, "Dear Lord Jesus, is everybody going to be blessed but me? Would You not forgive my coldness and my sin?" And the dear Lord did forgive and gave again the joy and assurance that I was a child of God, that my sins were all forgiven.

And walking home across the prairie, under the stars at night, I promised God I would never sin again! And wasn't that an ignorant and foolish promise? No doubt the dear Lord smiled about it, but He knew my good intentions. And I felt that if I failed God again He might not forgive me the next time. Oh, but how little I knew of the patience and grace of God.

1. Consider How the Lord Jesus Loved and Restored
Peter; How David Was Restored

It was a sad man, Simon Peter, who went away in the gray dawn of that Easter Sunday morning and wept bitterly after he had denied the Saviour three times, when the crucifixion was over. Then after the crucifixion, in horror at what he had done, in utter discouragement, he went back to Galilee, gave up the idea of preaching the Gospel and went back to the fishing business again!

Peter had earnestly denied that he was a disciple of Jesus. But when Jesus arose from the dead He sent the angels to say, "But go your way, tell his disciples AND PETER that he goeth before you into Galilee: there shall ye see him, as he said unto you" (Mark 16:7). Well, if Peter did not claim to be a disciple, Jesus still wanted him. So Jesus went in person to the Sea of Galilee, as we learn in John 21. He had Peter and the others to cast the net on the other side of the boat and they caught the great load of fish and Peter came to the shore. He challenged him again to "feed my sheep." Oh, Peter, if you love Jesus, He wants you still!

Isn't it wonderful that God restores the backslider, that He seeks and will not let us go!

David was a great sinner as well as a great saint. After murder and adultery and terrible payment for his sins, yet David prayed the brokenhearted prayer, in Psalm 51, for restoration and joy of salvation, and he got it. And David could close that prayer saying, "For thou desirest not sacrifice; else would I give it: thou delightest not in burnt-offering. The sacrifices of God are a broken spirit: a broken and a contrite heart, O God, thou wilt not despise" (Ps. 51:16, 17).

We remember how gracious was God to Israel. He says, "Go and proclaim these words toward the north, and say, Return, thou backsliding Israel, saith the Lord; and I will not cause mine anger to fall upon you: for I am merciful, saith the Lord, and I will not keep anger for ever. Only acknowledge thine iniquity, that thou hast transgressed against the Lord thy God, and hast scattered thy ways to the strangers under every green tree, and ye have not obeyed my voice, saith the Lord" (Jer. 3:12, 13). And in verse 14 following He says, "Turn, O backsliding children, saith the Lord; for I am married unto you. . . ." And in verse 22 following He said, "Return, ye backsliding children, and I will heal your backslidings." To backsliding Israel again God had the Prophet Hosea saying, "I will heal their backsliding, I will love them freely: for mine anger is turned away from him" (Hos. 14:4).

Oh, love and forgiveness are offered to the backslider and God will not let him go.

So, to the Christian the Lord says, "If we confess our sins, he is faithful and just to forgive us our sins, and to cleanse us from all unrighteousness" (I John 1:9). That is it! Forgiveness and cleansing just for honestly confessing we have sinned. The arms of the loving Father are open to the returning prodigal. That prodigal may represent a lost sinner or a Christian. So the Father rather goes to get the backslidden Christian even as He went after Peter and would not let him go without cleansing and forgiveness and a new commission.

2. Even the Wayward Christian Is Kept Forever Safe in God's Family

It is true that Christians sin. The plain statement is: "If we say that we have no sin, we deceive ourselves, and the truth is not in us" (I John 1:8). And God may chastise His children and often does, but He never forsakes them.

Here we need to understand that salvation is wholly by the grace of God, that God saves people who do not deserve it, and keeps people who do not deserve it, because of His wonderful grace. We should remember that Christ died for our sins, all of them, and that His death on the cross settled for all of our sins before we were ever born and the forgiveness became effective as soon we would trust the Saviour. The only righteousness that will do a Christian any good is the righteousness of Christ and that righteousness is freely given to all who will trust in Him.

"For by grace are ye saved through faith; and that not of yourselves it is the gift of God: Not of works, lest any man should boast."—Eph. 2:8, 9.

So the promise of God is that the Christian has everlasting life. John 5:24 says, "Verily, verily, I say unto you, He that heareth my word, and believeth on him that sent me, hath everlasting life, and shall not come into condemnation; but is passed from death unto life." Then that promise is repeated many, many times. And Jesus said, "My sheep hear my voice, and I know them, and they follow me: And I give unto them eternal life; and they shall never perish, neither shall any man pluck them out of my hand. My Father, which gave them me, is greater than all; and no man is able to pluck them out of my Father's hand" (John 10:27-29). No, a child of God will never perish. He did not deserve salvation. But Jesus deserved it for him. And the promise of Jesus is, "All that the Father giveth me shall come to me; and him that cometh to me I will in no wise cast out" (John 6:37). Jesus has never cast out one who has come seeking mercy and forgiveness. He did not cast one out when he came nor later when he failed to be all he ought to be. Thank God for His love and for the atoning blood of Jesus and for the everlasting promises that we are born into the family of God and He will never leave us nor forsake us.

3. The Christian Worker Who Fails, God Calls Wonderfully to Serve Again

I would not call John the Baptist in prison a backslider because he had doubts about Jesus. And Jesus had no rebuke for him. And I do not feel that he had in any wise turned away from the wonderful ministry God had for him for a limited season. He was in prison, not through any fault of his own but for Jesus' sake.

However, let us get sweet encouragement from the way Jesus dealt with this doubting forerunner. When a Christian worker fails God, God is so quick to forgive and to renew his call.

Jonah is a wonderful example of that. The book starts off with this statement: "Now the word of the Lord came unto Jonah the son of Amittai, saying, Arise, go to Nineveh, that great city, and cry against it. . . ." But Jonah was rebellious. He fled away. He would take a ship to a foreign shore. But God interrupted, but God sent a storm at sea. God prepared a great fish or sea monster to swallow Jonah. And the chastened Jonah cried to God from the belly of the whale and was delivered. Now he was back on land smelling, we suppose, very fishy, but certainly feeling more like preaching than before.

Now, after the chastening and sorrow, the third chapter starts again with these words, "And the word of the Lord came unto Jonah the SECOND TIME, saying, Arise, go unto Nineveh, that great city, and preach unto it the preaching that I bid thee." I am so glad God called Jonah the second time! And that God blessed him and did not lay him aside because of his rebellion and failure before.

We find that John Mark went with Paul and Barnabas on their first great missionary journey (Acts 13:5). He was a helper but that first missionary journey was too rough for the young Mark and after the first journey he left them and went back to Jerusalem (Acts 13:13). Later Barnabas determined to take John Mark (his nephew) with them again but Paul objected strenuously and would not have him (Acts 15:37-40). Many a young preacher has found the poverty, the persecution, the hardships of the ministry too much and turned back, as did John Mark.

But how glad we are to hear later that Mark redeemed himself. Paul, in prison at Rome, wrote to Timothy and said, "Only Luke is with me. Take Mark, and bring him with thee: for he is profitable to me for the ministry" (II Tim. 4:11). Oh, God will use a man again, just as He used Peter and just as He used Jonah, and just as He used John Mark, and just as He used David, after sin and backsliding and failure had marred their ministries.

III. God Calls Lost Sinners Again and Again

It is almost too trite to say it, but God seeks sinners and calls them and warns them and offers mercy again and again and again.

1. Most Sinners Would Never Be Saved if God Did Not Pursue Them Repeatedly

A famous preacher has a way of saying, "Why should one

person hear the Gospel twice when others have never heard it once?" That sounds like a smart saying but really it is not. The simple truth is that hardly anybody is ever saved the first time they hear the Gospel. I was saved when I was nine years old. But even then I could remember again and again the conviction of God that came upon me. When I was four years old I heard the story of the birth of Jesus and that there was no room in the inn. How guilty I felt that people had no room for Jesus. When I was five my mother sang sweet gospel songs and I wept as I thought what if Mother and Dad should go to Heaven and I were left outside. A little later I lied to my mother and she wept and warned me how wicked it was to lie. And when my mother died she made us all promise to meet her in Heaven, and, oh, I never forgot the scene or the words in that sad but glorious hour when my mother went to Heaven praising God.

I remember when I was seven or eight and a Sunday school teacher told me she would never give up praying for us all till we were saved. Oh, God called many, many times before I turned to Him as a nine-year-old boy.

Is it not the mercy of God that He calls and calls again and again!

Oh, a thousand sweet invitations, a thousand benefits, a thousand warnings does God give to every poor lost sinner.

2. And Jesus Would Not Only Receive the Sinner but He Will Remake the Ruined Life

Once God had Jeremiah go down to the potter's house to learn a lesson of God's mercy, as he watched the potter on the potter's wheel mold a vessel of clay: "And the vessel that he made of clay was marred in the hand of the potter: so he made it again another vessel, as seemed good to the potter to make it. Then the word of the Lord came to me, saying, O house of Israel, cannot I do with you as this potter? saith the Lord. Behold, as the clay is in the potter's hand, so are ye in mine hand, O house of Israel" (Jer. 18:4-6). And so He would make Israel, carried captive, punished for their sins, a scandal to all the centuries—yet He would make Israel into a new nation again. And God meant that lesson not only for Israel but for every ruined life, every marred vessel. God can take that vessel that is marred and make it again.

So we sing:

Have Thine own way, Lord! Have Thine own way!
Thou art the Potter; I am the clay.
Mould me and make me after Thy will,
While I am waiting, yielded and still.

In Evansville, Indiana, "Old Bill" was a drunken bum who came sometimes to the rescue mission for a cup of coffee. He would paint mailboxes at five cents each to get beer to drink. Once when he was drunk and had a fight he lost an eye. But Bill was wonderfully converted and changed. He, being a great Christian, insisted, "I am not 'Old Bill' any more. I am 'New Bill.' " So, everybody called him "New Bill." What a name that was! I do not even remember what his other name was. He was, to thousands of people who heard him testify in churches all around the area, simply "New Bill." God took the marred vessel and made it again.

I talked to a young man in Amarillo, Texas, who was making lots of money but had become, at twenty-six, an incurable alcoholic. His wife had left him as a hopeless case. He, in despair, had jumped from a third-story window trying to kill himself. But one night in a room in the Capitol Hotel, as we prayed and taught him to trust the Lord, he was wonderfully save and changed. In two days his wife was back with him again. He left liquor alone and went on to serve the Lord. God took the marred vessel and made it again.

In Sherman, Texas, in a blessed revival, a poor alcoholic, J. D. Welsh, a man who had lost his friends and lost respect of the crowd, had broken the heart of his wife and others, sat in a revival service. He was stirred beyond measure as he saw gray-headed men, as well as younger ones, come to Christ.

We had organized a new church and on the courthouse lawn in open-air meetings, we put up a baptistry and dressing tents and one night twenty-eight of the new converts were baptized. The effect was electric. He turned with deep emotion to his wife who sat beside him and said, "If I had my other clothes I would go and be baptized myself right now." His wife said, "Well, if you have the rest of it settled in your heart, we will have your clothes here tomorrow night." And he said, "I have it settled!" The next night he was baptized. He went back to Houston, Texas, to all the bars and saloons where he drank and cursed and wasted his money and now he went to tell again and again how God had saved and changed him. The marred vessel was made again. His health had been so ruined by his drunken life that he only lived about six months, but how triumphant they were!

I remember the heroin and morphine addict, the drunkard, the criminal, the pusher, who was saved in Sherman, Texas. I remember the panderer who had made love to girls, seduced them, led them in sin and then got $100 each as he took them to a house of ill fame to live. I saw him cowering, weeping, under the Gospel and pleading for mercy. I saw him changed. God took a marred vessel and made it again.

I remember the man who had become so obsessed with lust and sex till he found himself uncontrollable. He had approached women on the street. He told me that unless God fixed him he would soon be dragging some woman in an alley for rape. Would God save such a man and deliver him from the chains that bound him? God did. God gave peace to a tormented heart. God gave victory to an enslaved mind. The marred vessel was made again.

I saw a woman who came to Christ in a rescue mission after a life of awful sin. Then she was saved and her husband was saved. I remember how the results of sin had made her ugly in the face. But she was saved and her husband was saved and then he was called to preach and they set out to love the Lord and with all their hearts to serve Him and to win souls. I saw her some years later and her face had become beautiful. There was such kindness, such love, such compassion, such sweet peace. God had taken the marred vessel and made it again.

Oh, He can restore the years that the locusts have eaten. He can bring peace to the tortured heart. He says to the sinner,

"Come now, and let us reason together, saith the Lord: though your sins be as scarlet, they shall be as white as snow; though they be red like crimson, they shall be as wool" (Isa. 1:18).

And, oh, when one day the trumpet sounds and the dead in Christ arise and we Christians who are living shall be changed, then we will see all the glory of the unmarred vessel that God will make perfectly new, when the taint of sin is gone, when the marks of sin in our bodies are gone, when we are made whole and awake in the likeness of Jesus Christ, how wonderful it will be!

In 1957 I fell into a basement on my head. I have never been able to smell a flower since then, nor the shaving lotion I put on my face, nor my wife's perfume, nor smell bread baking. I will one day. These eyes are frail. I must wear glasses to read. I will throw them away one day.

I have had a wonderfully strong body. I rode broncs in West Texas. I played college football, marched in the Army. But now I find when I climb the stairs I have a tendency to pull on the banisters to help my legs lift the load.

I played college football and got a broken nose. And so now if I sleep on my right side, I often get so I cannot breathe well. In Heaven there will be no need for sleep and rest and there will be no night there, but thank God one side of my nose will not be stopped up!

I have scars on my body such as an active man has, with a knot under one knee, the gash of an ax on the right wrist, the slash of barbed wire on my left elbow, the scar of a falling brick on my scalp. And, oh, the scars of sin and failure on my soul, too. But, thank God, every mark will be removed one day. God will take the marred vessel and every imperfection He will correct and make the vessel new and glorious.

3. But God Sometimes Quits Calling Sinners
and Lets Them Go to Hell

Before the flood God said, "My spirit shall not always strive with man, for that he also is flesh: yet his days shall be an hundred and twenty years" (Gen. 6:3). And so that wicked generation, millions of people, before the flood, He gave up and with only Noah and his family in the ark, God destroyed the rest of the race. God's patience does wear out sometimes!

In the first chapter of Romans God tells how, after the flood, people did not glorify God, did not like to remember God, went worse into sin, worshiped idols: "Wherefore God gave them up to uncleanness," and "For this cause God gave them up unto vile affections," and "God gave them over to a reprobate mind" (Rom. 1:24, 26, 28). Oh, it is bad when men so long grieve God, so long resist the call of the Spirit of God that God gives them up, turns them over to a wickedness of mind and lets them go on to Hell.

The Lord Jesus called sinners again and again in Jerusalem. And then in the last week of His life before the crucifixion He looked upon the city and lamented, "O Jerusalem, Jerusalem, thou that killest the prophets, and stonest them which are sent unto thee, how often would I have gathered thy children together, even as a hen gathereth her chickens under her wings, and ye would not! Behold, your house is left unto you desolate. For I say unto you, Ye shall not see me henceforth, till ye shall say, Blessed is he that cometh in the name of the Lord" (Matt. 23:37-39). So the Shekinah glory, that living flame that has been with Israel, in the wilderness, and the pillar of fire, at night, and had dwelt over the mercy seat in the Holy of Holies in the Temple, now departed. The veil of the Temple is torn in two. God had forsaken the Temple. And in some sense He forsook thousands of people. Those who went on to the crucifixion, no doubt, many of them were never called again by the Spirit and many of them died and went to Hell. Yes, sadly, because He longs to see people saved, God gives people up who resist too long.

God loves you and wants to save you. But do not trifle with His pleading. One day the door of the ark was closed and none of that wicked generation could go in. One day Jesus quit calling the people of Jerusalem. And one day God's blessed Spirit may quit pleading with your heart, lost sinner! Oh, be saved now while you can. God calls you still. His arms of mercy are outstretched. He died for you. He says, "Behold, I stand at the door, and knock: if any man hear my voice, and open the door, I will come in to him, and will sup with him, and he with me" (Rev. 3:20). He says now, "Whosover will, let him take the water of life freely" (Rev. 22:17). Will you come today?

You have read the sermon, "In Doubt or Failure Christ Jesus Still Loves and Keeps," by our beloved Dr. John R. Rice. I, with him, urge you to come to Jesus today. If you will take "the water of life freely" by receiving Jesus Christ as your Saviour, simply tell God you will. In prayer tell the dear Lord that you are a sinner and deserve hell but you will accept Jesus and His payment for your sin. If you will trust Christ and write to tell me, I will send you some free literature that will help you as you set out to live the Christian life. Fill out the decision form below and mail it today.

Decision Form

Dr. Shelton Smith
Sword of the Lord Foundation
P. O. Box 1099
Murfreesboro, TN 37133

Dear Dr. Smith:
I have read Dr. John R. Rice's sermon, "In Doubt or Failure Christ Jesus Still Loves and Keeps." I am glad God calls sinners again and again—I am glad He called me. I have now accepted Jesus as my Saviour, trusting Him to forgive my sins and give me a home in Heaven. Please send me the free literature that will help me in the Christian life.

Name _____

Address_____

_____

City_____ State _____ Zip _____

CHAPTER VI

Abiding in Christ for Fruit-Bearing

With infinite grace the Saviour taught His disciples the night He was betrayed. He gave them the Last Supper that would picture His death until He should come again. He told them of the Father's house of many mansions that He was going to prepare and that He would come again and receive His saints unto Himself. He gave the marvelous teaching of the Comforter, the Holy Spirit, who would abide with and in the disciples forever. He prayed for the disciples in the 17th chapter of John. He gave blessed promises concerning prayer in His name. And in John the 15th chapter He gave us the remarkable discourse about how Christians should bear fruit—that He had ordained them and sent them forth for this purpose of bearing fruit. He said that the Father would be glorified in Christians as they bore much fruit and that fruit-bearing was by abiding in Him.

The Christian will do well to read prayerfully here the first seventeen verses of John, chapter 15.

"I am the true vine, and my Father is the husbandman. Every branch in me that beareth not fruit he taketh away: and every branch that beareth fruit, he purgeth it that it may bring forth more fruit. Now ye are clean through the word which I have spoken unto you. Abide in me, and I in you. As the branch cannot bear fruit of itself, except it abide in the vine; no more can ye, except ye abide in me. I am the vine, ye are the branches: He that abideth in me, and I in him, the same bringeth forth much fruit: for without me ye can do nothing. If a man abide not in me, he is cast forth as a branch, and is withered; and men gather them, and cast them into the fire, and they are burned. If ye abide in me, and my words abide in you, ye shall ask what ye will, and it shall be done unto you. Herein is my Father

glorified, that ye bear much fruit; so shall ye be my disciples. As the Father hath loved me, so have I loved you: continue ye in my love. If ye keep my commandments, ye shall abide in my love; even as I have kept my Father's commandments, and abide in his love. These things have I spoken unto you, that my joy might remain in you, and that your joy might be full. This is my commandment, That ye love one another, as I have loved you. Greater love hath no man than this, that a man lay down his life for his friends. Ye are my friends, if ye do whatsoever I command you. Henceforth I call you not servants; for the servant knoweth not what his lord doeth: but I have called you friends; for all things that I have heard of my Father I have made known unto you. Ye have not chosen me, but I have chosen you, and ordained you, that ye should go and bring forth fruit, and that your fruit should remain: that whatsoever ye shall ask of the Father in my name, he may give it you. These things I command you, that ye love one another."

Verse 5 pretty well sums up the entire passage. Christ is the Vine, we are the branches. If we abide in Him and He in us, we bring forth much fruit; without Him we can do nothing.

Here is a beautifully intimate picture of the relation of Christ and His saints. We are really a part of Christ. There is a living connection between Christ and every child of God and the life of Christ flows through the Christian just as sap comes from the vine into the branch. Jesus teaches the same thing when He says that we are members of His body. There is as much connection between Christ and His saints as there is between head and hands. We are the members of Christ.

The whole object of the vine is to bear fruit. Grapevines are kept for the grapes. They are created by the Maker of Heaven and earth to take the mineral elements of the soil in solution, carry them up into the plant and by the combination of sunshine and air and sap to produce grapes. Roots, vine, branches all have one aim. The aim of the husbandman is to have fruit from the vine and branches.

So all the dealings of Christ with the human race were intended to result in souls being saved. To this end the Bible was written. To this end Christ came into the world, was born of a virgin, lived a sinless life, died on the cross and rose from the dead and now intercedes for us at the right hand of God as our High Priest—all this for the one purpose of saving sinners. Souls saved are the fruit that God expects of His Vine, Jesus Christ, and of us Christians since we are the branches. "The fruit of a Christian is another Christian."

We are partners with the Lord Jesus in soul winning. Jesus told Peter, James, and John, "Follow me, and I will make you fishers of men" (Matt. 4:19). Every Christian who really follows Christ will be fishing for men.

Christian, God wants you to bear fruit! Your happiness as a Christian will depend upon your victory over temptation, your enjoyment of the Holy Spirit's presence, and will depend on your bearing fruit. And here the Saviour tells us of the conditions under which you can bear fruit.

The Word Essential in Fruit-Bearing

The first condtion of a fruitful Christian life is that the Word of God have its effect upon a Christian. We know, of course, that the soul winner needs to use the Scripture to be effective in dealing with lost souls. "The word of God is quick and powerful and sharper than any twoedged sword, piercing even to the dividing asunder of soul and spirit, and of the joints and marrow, and is a discerner of the thoughts and intents of the heart" (Heb. 4:12). Psalm 126:6 says that, "He that goeth forth and weepeth, BEARING PRECIOUS SEED, shall doubtless come again with rejoicing, bringing his sheaves with him." You must use the Word of God on sinners, but that is not what this Scripture here means. If you are to bear fruit you must use the Scripture *on yourself!* In verse 3 of the passage above, Jesus said, "Now ye are clean through *the word* which I have spoken unto you." And that is just after verse 2 which says, "Every branch in me that beareth not fruit he taketh away: and every branch that beareth fruit, he purgeth it, that it may bring forth more fruit." Purging, cleansing, is essential if the branch is to bear fruit and this purging is done by the Word of God.

Every kind of fruit has its natural enemies, part of the curse put upon the world through sin. Various kinds of scale, rust, borers and insects infest every fruit tree and grapevine. The vine must be sprayed and purged and cleansed and pruned if it is to bear fruit. That is what the Word of God does for a Christian. You remember that the psalmist said, "Thy word have I hid in mine heart, that I might not sin against thee" (Ps. 119:11). Again Psalm 119 asks the question, "Wherewithal shall a young man cleanse his way?" And the divinely inspired answer is given; "by taking heed thereto according to thy word." It is only as a Christian knows the Bible that he is able to overcome sin and live a victorious life. Sin separates us from communion and fellowship with Christ, and the only way to a victorious life, overcoming sin, is by daily use of the Word of God. The Bible points out sin we had never seen, is used of the Spirit to convict us of sin, shows us the remedy for sin, points us to Jesus, leads us to prayer and trust. To the surrendered and anointed soul winner the Saviour says, "Now ye are clean through the word which I have spoken unto you." Christians who do not know the Bible are unsteady Christians who stumble along in the dark, constantly falling into sin.

One of the most blessed promises in the Bible is in verse 7, "If ye abide in me, AND MY WORDS ABIDE IN YOU, ye shall ask what ye will, and it shall be done unto you." The soul winner must be able to pray. There is no hope of victory over Satan in the Christian work except as we can make connection with God in prayer, and successful prayer, answered prayer depends on having the words of Christ abiding in us. In other words, by memorizing the Scripture, meditating upon it, study- ing it, absorbing it, getting the true meaning of the Scripture, we learn the mind of God and the will of God and are able to ask according to His will so that our prayers will be answered. How important it is for the soul winner to know the Scriptures and not only to know the Scriptures, but to have the Scriptures, abiding in his heart. Not only must he have the Scriptures, but have the Scriptures abiding in his heart.

The Christian needs pruning just as the grapevine does, and the sharp knife of the Scripture does the work. The Christian needs to be guided just as the grapevine is led upon a trellis or pole. The Word of God is the strong support and guide for the Christian.

And besides, how are we to abide in Christ without abiding in His Word? In the Bible we have all His commands, all His desires expressed. In the Bible we have the entire story about how Jesus lived and died, how He overcame Satan and lived a holy life as our pattern. The will and character of Christ are revealed in the Bible, and so daily feeding on the Word of God, judging self by the Word, claiming the promises of God, following the instructions of the Word, are necessary if we are to abide in Christ and bear fruit.

Consciously Abiding in Christ

Everything good for the Christian is involved in abiding in Christ. This is the central thought of the entire passage in John 15:1-17. In some sense Bible reading and prayer are a part of abiding in Christ, but besides these, there should be a very deliberate effort to be conscious of the continual presence of Christ. To read the Bible is not enough. We should read it in the presence of Christ, with Him pointing out the meaning and speaking to our hearts as we read. To pray is not enough. We should be conscious of the very near presence of Christ as we pray, to talk to Him personally and have Him speak to us just as definitely as we speak to Him. We should practice the presence of Christ.

A branch may be grafted into a vine but if it is to bear fruit it must grow into the vine and have a constant supply of sap, becoming a part of the vine. If a branch is grafted into a vine today and then tomorrow pulled apart and then later on grafted back in, it cannot bear fruit. The branch that is green and fresh today but withered tomorrow cannot bear fruit. Just occasionally to be in touch with Christ will not do for the soul winner. He must learn to "abide in Christ."

Oh, how we need to be conscious of the presence of Christ day and night! How we need to watch so that we never grieve the Spirit by sin, never quench Him by rebellion.

This is what the Scripture means when we are commanded to

"pray without ceasing" (I Thess. 5:17). How can one pray without ceasing? Sometimes he must concentrate his entire time on the work he is doing. Sometimes he must eat and sleep. Is it really possible to pray without ceasing?

Yes, it is! A mother can watch after her baby without ceasing. She goes about her housework and suddenly, when no one else heard a sound, she says, "My baby!" and runs to the little one and then others notice that the child is fretting. The mother's ear has been tuned to hear the cry of the child no matter how absorbed she must be in something else.

Sometimes a mother sleeps and yet the subconscious mind gives constant attention to the little one, and the faintest stir or sound will awaken the mother. When the conscious mind lays down its burden in rest, yet the subconscious mind is still aware and watching, listening. So we may be continually conscious of the presence of Christ.

Many a time on the coldest winter nights I have had a strange urge to see after my little girls, when they were at home, to make sure they were covered and comfortable and safe. That urge waked me out of the soundest sleep when I had not planned to wake and when there was not a sound or movement to arouse me as far as I knew. Part of the personality does not sleep but can be held in attention on some one matter.

I know that sometimes in the night I have reached my hand out to the pillow beside me and touched my wife's face or shoulder. I was aware that she was there even though I was not awake. This awareness of the subconscious mind that can center itself on some object or purpose even when we sleep, ought to be centered on Christ so that literally we could always, day and night, abide in Christ and be conscious of His presence, eager to please Him, to have His favor and do His will!

Many people can wake without an alarm clock at approximately whatever time they wish to awake. I have known several who never relied upon an alarm clock but would simply definitely set their mind to awaken at a certain time and never miss it far. For months, while in Baylor University, I awoke each morning at 5:20 to begin my heavy duties. Most of that time I got not over six hours of sleep a night and oftentimes I was desperately sleepy. If I got a chance during the day, I could go to sleep almost instantly, but my will to arise at a certain time pulled me from the depths of slumber and sent me about my work.

Oh, how I would to God I could have such a continual will to please Christ and know His presence and blessing and power! It is a wonderful thing what love will do. When Mrs. Rice and I were sweethearts in college I was conscious of her every moment we were in recitations together, no matter whether I was reciting or concentrating on the lesson. When I entered an oratorical contest and spoke rapidly and from memory a prepared address, I was continually conscious that she heard me. I knew where she sat and knew she was interested in what I did. When I played college football, which is a most strenuous game, exacting the most vigorous concentration of mind, will and muscle, again and again I saw from the corner of my eye the flash of an orange-colored blouse and knew she was there. It is not hard to abide in the consciousness of those we love.

I am proving to you, dear reader, that you can abide in Christ. You can be conscious of Him whether you work or play or eat or sleep. You can really "pray without ceasing." You can "rejoice in the Lord *alway.*" You can "ABIDE under the shadow of the Almighty" (Ps. 91:1). "The peace of God, which passeth all understanding" can really "KEEP your hearts and minds through Christ Jesus." Christians may have the joy and safety and certainty and power of abiding in Christ.

Sometimes I have gone to sleep with Christ very, very near and in the night I would wake praying, or I could hear the refrain of some sweet Christian song that had blessed my heart. How happy is the Christian whose dreams are of God and Heaven! The happiest dreams I have ever had have been when I dreamed of great revivals and hundreds saved, dreamed I was preaching with the power of God upon me.

All of the men and women, who are my assistants in the blessed work of getting out the Gospel, are devout Christians, prayerful, useful, Bible-studying, soul-winning Christians. One of them dreamed one night of the coming of the Saviour. When she told all of us about it the next day we rejoiced together with tears. How real it seemed when she told of seeing Jesus and the glory of the resurrection and of meeting all the saints of God and of the old sinful nature and mortal body left behind! For days she seemed transformed and could think of little else. I have thought many times of it since and wondered what glories there would be for Christians if we would really abide in Christ so that our thoughts and emotions were absorbed in Him! How sweet would be the rest, how pleasant the dreams, how joyful the waking of those who abide in Christ! How easy would be our burdens if always we knew and felt the presence of our Burden-Bearer standing by our side. What sweet comfort in our sorrows if we were always conscious of His comfort and that His will was being done! How safe would be our refuge in every trial, temptation and persecution if we always felt the safety of His arms and protection of His power! May God help us to abide in Christ.

And such abiding is, my Christian friend, essential to the fullest fruit bearing. We need to "take time to be holy." We need to learn to wait on God. We need to be so close to the Saviour that we can be absorbed in His will. Then we can receive His power. I do not have any idea that the branches of a grapevine have any sense of strain and toil. Rather, they are passive and the sap flows through them. God works the miracle of grapes through the combination of sap and sunshine and air. So when we toil and fret and worry about our work, trying to bear fruit, our trouble is that we are not abiding in Christ as much as we ought. Fulness of power comes with fulness of association with Christ and identification with Him.

Asking: Definite Prayer Has a Place in Fruit-Bearing

John 15:7 says,

"If ye abide in me, and my words abide in you, ye shall ask what ye will, and it shall be done unto you."

One who abides in Christ and feeds on the Word of God, is then ready to pray, to pray for results, to pray for power. Some people have an idea that simply to live an upright Christian life will result in people being saved, but they are mistaken. You may pay your debts, control your tongue, give of your money, and be kind to your neighbor: I suppose the Pharisees did all that and yet they never won a soul. The fruit does not proceed from the branches alone, it comes from the vine. So if souls are to be won, we must seek them from God. It is God who convicts sinners. God alone can change wicked hearts. Only God can make children of Hell into children of God. The most important part of the ministry is prayer. The apostles said, "We will give ourselves continually to prayer, and to the ministry of the word" (Acts 6:4).

Notice that now we are not speaking of prayer as meditation or as feeling after God but prayer as definite asking, objective praying. Praise and thanksgiving have their place with prayer but here the Lord says, "*Ask* what ye will." I am sure I have preached many sermons that were not as fruitful as they ought to have been because I did not ask God for particular and definite results. In prayer God will give you wisdom about where to go, whom to see, what to say. Prayer gets results for one who abides in Christ.

If you abide in Christ then you will want the will of God done. With your will surrendered to the will of God, you will be anxious to please Him. You will earnestly strive not to grieve the Spirit nor quench His leading. You will want the will of God done. And if his Words abide in you, you will KNOW the will of God and can pray according to His will. Verse 15 then means that abiding in Christ and with His Word abiding in you, you will be anxious to please God and will know how to please God so that you will ask only the things that can honor Him and God can give you whatsoever you desire. That is kin to the Scripture in I John 3:21 and 22 which says, "Beloved, if our heart condemn us not, then have we confidence toward God. And whatsoever we ask, we receive of him, because we keep his commandments, and do those things that are pleasing in his sight." One who abides in Christ and is saturated in mind and heart with the Word of God, can ask whatsoever he will and shall receive it.

Again, in Psalm 37:4 we are told, "Delight thyself also in the Lord; and he shall give thee the desires of thine heart." That verse means almost exactly the same, I think, as John 15:7. Delighting in the presence and will of God and delighting in His Word make it so that God will gladly give you the desires of your heart. Your desires will fit into God's desires and it will be perfectly safe for God to give you carte blanche. How free is the Christian who is filled with the Spirit! How rich our inheritance when we abide in Christ! What limitless powers are ours to bear fruit if we truly abide in Christ, our Branch. It is not surprising that in the same passage, verse 5, Jesus says, "He that abideth in me, and I in him, the same bringeth forth MUCH FRUIT," and verse 2 says, "Every branch that beareth fruit he purgeth it, that it may bring forth MORE FRUIT," and verse 8 says, "Herein is my Father glorified, that ye bear MUCH FRUIT." If you abide in Christ you will have a right to make big requests and get them answered. God ordained us to bring forth fruit and therein is He glorified. Therefore, dear Christian, abide in Christ and ask anything you want in the way of fruit-bearing.

Love's Relation to Fruit-Bearing

How fitting that the dear Saviour here would give an extended passage on love. In verses 9 to 17 love is mentioned nine times and that right in the midst of the discussion on fruit-bearing. Fruit is possible because the Father loves the Vine and the Vine loves the branches and we are all to join in this love. Soul winning is a work of love. There is no hope of the soul winner being properly rewarded in this world. "He that winneth souls is wise," it is true, because "they that be wise shall shine as the brightness of the firmament; and they that turn many to righteousness as the stars for ever and ever." You will never win souls for money or hope of earthly reward. "God so LOVED the world that he gave" Jesus. Love was the Father's motive. "God commendeth his LOVE toward us, in that, while we were yet sinners, Christ died for us. Love was the motive of the Saviour. So love must be the motive of the Christian who would win souls. Otherwise, we cannot go weeping. Otherwise, we cannot "compel them to come in."

The relation of one soul winner to another is very sweet. Those who have worked together, prayed together and rejoiced together in the salvation of sinners have a fellowship that is partly of Heaven. Indeed angels themselves out of the very love of sinners and love of God, rejoice more over one sinner that repents than over ninety-nine just persons that need no repentance. What perfect love and cooperation between God and Christ and the Holy Spirit and the angels in winning souls! Jesus could say, "I and my Father are one." Here He says, "As the Father hath loved me, so have I loved you: continue ye in my love." The love of the Father and of Christ for sinners unite in their love for each other. When you and Christ can unite in the work of saving sinners, you will love Him better. And then if you join other Christians in the same holy task of abiding in Christ, you will love other Christians better.

First Corinthians tells us that love is the greatest thing in the world, greater that faith, greater than the gifts of the Spirit, greater than knowledge, greater than sacrifice. You would certainly not expect love to be left out in fruit-bearing. Love is the mark of a Christian, for Jesus said, "By this shall all men know that ye are my disciples, if ye have love one to another" (John 13:35). The very nature of God is essentially love—"God is love." We are told that, "Beloved, let us love one another: for love is of God; and every one that loveth is born of God, and knoweth God. He that loveth not, knoweth not God; for God is love" (I John 4:7, 8).

It is evident on the face of it that abiding in Christ would involve brotherly love. If Christ so loves my brother and I abide in Christ, how can I avoid loving my brother like Christ does? If God is love and I so abide in Christ and His Word abides in me, as to make me like God, then I, too, will be moved by love. If the answers to our prayers depend upon our asking according to His will and upon keeping His commandments, then love must be essential, because, "And whatsoever we ask, we receive of him, because we keep his commandments, and do those things that are pleasing in his sight. And this is his commandment, That we should believe on the name of his Son Jesus Christ, and love one another, as he gave us commandment" (I John 3:22, 23).

Brotherly love then is necessary to fruit-bearing. Love is both cause and result of fruit-bearing. Love goes before and accompanies and follows abiding in Christ. No one will be received into that inner circle with Christ who does not love others in the same circle, and other branches of the same vine. If the branch is joined into the vine and becomes one with the vine, then it becomes one with the other branches. A unity with Christ means a unity with other believers too, and fellowship in fruit-bearing makes for further fellowship. The branch that bears fruit is purged that it may bear more fruit. So the Christian who wins souls will so learn to love other Christians that he may win souls. Brotherly love is one of the essentials of fruit-bearing. In fact it is the great characteristic of a Christian who is close to Christ.

Did you ever know of a young married couple who found it hard to get along, hard to adjust themselves to each other, as each one wanted his own way and divorce seemed likely? And then did you ever know of such a couple when God sent a little, tiny baby into the home so that their hearts were knit together in unselfish love of a third person? The husband and wife have much more chance of happiness and perfect unity of heart and life when they are compelled to think and plan together for children. When a man begins to call his wife "Mother" and she calls him "Dad," it is a good sign. Little baby fingers take hold like grips of steel and bind together hearts that would otherwise not be able to stand the strain of selfishness and self-will.

Just so, we Christians are such frail and worldly mortals, falling so far short of what we ought to be there are natural tendencies to disagree. Unless we are absorbed in the love of Christ and melted to His will united in the winning of other souls, we are likely to sin. But the branch who is in perfect touch with the Vine will love the other branches. Brotherly love is one of the essentials of fruit-bearing.

I am reminded that D. L. Moody, R. A. Torrey, and other great evangelists were essentially undenominational in their attitude. They loved all Christians. Moody said, "If I knew that I had one drop of sectarian blood in my veins, I would have a doctor take it out." That did not mean that those great men of God lacked convictions. It meant that they loved all Christians and would not be bound by arbitrary denominational lines. Moody would never go to a city for a revival unless the Bible-believing Protestant ministers of the city were united in agreement about the revival. The greatest revivals that Billy Sunday ever had were on the same basis.

Fundamentalists do well when they insist on certain great essentials of truth such as the deity of Christ, His blood atonement, salvation by grace through faith, Hell, Heaven, and the second coming of Christ. But fundamentalists do wrong when they are impatient and hateful to their brethren of like faith, and when they split hairs and divide congregations over lesser matters not one-thousandth part as important as brotherly love! One of the greater fundamentals of the faith is brotherly love. One is to be known as a Christian not because he is sound in doctrine but because he loves other Christians. Remember, "By this shall all men know that ye are my disciples, if ye have love one to another." Brotherly love looms much larger in the Bible than it does in other Christian literature. It is much more important in the mind of God than it is in the mind of preachers. Let every Christian be true to great convictions in truth, but I beg you, my Christian brethren, do not be like the Pharisee who tithed mint, anise, and cummin and neglected the weightier matters of mercy, judgment and faith. Every Christian who is really close to God can say, "Blest be the tie that binds our hearts in Christian love!" It would be well for every Christian to memorize the 13th chapter of First Corinthians and earnestly seek the grace of God to be able to love as he should.

If you long to be used of God and win souls, then I beg you, let love have a greater place in your life. You may seek to be a great preacher when God is more concerned that you be a great lover! Though you may understand all mysteries and speak with tongues of men and angels and have faith to remove mountains and give your body to be burned, there is no real Christian character and no reward in Heaven except as the love of God is shed abroad in your heart until you love others. Abiding in Christ means love, oceans of love, love like Christ's for us.

The Joy of Fruit-Bearing

And now, dear reader, let me call your attention to the soul winner's joy. As Christ rejoiced in the sinner's salvation, and as the angels rejoice in Heaven, so you can rejoice too. This entire passage of Scripture is given to make you happy, for verse 11 says, "These things have I spoken unto you, that my joy might remain in you, and that your joy might be full" (John 15:11). Fulness of joy is found in abiding in Christ, in doing His will, and seeing the precious fruit which results.

The fruit-bearer's joy comes from communion with Christ, your lovely Saviour. What a joy to know Him better! Remember that Paul said, "—I have suffered the loss of all things, and do count them but dung, that I may win Christ" (Phil. 3:8). Christ Himself is joy enough for every Christian. His beauty, richness, and fellowship are enough to repay the loss of all things on earth.

The fruit-bearer's joy is the joy of answered prayer. Elsewhere (John 16:24) Jesus told the disciples, "Ask, and ye shall receive, that your joy may be full." Fullness of joy comes when God answers prayer. Answered prayer proves there is a God, proves the Bible is true, proves that God loves us. Christians, ask and be happy!

The fruit-bearer's joy is the joy of fellowship with other "branches." I have known Christians who had known each other not one hour, put their arms around each other and rejoice in the sweetest fellowship over some sinner being saved.

The sweetest joy of all, I think, when one abides in Christ and lives in His will is to know that Christ Himself rejoices in sinners being saved. I should have more joy, far more, and do have, I think, in the thought that sinners in Heaven will glorify Christ, than in the thought that I will have reward in Heaven for winning them.

Dear Christian, are you abiding in Christ and bearing fruit? If you are, ask what you will and bear much fruit. If you are not, then today set out to please Christ, abide in Him and bear much fruit so that your Father in Heaven will be glorified and that your own joy may be full!

CHAPTER VII

"Honour Thy Father and Thy Mother"

The first command with a promise is the fifth of the Ten Commandments. So part of God's program for a long, successful life is this, "Honour thy father and thy mother." Personal and national spiritual prosperity depend upon a proper relationship between godly parents and obedient, reverent children. A good Christian cannot be a rebel in the home.

The Ten Commandments sum up all law and all duty. The first three commandments tell our duty to God. The fourth commandment summed up for the Jew all ceremonial law. The last six commandments picture man's duties to all mankind. And the very first of those commandments about our duty to others is this blessed law:

"Honour thy father and thy mother: that thy days may be long upon the land which the Lord thy God giveth thee."— Exod. 20:12.

The sixth commandment says, "Thou shalt not kill," but before that comes the commandment, "Honour thy father and thy mother." ·

The seventh commandment says, "Thou shalt not commit adultery," but before that comes the command, "Honour thy father and thy mother."

The eighth commandment says, "Thou shalt not steal," but before that comes the command, "Honour thy father and thy mother."

The ninth commandment says, "Thou shalt not bear false witness against thy neighbour," but before that comes the command, "Honour thy father and thy mother."

The tenth commandment says, "Thou shalt not covet"—and all the booze selling, all the harlotry, all the corruption in public office, and nearly all the crime in the world are caused by covetousness. Yet before that command comes this plain law, "Honour thy father and thy mother."

In God's sight, then, the first duty of every living person is toward father and mother. One cannot be a good husband, or a good wife, or a good citizen, or a good friend, or a good servant, or a good master, or a good Christian until first he is a good son, or she is a good daughter. In God's sight the first duty is not of parent to child, but child to parent. The first duty is not toward the state, nor toward the church, nor toward the job, but toward father and mother. The heart of all morality, all virtue, all righteousness in our action is based upon obedience to this command, "Honour thy father and thy mother."

This command is quoted twice in the Old Testament: in Exodus 20:12 and in Deuteronomy 5:16. It is repeated six times in the New Testament. Jesus twice quoted it in Matthew —in Matthew 15:4 and Matthew 19:19; and twice in Mark— in Mark 7:10 and Mark 10:19; and once in Luke—Luke 18: 20. The commandment is also repeated in Ephesians 6:2. It is referred to in I Timothy 5:3, 4: "Honour widows . . . children . . . requite their parents. . . ." Ephesians 6:1 and Colossians 3:20 command children to obey their parents, and the plain teaching of this command is borne out throughout the Old and New Testaments. It is difficult to exaggerate the enormous importance of this commandment.

"Honour thy father and thy mother" is the first commandment with promise. No promise was given with the command to have one God, to avoid graven images or idols. Taking God's name in vain brings a stern warning that "God will not hold him guiltless," but no promise. No promise is given to those who keep the Sabbath in the fourth commandment. But Ephesians 6:2 reminds us this is the first commandment with promise. And the promise is "that thy days may be long upon the land which the Lord thy God giveth thee."

There is a reason why the Chinese are an unconquerable people who have for thousands of year maintained themselves and their civilization. They had learned scholars and classic writings; they made gun powder, made the finest porcelain and the most delicate silk long before the empires of Greece and Rome arose and when all of Europe was populated by savages. Even though they are heathen people, God has fulfilled His promise that their days should be long in the land. But the cardinal virtue of the Chinese is reverence, honor, respect and obedience to parents. They have sometimes even carried it to worship. They have sometimes perverted the doctrine. But they have in the past honored parents more than any nation in the world, and God has kept to them His blessed and unfailing Word.

It pays to honor father and mother. It pays in long life for individuals and in long life for nations.

Thus we can see that honoring our parents involves all the virtues that men admire and begets all the blessings men crave. Obedient sons and daughters could not be criminals, could not be godless, could not be traitors. To honor father and mother disciplines the mind and will, corrects errors, and inevitably develops character and virtue. To honor father and mother kills lawlessness at its source and naturally brings peace and prosperity. No wonder God put this command first of all in revealing our duties to others of mankind.

Our duty to father and mother does not come before our duty to God, but it comes before any other duty to mankind and could not contradict our duty to God.

The greatest possible fight against crime would be to start in the home and demand everywhere that children be strictly taught and compelled to honor father and mother.

How may we honor father and mother? The Scriptures tell us very plainly and here I will name some of the ways that the Bible commands us to honor father and mother.

I. By Obedience

Obedience is the first meaning of the command, "Honour thy father and thy mother." In Ephesians 6:1 we are commanded, "Children, obey your parents in the Lord: for this is right." In

Colossians 3:20 the Word of God says, "Children, obey your parents in all things: for this is well pleasing unto the Lord."

Note that the obedience of children to parents is to be un-limited. Children are to obey their parents "in all things." And we are particularly told that the duty of a Christian to His God does not interfere with this duty to parents. Christian children are still to obey their parents in all things, and this is well pleasing to the Lord.

Sometimes parents will be unconverted, but Christian sons and daughters must obey them. Sometimes mothers and fathers will be illiterate or ignorant, or drunkards, or ungodly, but children are to obey them. It would be the rarest thing imagina-ble if it should ever occur that any child could please God by being disobedient to parents.

Even about the matter of a vow to God, the daughter is plainly commanded that she is to let her father hear her vow, and then pass upon it. If her father should allow her vow to God, then the vow would stand. If her father should "disallow" her vow to God, then the vow would not stand (Num. 30:3-5). And notice that this command is about a *woman* in her father's house, and not a little girl. Grown daughters are to be subject to their fathers, even in the matter of religion and vows to God.

The Rechabites, a certain family who lived in Judaea in the time of Jeremiah, obeyed their father Jonadab even to the ex-tent of refusing to drink wine or build houses or sow seeds or plant vineyards or own them. They took this as a solemn duty to Almighty God, since it was commanded by their ancestors. And God commends them for it! (Jer. 35:1-14).

Jacob obeyed his father and mother even as to where he should go to find a wife (Gen. 28:7).

These are but illustrations of the command of God that children are to obey their parents in all things. Certainly there will come a time when the daughter must leave father and mother and put her husband first. There comes a time when the son is no longer a child and must be a man. The honor must continue then. But certainly every child must obey father and mother. And if a son were thirty years old and still lived at home with his parents, he would owe them a certain duty of obedience that he could not refuse without dishonoring God and breaking this commandment.

Parents are duty-bound to enforce this obedience. There can be no obedience without commands. So it is the Christian duty of parents to demand and enforce strict obedience.

The extent of the parents' authority and responsibility to their children is made clear to us in Deuteronomy 21:18-21:

"If a man have a stubborn and rebellious son, which will not obey the voice of his father, or the voice of his mother, and that, when they have chastened him, will not hearken unto them: Then shall his father and his mother lay hold on him, and bring him out unto the elders of his city, and unto the gate of his place; And they shall say unto the elders of his city, This our son is stubborn and rebellious, he will not obey our voice; he is a glutton, and a drunkard. And all the men of his city shall stone him with stones, that he die: so shalt thou put evil away from among you; and all Israel shall hear, and fear."

This command was given, the Scripture says, for this purpose: "So shalt thou put evil away from among you; and all Israel shall hear, and fear." For a father and mother to have their own son beaten to death with stones seems horrible. But in God's sight it is not nearly so horrible as to have such a boy grow up disobedient to parents, lawless toward government, irreligious and wicked toward God. Sin is far worse in God's sight than it is in our sight. And disobedience and rebellion is the very heart and substance of sin.

Many, many times the Bible plainly commands that children are to be whipped or beaten in order to make them mind. It is true that beating with a rod is not the *whole* duty of parents to children. Many other things parents ought to do, too. But it is equally certain from the Bible that beating with the rod is certainly a duty of parents toward children in many, many, many cases.

Consider prayerfully the following Scriptures, and remember that these are the plain commands of God in His inspired Word.

"He that spareth his rod hateth his son: but he that loveth him chasteneth him betimes."—Prov. 13:24.

"Chasten thy son while there is hope, and let not thy soul spare for his crying."—Prov. 19:18.

"The blueness of a wound cleanseth away evil: so do stripes the inward parts of the belly."—Prov. 20:30.

"Foolishness is bound in the heart of a child; but the rod of correction shall drive it far from him."—Prov. 22:15.

"Withhold not correction from the child: for if thou beatest him with the rod, he shall not die. Thou shalt beat him with the rod, and shalt deliver his soul from hell."—Prov. 23:13, 14.

"The rod and reproof give wisdom: but a child left to himself bringeth his mother to shame. . . . Correct thy son, and he shall give thee rest; yea, he shall give delight unto thy soul."—Prov. 29:15, 17.

Here as plainly as it can be said in human language, God tells us that to chastise children bodily is a mark of parental love, that it cleanses the heart, that it drives away foolishness, that it keeps children from going to Hell, that it gives wisdom to the child and rest and delight to the parent.

All the foolish thoughts that children would not love parents who whipped them are belied by the Word of God. And the experience of past generations proves that a real respect of children for parents cannot be had without punishment for sins. Really, children that are corrected and whipped when necessary; made to mind, made to speak respectfully, and to work honestly, will rise up in later years and call the father and mother blessed who helped them to form noble character by scriptural punishment, as well as by prayer and teaching and example.

I say, the parents must enforce obedience as well as deserving it. God holds parents to blame when children are disobedient.

Abraham was commended because, God said, "I know him, that he will command his children and his household after him, and they shall keep the way of the Lord, to do justice and judgment; that the Lord may bring upon Abraham that which he hath spoken of him" (Gen. 18:19).

But contrasted to Abraham is the case of Eli. His grown sons were wicked and adulterous, though in the priesthood. And God brought a curse upon the whole house of Eli, and sent him word by the boy Samuel in these words:

"For I have told him that I will judge his house for ever for the iniquity which he knoweth; because his sons made themselves vile, and he restrained them not. And therefore I have sworn unto the house of Eli, that the iniquity of Eli's house shall not be purged with sacrifice nor offering for ever."— I Sam. 3:13, 14.

Here God held Eli responsible for the restraint of his grown and wicked sons and brought a curse upon him and all his descendants.

All over the land there are young people claiming to be Christians, and in many cases sincerely longing to please God and live moral and upright lives, but who utterly fail to please God because they do not obey father and mother. Remember that God said, "Behold, to obey is better than sacrifice, and to hearken than the fat of rams" (I Sam. 15:22).

There is no way to obey God unless you obey those God put over you. One who cannot bow to the will of father and mother and give loving obedience to the ones to whom he owes more than to anyone else in the world, cannot obey God. No doubt in many, many cases Christian young people find they have no peace and they wonder why they cannot feel the Lord's nearness, and the joy of the conscious communion of the Holy Spirit. In many such cases the Holy Spirit is grieved by this wicked sin of rebellion against fathers and mothers. "Children, obey your parents in the Lord: for this is right" (Eph. 6:1).

And again hear the Word of God: "Children, obey your parents *in all things:* for this is well pleasing unto the Lord" (Col. 3:20).

II. Heart Reverence and Respect Demanded

When the Lord said, "Honour thy father and thy mother,"

He meant an honor that really comes from the heart. The outward form of obedience is not enough. Just as the Pharisees who brought sacrifices and tithes, who fasted, who made long prayers, and who made clean the outside of the cup and the platter to be seen of men, did not really please God; just so an outward form of obedience to parents is wicked. God demands that the son and daughter honor father and mother from the heart.

The shame and sin of disrespect for parents are indicated by Leviticus 20:9 where the Lord commanded: "For every one that curseth his father or his mother shall be surely put to death: he hath cursed his father or his mother; his blood shall be upon him." Disrespectful words to or about parents are sinful and wicked and worthy the death penalty in the sight of God.

Even so, in Proverbs 15:5 we are told that one is a fool who "despiseth his father's instruction," but a reverent respect for the father's instruction is a matter of wisdom, in God's sight. And on the same theme, Proverbs 30:17 tells us, "The eye that mocketh at his father and despiseth to obey his mother, the ravens of the valley shall pick it out and the young eagles shall eat it."

Not only outward rebellion, but a disrespectful glance of a son or daughter toward father or mother is horrible sin in God's sight and will bring sure punishment from God.

Children should respect the physical body of father and of mother with a holy reverence. Leviticus 18:7 says, "The nakedness of thy father, or the nakedness of thy mother, shalt thou not uncover: she is thy mother; thou shalt not uncover her nakedness."

Women who appear before their children three-quarters naked sin against God and help to break down the proper respect of children for parents.

In Genesis 9:20-22 we are told how soon after the flood Noah planted a vineyard and drank of the wine and was drunken, and lay uncovered in his tent. "And Ham, the father of Canaan, saw the nakedness of his father, and told his two brethren without," we are told. Noah's drunkenness may have been unintentional; let us hope that it was. At any rate, this Scripture does not stress Noah's mistake; rather, it impresses upon us the horrible sin of Ham who saw his father's nakedness. With the Spirit of prophecy that was upon him, Noah, when he learned what his younger son had done in seeing him stretched out naked in his tent, pronounced a horrible curse upon Canaan, Ham's son. And to this very day the descendants of Ham are to be servants of the descendants of Shem and of Japheth.

May God help us to take fully to heart the lesson. Children ought to have a reverential respect toward fathers and mothers.

Some parents very foolishly teach their children to call them by their first names. In the first place that is a sin, and in the second place it is folly. If Sarah was commended for calling her husband, Abraham, "Lord," then how much more important it is that children should address their parents only in the most reverential, respectful terms!

A girl goes away to college. She does not write mother with any regularity. And father, perhaps, only gets a brief note when there is need for more money. How wicked! And many a boy goes off to the city to work, and is so occupied with his companions that he does not even answer mother's letter. If you are that kind, then you are a cheat, and guilty of the basest ingratitude. The hearts of mother and father long to know all about their children. But even more, they long to have the love and respect and reverence that are their proper due.

If one reads this who has been guilty of neglect of father or mother, I hope that today you will remedy that error and confess and forsake that sin. Letters, words of endearment, a chaste kiss, pictures, telegrams, flowers, and gifts—how much they mean to parents when sons and daughters begin to break the home ties or even when they are far away. No son or daughter really honors father or mother who does not day by day remember, and with reverential and loving respect, seek to make the days happy and make mother and father proud and glad. To honor father and mother is more than deed; it is an attitude of heart.

III. To Honor Means Financial Support and Provision for Father and Mother

"God so loved . . . that he gave. . . ." Love always gives. And so it is with a real honor for father and mother in the heart of any son or daughter. To pretend to honor father and mother and yet to let them go hungry or to fail to provide for their comforts and happiness in material things is hypocrisy. It is God's appointed way that "Honour thy father and thy mother" means to support father and mother when they need it.

Note that this is the meaning the Saviour Himself gave to this commandment. In Mark 7:10-13 are the following words of Jesus:

"For Moses said, Honour thy father and thy mother; and, Whoso curseth father or mother, let him die the death. But ye say, If a man shall say to his father or mother, It is Corban, that is to say, a gift, by whatsoever thou mightest be profited by me; he shall be free. And ye suffer him no more to do ought for his father or his mother; Making the word of God of none effect through your tradition, which ye have delivered; and many such like things do ye."

Jesus is discussing the command, "Honour thy father and thy mother," the sixth of the Ten Commandments. And He plainly says that when the Pharisees, or religious leaders, encouraged young people to dedicate their money to God, saying, "It is Corban," and then allowing such young people to do no more for father and mother, they were guilty of wicked perversion of Scripture. They were putting their tradition in the place of the Word of God, and making the Word of God of none effect, Jesus said, because "Honour thy father and thy mother" means to support father and mother.

There are two lessons which are plainly indicated here. One is that while all of us should give to the Lord's cause in proportion as He has prospered us, yet it is wicked to make that an excuse for not supporting parents. If a son can eat, then father and mother should eat. If he has a shelter over his head, then father and mother should have a shelter also. It is wicked and unchristian for sons and daughters not to provide for fathers and mothers when they are old.

And another lesson is this: The Saviour seems to have fore-known that in these days there would be great pressure on various groups to take care of old people. The churches are besieged to care for the old and poor and unemployed. And the government is urged to give them pensions.

A foolish and wicked plan proposed to take the responsibility away from children and saddle it upon an overloaded govern-ment. That is absolutely contrary to the Word of God. God's plan is that sons and daughters should care for their mothers and fathers. That is involved, Jesus tells us here, in the com-mand to "Honour thy father and thy mother." And the prom-ise, "That thy days may be long upon the land which the Lord thy God giveth thee," is not to governments which furnish an old-age pension, but to a people whose parents are supported by their children, whenever necessary.

This teaching, that children are responsible to God to take care of their elders, is repeated in I Timothy 5:3, 4. The ques-tion under discussion is this: Shall the local church be respon-sible for the financial support of widows in the congregation? And in answer, this chapter plainly tells us, "Honour widows that are widows indeed. But if any widow have children or nephews, let them learn first to show piety at home, and to requite their parents: for that is good and acceptable before God."

And here *honor* means to provide for. But the church is not to provide for widows who have children, or even those who have nephews. It is a shame for parents to be supported by a church when there are children. It is true piety, says this Scripture, for children to "requite their parents."

Note the word *requite*. It means to pay back. Every child owes an honest debt, and he is dishonest if he does not requite his parents, and earnestly try to make up to them the money and the care which have been so unselfishly poured out on him by father and mother.

Then that passage in I Timothy 5 continues (verse 8): "But

if any provide not for his own [his own widows or his own parents], and especially those of his own house, he hath denied the faith, and is worse than an infidel." And the chapter expressly commands that younger widows are not to be supported at all by the church, and no old people are to be supported by the churches who have saved children. In other words, real Christians take care of father and mother in old age, and those who do not are worse than infidels, says the Scripture.

Many people have thought that I Timothy 5:8 referred to a man providing for his wife and children, but it is not so. It plainly teaches that if children do not requite their parents, and if younger people do not care for the widows and dependent older ones of their families, that they are worse than infidels. A heathen Chinese supports his aged parents; why should not a Christian do far more?

Let every reader consider well the reasons for supporting father and mother. First, honesty requires it. One who is not willing to pay back the care and support that was lavished on him is crooked and dishonest. Second, gratitude would compel anyone with a tender heart to rejoice at the privilege of providing for father and mother who have done so much for him. Third, it is nature's law, that the productive period should be in youth and middle life. Little children need someone to care for them. Older people who have passed the years of employability and productivity should be supported. Parents should first care for children and then children should care for parents: That is nature's law, and God's law.

Great blessings will come when children support their aged parents who are unable to support themselves. First, it will relieve the government and relieve business of the burden of pensions. God did not command the government to care for old people. God did not command business firms to care for retired employees. But certainly God did command children to care for their parents.

Second, a far greater blessing would be that it would make the family tie again strong. It would encourage large families. Children would be regarded as a blessing and not as a liability.

It would give peace of mind and trust in God to old people. It would eliminate enormous social and economic problems and make for a widespread general peace and prosperity. In other words, it would lead to the fulfillment of the blessed promise of God: "That thy days may be long upon the land which the Lord thy God giveth thee."

To honor father and mother means to provide for them in old age, as the Scriptures clearly teach.

IV. True Godliness Honors Parents Best

Honoring father and mother is a matter more of the heart than of the hand. Thus true godliness on the part of children brings the greatest honor to father and mother and the greatest joy to their hearts.

Proverbs 23:24 and 25 says:

"The father of the righteous shall greatly rejoice: and he that begetteth a wise child shall have joy of him. Thy father and thy mother shall be glad, and she that bare thee shall rejoice."

How many times I have known of mothers who would lie awake at night weeping over sons or daughters who were dutiful in outward matters but unsaved. Such sons and daughters go through the outward form of obedience, in their hearts they rebel against God and bring shame and heartache and grief to parents.

We are told: "A wise son maketh a glad father: but a foolish son is the heaviness of his mother" (Prov. 10:1).

And again: "A wise son maketh a glad father: but a foolish man despiseth his mother" (Prov. 15:20).

And: "A foolish son is a grief to his father" (Prov. 17:25).

And, "A foolish son is the calamity of his father" (Prov. 19:13).

And, "A companion of riotous men shameth his father" (Prov. 28:7).

Certainly it is clear that a child cannot honor his father and go into sin or turn away from God.

How Timothy's unfeigned faith and great usefulness must

have pleased his godly mother, and his good Christian grandmother, Lois!

And how the prodigal son brought grief and shame to his father! The father's money was wasted, the father's heart was broken, and the reproaches of the elder brother made the father's lot harder yet.

My own mother gave me to the Lord when I was born. I didn't learn of it until years later, after she had gone to Heaven. And now it makes me happy to feel that she rejoices, knowing that I love the Lord, knowing my labors and how earnestly I am trying to get out the Gospel to a dying world.

Even in Heaven our mothers know about us. The Bible tells us that there are tears in Heaven (Rev. 21:4). Parents even in Heaven are honored or dishonored by their children.

Years ago the song, "Tell Mother I'll Be There," touched thousands of hearts. Many a prodigal boy and many a wayward girl came to the Saviour under the moving impulse of the thought that a mother in Heaven would be honored and pleased at the joyful news of her child's conversion. And surely when "joy shall be in heaven over one sinner that repenteth, more than over ninety and nine just persons, which need no repentance" (Luke 15:7), the mother would have a large part in the rejoicing.

How can you honor your mother or father without making sure of meeting them in Heaven, How can you honor father and mother without trusting in their Saviour and serving their God? It is my humble prayer that today some reader may resolve: "I will trust in the Saviour my mother loved and believed in. Today I will follow in the footsteps of my godly father or my Christian mother."

If you will decide that today, then will you let me hear from you? I will write you a personal letter and answer any questions and will send you free some gospel literature that will give sweet assurance so you may know your sins are forgiven and your soul saved.

Then one glad day in Heaven the circle will be unbroken and the whole family can gather and praise God together!

And if your parents are unsaved, it will certainly not honor them to go on in sin, for the Scripture says, "Sin is a reproach to any people." Even when mother and father are not saved, they do not want their son to be a drunkard nor their girl to be a harlot. Your unbelief, your worldliness, your rejection of Christ will bring shame and heartache to them in the long run. So the best thing you can ever do to honor father and mother will be to take Christ as your own Saviour, trusting Him with all your heart, depending on Him to forgive your sins and save your soul. Will you do that today?

"Honour thy father and thy mother: that thy days may be long upon the, land which the Lord thy God giveth thee."— Exod. 20:12.

Dr. Shelton Smith
Sword of the Lord Foundation
P. O. Box 1099
Murfreesboro, TN 37133

Dear Dr. Smith:

I have read Dr. John R. Rice's sermon on "Honour Thy Father and Thy Mother." I see that my rebellion against my parents and against society is fundamentally rebellion against God. And I admit that I am a poor, lost sinner who has not been saved and who needs forgiveness and salvation. I believe that Jesus Christ died for me and wants to save me, as the Bible says; so here and now I come to Him in my heart, confessing my sinfulness and asking Him for forgiveness and mercy. I here and now surrender my heart to Him and trust Him to forgive me. I will claim Him openly as my Saviour and will set out to live for Him. Now that I am taking Christ as my own personal Saviour, please send me some free literature that will encourage and help me as I live for the Lord.

Name _____

Address _____

_____

City_____ State_____ Zip_____

CHAPTER VIII

Five Bible Rules About Fellowship

1. Christians Should Avoid the Fellowship of the Unsaved, the Ungodly.

2. The Christian Must Always Act in Love, Abhoring Evil, Cleaving to the Good.

3. Those Weak in the Faith Are to Be Received in Fellowship, "but Not to Doubtful Disputations."

4. Those Denying Essential Doctrines About Christ Are Not Saved, Are Not to be Received as Christians nor Supported.

5. God's Preachers and Teachers Must Rebuke and Reprove Sin, Though It Will Offend Some.

Every real Christian is a child of God, is born again, is going to Heaven. He then should live to show that. The companionship of those who are not Christians would tend to influence Christians wrong, to lead them to sin, to hinder their spiritual life and growth and usefulness.

1. Christians Should Avoid the Fellowship of the Unsaved, the Ungodly

This is made very clear in the Scripture. Psalm 1:1 says, "Blessed is the man that walketh not in the counsel of the ungodly, not standeth in the way of sinners, nor sitteth in the seat of the scornful." So the counsel, the walk and the fellowship with the ungodly, the sinful, the scoffers are forbidden for the Christian.

Again, Ephesians 5:11 says, "And have no fellowship with the unfruitful works of darkness, but rather reprove them."

One of the plainest Scriptures on this matter is in II Corinthians 6:14-18. There the inspired Word of God says:

"Be ye not unequally yoked together with unbelievers: for what fellowship hath righteousness with unrighteousness? and what communion hath light with darkness? And what concord hath Christ with Belial? or what part hath he that believeth with an infidel? And what agreement hath the temple of God with idols? for ye are the temple of the living God; as God hath said, I will dwell in them, and walk in them; and I will be their God, and they shall be my people. Wherefore come out from among them, and be ye separate, saith the Lord, and touch not the unclean thing; and I will receive you, And will be a Father unto you, and ye shall be my sons and daughters, saith the Lord Almighty."

So the first rule about Christian fellowship is that a Christian should avoid the fellowship of the wicked, seek the fellowship of godly people.

Always, of course, we should love lost sinners, seek to know them, seek to love them, to help them, to win them. But we should not take up their ways, should not join in their sin, should not condone nor take any part in their actions, their viewpoints and their teachings that are sinful and wrong.

First of all, Christians should marry Christians. The closest tie on earth between two people is the marriage bond. Misery and trouble and failure in the Christian life often follow when a Christian disobeys God's plan here and marries the unsaved.

That means that Christian young people should not date unsaved people and so fall in love nor ever condone a marriage of a saved person with a lost person.

Of course, after the marriage is sealed it should not be broken. Vows and contracts should be kept. And the converted man and woman should seek to win the unconverted mate. How happy when both the husband and wife love and serve the same Lord, read the Scriptures together, have the same great principles to live by and can pray together over their family, their needs, their usefulness, their children! Marriage ought not be an unequal yoke.

In secret orders, sometimes people take bloody oaths, oaths forbidden in the Scriptures, to bind themselves to support, to patronize, to defend others in the secret order who are unconverted. Thus they put a tie with an unsaved lodge member more binding than the tie of pastor and people or the tie of Christian brotherhood or Christian influence. That is wrong. Any yoke that binds us in spiritual matters to unsaved people is wrong.

Thus Christians should not belong to churches where people who do not claim to be converted or who do not believe the Bible are regarded as Christians, along with born-again Bible believers. That is wrong. A Christian should be in a church where people believe the Bible, where one must claim to trust Christ as Saviour before he is admitted as a member.

So with the ministerial association or other religious organizations. Christians ought not give Christian recognition to those who are not Christians. They ought not call those "brethren" who are not really spiritual brethren. One who does not hold the historic Christian faith, does not accept the deity of Christ, the infallible inspiration of the Bible and has not trusted Christ personally as Saviour, is not a Christian and ought not be called a Christian. The yoke is unequal when born-again people and unconverted cultists or liberals and modernists are in the same organization, calling each other brethren.

That means, too, that a Christian ought not support any denominational program where part of the money goes to support unbelievers in Christ and the Bible—liberals, modernists, and those who do not hold the historic Christian faith.

So the first rule of fellowship is that Christians should have fellowship with born-again Christians. He should love outsiders but remember they are outsiders. He should earnestly seek to save the lost sinner with fear "pulling them out of the fire; hating even the garment spotted by the flesh."

In the business world we necessarily must buy in stores and travel on buses and sometimes work in schools along with unsaved people, but when the tie is spiritual and moral it should be with saved people, not with unsaved people.

2. Christians Ought to Act and Speak in Love

Romans 12:9 commands us, "Let love be without dissimulation. Abhor that which is evil; cleave to that which is good." Christians ought not to act out of malice, ought not to hate people, ought not to try to do evil, but always to do good with love and kindness.

However, remember that Scripture says that love is to be without dissimulation or hypocrisy, not pretense. The right kind of love which is from God means that we are to "abhor that which is evil; cleave to that which is good." Parents who love a child will yet whip a child to make him do right. Pastors who love sinners will preach against sin and warn them of coming judgment. A policeman may love the wrongdoer when he arrests him, and the judge may love the criminal when he sentences him. Love must be without hypocrisy and pretense. For anybody to pretend that it is love when he puts up with sin and does not condemn it and does not punish evil and does not want sin punished, then that is love with dissimulation. The right kind of love is to abhor that which is evil and cleave to that which is good. So the preacher who loves God the most and loves people the most will be the plainest in his preaching. But a Christian ought never to act from malice or hate of people.

3. The Weak "in the Faith" Should Be Received but Not to Doubtful Disputations

In Romans 14:1 we are commanded, "Him that is weak in the faith receive ye, but not to doubtful disputations." That means that I am to receive those who are in the faith, but who are not necessarily grown up and strong in the faith. It does not mean I am to receive a man as a Christian who is not a Christian, who does not believe the Bible, who has not been converted, who does not believe Jesus Christ is all He claimed to be, the virgin-born Son of God. But those who "are in the faith," that is, who are real Christians, we ought to receive even if they are weak. I ought to count such a man a brother, even if he talks in tongues or if he believes in falling from grace, or if he does not know what the Bible teaches about Christ's second coming.

However, there is a Bible limitation here. "Him that is weak in the faith receive ye, *but not to doubtful disputations.*" I should not keep company with one who makes a great division and strife over some lesser matter. A born-again Christian who believes in sprinkling is my brother and I can have fellowship with him as long as he does not make division and strife over sprinkling or other lesser matters. A man may not understand the Bible teaching that the preacher of God must condemn sin and rebuke unbelief, but if he does not make division and strife in his ignorance, then I will count him a Christian brother and will have fellowship with him.

4. But We Are Not to Fellowship With Those Who Deny the Bible Doctrine About Christ

There is a clear Bible rule in II John, verses 7-11 which says, "For many deceivers are entered into the world, who confess not that Jesus Christ is come in the flesh. This is a deceiver and an antichrist. Look to yourselves, that we lose not those things which we have wrought, but that we receive a full reward. Whosoever transgresseth, and abideth not in the doctrine of Christ, hath not God. He that abideth in the doctrine of Christ, he hath both the Father and the Son. If there come any unto you, and bring not this doctrine, receive him not into your house, neither bid him God speed: For he that biddeth him God speed is partaker of his evil deeds."

So one might differ on other doctrines and be a Christian, but he cannot be far wrong on the doctrine about the person of Jesus Christ, His deity, His virgin birth, His bodily resurrection, His blood atonement—a man cannot deny these truths and be a Christian. One can be wrong on baptism and be a Christian, but he cannot be wrong on "the doctrine of Christ." That is what the Bible teaches about Christ.

And on this matter a good Christian has to obey the Scripture. He is simply to know that such a man "hath not God," is not saved. And such a man we are not to have in fellowship, not to receive him in our houses or pulpit, not to bid him Godspeed. If such a man teaches in a Baptist school, we are not to give any money to that school. If such a man preaches in the pulpit, we are not to go to hear him and endorse him. A Christian is clearly forbidden to yoke up with or to offer Christian recognition to a man who is wrong on the essential doctrine of who Jesus Christ is, His virgin birth, His blood atonement, His bodily resurrection, etc.

We are not left to choose for ourselves whether we have fellowship with such people or not.

Second Corinthians 6:14-18 commands us: "Be ye not unequally yoked together with unbelievers: for what fellowship hath righteousness with unrighteousness? and what communion hath light with darkness? And what concord hath Christ with Belial? or what part hath he that believeth with an infidel? And what agreement hath the temple of God with idols? for ye are the temple of the living God; as God hath said, I will dwell in them, and walk in them; and I will be their God; and they shall be my people. Wherefore come out from among them, and be ye separate, saith the Lord, and touch not the unclean thing; and I will receive you, And will be a Father unto you, and ye shall be my sons and daughters, saith the Lord Almighty."

So brotherly love is no excuse for running with people who are not saved, supporting people through churches who do not believe the Bible and who have not been converted, etc.

USUALLY THOSE IN FALSE CULTS ARE NOT SAVED. Someone says, "Brother Rice, I can't believe that other Christians who are true to their faith and beliefs, whether they are Catholics, Mormons, Jehovah's Witnesses, Methodists, Churches of Christ, Episcopalians, Presbyterians, Baptists, or any other, as far as they are in the will of the Lord, that they are going to miss Heaven. . . ." But here, dear friend, you show that you are mixed up and uninformed. You indicate that God reveals to one man he is to be a Catholic and pray to Mary, depend on the priest for forgiveness; you indicate that another man is to go by the Book of Mormon instead of the Bible and that he is to depend upon baptism and the laying on of hands of elders of the Mormon Church to get him to Heaven. You indicate that God led Jehovah's Witnesses to deny the actual deity of Jesus. You feel that Churches of Christ, people who teach baptismal regeneration and do not teach being born again by faith in Christ, are Christians just like anybody else. Now, we know that some individuals in all these groups have been converted, but they are not converted by those doctrines which are wrong. It is obvious to one who has had contact with thousands of Catholics that most of them know nothing in the world about salvation. They have never personally trusted Christ. They are depending on the church, the priest, and on Mary, and have not personally taken Christ as Saviour. And so I have seen the same thing with Jehovah's Witnesses and Mormons. There are multitudes of them who never heard of being born again, and know nothing about personally trusting Christ for a new heart.

Now the simple truth is that one who does not take Jesus as his only Saviour and rely on Him simply is not saved; so the Bible teaches. And I would sin if I should call people saved who openly admit they have not been converted, born again, admit they are not depending on Jesus Christ to save them. You seem to feel there is no difference between any heathen religion and the historic Christian faith, but you are certainly mistaken. You think that just so a person is sincere he is saved, but that is certainly not true according to the Bible. Those who depend on Jesus Christ for forgiveness are saved. Those who do not know Jesus as Saviour and do not trust Him to save simply are not saved. And according to plain statements in the Bible, one who does not believe that Jesus Christ is God has not trusted Him and is not saved.

5. *Preachers and Christians Must Take Sides Against Sin*

There is another Bible rule which Christians ought to observe in matters of fellowship with others. That is those who take any place of leadership for Christ ought to condemn sin. God commanded in Isaiah 58:1, "Cry aloud, spare not, lift up thy voice like a trumpet and shew my people their transgression, and the house of Jacob their sins." The preacher, the prophet, is to condemn the sins of God's people and do it openly. That does not mean lack of love; it does not mean ill will and trying to get even. It means that we should help people do right. Paul commanded Timothy, "Them that sin rebuke before all, that others also may fear" (I Tim. 5:20). And then in his farewell message Paul commanded, "Preach the word; be instant in season, out of season; reprove, rebuke, exhort with all long-suffering and doctrine." The preacher who does not "reprove, rebuke, and exhort with longsuffering and doctrine" does not obey the Bible.

In many cases an individual's mistake or sin is not leading others astray, and can be talked over with the Christian and he may be helped privately. And in other cases, when the sin leads many others wrong and is a public sin, it must sometimes be rebuked openly. That is the way Paul was led to rebuke Peter in Galatians 2:11-14. Barnabas and others were being led away by Peter's hypocrisy, refusing to eat and have fellowship with the Gentile Christians. So Paul says, "But when Peter was come to Antioch, I withstood him to the face, because he was to be blamed." The man who stands up against false doctrine or against yoking up with unbelievers or against outright scandalous worldliness is doing what God has commanded him to do. To have peace at the expense of morality, to have peace at the expense of truth, is never proper. That means that the man of God who is true to Christ will not always have everybody for him. He will suffer some persecution. That is why Jesus said, "Blessed are ye, when men shall hate you, and when they shall separate you from their company, and shall reproach you, and cast out your name as evil, for the Son of man's sake. Rejoice ye in that day, and leap for joy: for, behold, your reward is great in heaven: for in the like manner did their fathers unto the prophets" (Luke 6:22, 23).

The person who is true to Christ will not please all men. The preacher who has the most friends and the fewest enemies is thereby proved to be a poorer Christian and a sorrier preacher. The preacher who does not make many enemies and does not have many against him has failed to be true to Christ.

On the other hand, the person who honestly and in love and faithfulness rebukes sin and obeys the Bible in his preaching will have people say all manner of evil against him and separate from his company. A good Christian is to be known by his enemies as well as by his friends. The world hates Jesus Christ and the servant is no better than his master.

The above rules are God's rules, not mine. Let us go over them again.

1. Christians should avoid the fellowship of the unsaved, the ungodly.

2. The Christian is to love both saints and sinners and do right without malice, even when he must be against sin.

3. The Christians who are weak in the faith are to be received, and we are to have fellowship with those who differ with us as long as it is not "to doubtful disputations" and does not make divisions and strife.

4. We are not to count a man a Christian who does not believe the Bible, who does not believe that Christ is the virgin-born Saviour as He claimed to be, and who does not personally trust Him and His atoning blood for salvation. We are never to receive as a Christian brother one who is against the Christ of the Bible or against the authority of the Bible. We are not to receive him in our houses nor bid him Godspeed.

5. We are to rebuke sin lovingly but firmly and for Jesus' sake and for the good of those to whom we preach and teach.

CHAPTER IX

"Keep Yourselves From Idols"

"Little children, keep yourselves from idols. Amen."
I John 5:21.

Here is a plain command of God, written to Christians, God's "little children." Christians are warned to "keep yourselves from idols."

It is shocking that hardly ever does a preacher preach today on the sin of idolatry. Yet it looms very large in Scripture and in the warnings which God gives.

In the Ten Commandments, for example, the first two commands are: "Thou shalt have no other gods before me. Thou shalt not make unto thee any graven image, or any likeness of any thing that is in heaven above, or that is in the earth beneath, or that is in the water under the earth."

Two of the Ten Commandments deal with idolatry! The first two commandments use ninety-eight words in the King James Version, while the last five—including all man's duties to mankind—use only seventy-six words! Since the command about idols is first and since it is stressed more than any other and takes up two of the Ten Commandments, surely people ought to take it to heart.

In a tour of Cairo, Egypt, we went to the Museum where lies a giant carved statue of Rameses, perhaps ninety feet long. In a corner of that museum is a little squat idol, perhaps three or four feet high, big-bellied and naked. Someone remarked: "I don't see how anybody could worship that ugly, senseless thing!"

But people did not worship that little thing; they worshiped what that represented. People who worship idols have something that represents their god: what they love the most, what they think of most, and what they adhere to.

We read in I Corinthians 10:20, "But I say, that the things which the Gentiles sacrifice, they sacrifice to devils, and not to God: and I would not that ye should have fellowship with devils." You see, actually to the wooden or golden idol, before which heathens bow, they ascribe the virtues of some evil spirit that really is back of it. When a man carved an idol out of a log, it was not the wood he worshiped but some spirit that it represented, as the Scripture said—the worship of devils through some wooden or brazen or golden idol, perhaps.

Here we are commanded, "Little children, keep yourselves from idols." Let us take it to heart.

I. How Strong Is the Bible Emphasis on Idolatry

We have sinned in being careless about idolatry, and preachers, no doubt, have sinned in not warning people about idolatry.

1. In the Ten Commandments, Idolatry Is the First Thing Forbidden

Let us give here the first two commandments of the Ten Commandments:

"I am the Lord thy God, which have brought thee out of the land of Egypt, out of the house of bondage. Thou shalt have no other gods before me. Thou shalt not make unto thee any graven image, or any likeness of any thing that is in heaven above, or that is in the earth beneath, or that is in the water under the earth. Thou shalt not bow down thyself to them, nor serve them: for I the Lord thy God am a jealous God, visiting the iniquity of the fathers upon the children unto the third and fourth generation of them that hate me; And shewing mercy unto thousands of them that love me, and keep my commandments."—Exod. 20:2-6.

Notice again that there are ninety-eight words in these two verses about idolatry and only seventy-six words in the last five commandments of the ten!

And when the Lord Jesus sums up the Ten Commandments in two commandments, He gave the first commandment thus:

"Thou shalt love the Lord thy God with all thy heart, and with all thy soul, and with all thy mind. This is the first and great commandment."—Matt. 22:37, 38.

We can see at once that a simple acknowledgment that the God of the Bible is our God and we believe in Christ as Saviour is not enough. God wants not only love but wholehearted love that exceeds our love for anything else. He means an allegiance and loyalty that will please God before it will please anybody else. He means that the heart, soul and mind are all to be committed to God. Less than that would be a kind of idolatry, for Jesus here is summing up the commands about idolatry as well as other duties to God.

We would be foolish to suppose that this command about idolatry was simply a ceremonial command and meant we were not to make wood nor metal idols. Far more than that!

2. In the New Testament, Idolatry Is Mentioned Again and Again

Here in the text for today we are told, "Little children, keep yourselves from idols." Among the works of the flesh idolatry is named along with other awful and hateful sins. Galatians 5:19-21 says:

"Now the works of the flesh are manifest, which are these; Adultery, fornication, uncleanness, lasciviousness, IDOLATRY, witchcraft, hatred, variance, emulations, wrath, strife, seditions, heresies, Envyings, murders, drunkenness, revellings, and such like: of the which I tell you before, as I have also told you in time past, that they which do such things shall not inherit the kingdom of God."

And we are plainly told in verse 17 of that chapter that "the flesh lusteth against the Spirit, and the Spirit against the flesh: and these are contrary the one to the other: so that ye cannot do the things that ye would." So you who read this must beware of the hatred, wrath, strife, heresies, envyings, murders, drunkenness, revellings and adultery named in the same passage. Idolatry is a work of the flesh and comes natural to man, just as other sins do.

In Colossians 3:5 we are told again that idolatry comes natural to our old carnal nature and we are commanded,

"Mortify therefore your members which are upon the earth; fornication, uncleanness, inordinate affection, evil concupiscence, and COVETOUSNESS, WHICH IS IDOLATRY. . . ."

Every Christian needs to mortify his members and the tendency toward idolatry which all of us have.

First Corinthians 5:10, 11 tells us:

"Yet not altogether with the fornicators of this world, or with the covetous, or extortioners, or with IDOLATERS; for then must ye needs go out of the world. But now I have written unto you not to keep company, if any man that is called a brother be a fornicator, or covetous, or an IDOLATER, or a railer, or a drunkard, or an extortioner; with such an one no not to eat."

We are to withdraw fellowship from those who claim to be Christians, and probably are, but who are guilty of idolatry. How strange and yet how strong is that command!

And in I Corinthians 6:9, 10, when God is talking about the wicked, unregenerate sinners who cannot go to Heaven, He speaks of fornicators, IDOLATERS, adulterers, effeminate, abusers of themselves with mankind, thieves, covetous, drunkards, revilers, extortioners, etc., and says these "shall not inherit the kingdom of God." It is true, as He says following that, "And such were some of you: but ye are washed. . . ."

3. In the New Testament, the Warning Against Idolatry Is Often Given in Other Terms

It is true we have a clear command, "Little children, keep yourselves from idols." But that command appears in many other terms in the New Testament. And that is not surprising.

In the Ten Commandments the Lord commanded, "Thou shalt not kill," but in the New Testament we learn that "whosoever hateth his brother is a murderer . . ." (I John 3:15).

And we learn that "whosoever shall say, Thou fool, shall be in danger of hell fire" (Matt. 5:22).

In the Ten Commandments we are commanded, "Thou shalt not commit adultery," but Jesus puts it in these words, ". . . whosoever looketh on a woman to lust after her hath committed adultery with her already in his heart" (Matt. 5:28). So idolatry may be put in other terms also, and it often is.

The Lord Jesus could have said, "Whoever loves his father or mother more than he loves Me or puts their will before pleasing Me is an idolater." That is true all right, but the words with which Jesus stated it are these in Luke 14:26, 27, "If any man come to me, and hate not his father, and mother, and wife, and children, and brethren, and sisters, yea, and his own life also, he cannot be my disciple. And whosoever doth not bear his cross, and come after me, cannot be my disciple." And then again He said in Luke 14:33, "So likewise, whosoever he be of you that forsaketh not all that he hath, he cannot be my disciple." That is a command against idolatry, for one who puts his possessions before his love for God and serving God is thus an idolater.

The Lord Jesus could have said that one who puts his money and his business and his possessions ahead of his love for God and service to God is an idolater. But instead, Jesus said the same thing in other words. In Matthew 6:24 He said, "No man can serve two masters: for either he will hate the one, and love the other; or else he will hold to the one, and despise the other. Ye cannot serve God and mammon." Mammon means money, possessions, and you cannot serve God and your possessions too. And one who puts money or job or career, in that sense, ahead of God is thus an idolater.

Oh, the Bible, including the New Testament, has much to say in warning us about the sin of idolatry.

II. Religious Idolatry Is Prevalent

Yes, it is true that one may believe the true God and that Jesus Christ is His Son and that the Bible is true, and whether he has trusted Christ as Saviour or not trusted Christ as Saviour, he may be guilty of idolatry in religious matters.

1. An Object Lesson That God Himself Gave to Picture the Saviour, Became an Idol Hateful to God

We have an instance of that clearly recorded in II Kings 18:4. Good King Hezekiah had a blessed revival and did right in the sight of the Lord. And then we are told, "He removed the high places, and brake the images, and cut down the groves, and brake in pieces the brasen serpent that Moses had made: for unto those days the children of Israel did burn incense to it: and he called it Nehushtan."

Isn't it strange that the serpent of brass that God had so wonderfully used to picture the Saviour became an idol?

It was a serpent, illustrating the fact that those snake-bitten Israelites had been bitten by Satan the serpent and poisoned in sin. It was nailed upon a pole, showing that Christ had been made sin for us and bore our sins when He died upon the cross. But when Jesus talked to Nicodemus in the third chapter of John, He said, "And as Moses lifted up the serpent in the wilderness, even so must the Son of man be lifted up: That whosoever believeth in him should not perish, but have eternal life." It was a wonderful gospel message.

But this simple thing used in an illustration of salvation, used as an object lesson, became an accursed idol. Here people did not care about, or perhaps did not know about, the coming Messiah who would be put on the cross and bear the sins of men. They looked at that brass snake, and worshiped it, and burned incense to it! How perverse is the human heart, to make an idol out of beautiful things, out of good things! But often we do.

2. So Did Many Israelites Make an Idol Out of the Ceremonial Law

It is surprising and shocking that when Jesus came and healed people on the Sabbath, Pharisees and chief priests hated Him and wanted to kill Him! They were more anxious to keep the letter and traditions of ceremonies, than have any compassion, any outpouring of God's mercy. They did not even know the sweet meaning that the Jewish Sabbath was a ceremony picturing Heaven. Under the law it pictured that Heaven could only be reached by merit, by keeping perfectly the will of God in the six days which pictured a man's whole life. But in the passover supper, picturing grace and salvation through Christ, the first day of the unleavened bread was a holy Sabbath which pictured Heaven in the heart now, before we do any work at all, and then at last Heaven is pictured by the seventh day. But the Pharisees did not know or did not care.

So, when they hanged Jesus on the cross and mocked Him while He died, their hate was spit out like poison upon Him. But they were anxious that the ceremony be rigidly observed. People who did not mind killing the Son of God, spitting in His face, hating Him, blaspheming Him, were very particular to keep their interpretation of the ceremonial Sabbath. What idolatry is this!

I am reminded of a man who stole a horse on Saturday night in New York State. On Monday he was captured near the place where he stole the horse. When someone asked him why he didn't get away, he said, "Do you think I would ride that far on Sunday?" He cared about keeping Sunday, but he didn't care about stealing! So are those who make an idol of religious matters.

3. So Our Catholic Friends Make an Idol of Mary, the Mother of Jesus

Our Catholic friends call Mary "Queen of Heaven," "Mother of God," "Our Mediatrix," etc. Many Catholics love Mary far more than they love Jesus Christ. They pray to Mary. They ask Mary to intercede with God for them. As if Mary, who was simply a woman with the same frailties of all mankind, would be more merciful than the Lord Jesus who died for sinners! To pray to Mary, to honor her as if she were born without sin, "the immaculate conception," which they say, to claim that she went bodily to Heaven, and even to count her as a mediator between man and God all means that they put Mary before Christ. It is a big Mary and a little Jesus, and that is idolatry.

No wonder in the New Testament Mary is only mentioned

as being present in that prayer meeting in Acts 1:14, and thereafter she is never mentioned. God did not want her honored more. She was a good woman; she was greatly honored in being allowed to bear Jesus. But she was a sinner, saved by grace, as all others are. To exalt Mary thus is a kind of idolatry that is sinful. It puts something else between men and God.

4. And Thus People May Put Their Denomination Before God and Make of It an Idol

Our Catholic friends say that Peter and all the popes after him have the keys of the kingdom of Heaven. They say that only the Catholic church can interpret the Bible, and no individual has a right to interpret for himself. They make it so that only by coming to the priest can one get sins forgiven. They make a service in the church, the mass, as if it were another sacrifice, and thus they do discredit to the sacrifice that once for all paid for sins, so that God says, "There remaineth no more sacrifice for sins" (Heb. 10:26).

But Catholics are not alone in insisting that their great monstrous denomination, which has committed adultery with the kings, which has slain its thousands in persecution and still slays them, in South America and some other predominantly Catholic countries, is called the true church of Christ! It is an idol hateful to God.

One group will call themselves "the Church of Christ." They insist they have restored New Testament Christianity and that no other group has the right to call themselves the Church of Christ. They often say that only those baptized in one of their churches by one of their ministers, and attending can be a Christian. They also mean, of course, that one must hold out faithful, and go to church every Sunday, and take the Lord's Supper, and do right "in every thought, word, and deed." Actually they are making an idol out of the church, and it thus takes from the glory of Jesus Christ and the place of deity when He ought to stand alone.

Also, some Baptist people claim that "we are the true church." They say that "the Baptist church is the bride of

Christ." Actually there is no such thing as "the Baptist church." There are Baptist churches—plural—and a plurality of churches are never lumped in a sum as one church in the Bible. Local congregations were always listed separately as complete churches. And the word "church" in the Bible never did represent a denomination nor a group of churches as such. Sometimes it represents that assembly of all the saved who will be caught out at the rapture and assembled in Heaven, as mentioned in Hebrews 12:23. But no denomination or no local church has a right to claim it exclusively has some authority from God that others do not have. Thus people would take from Jesus Christ His rulership and His glory and His crown rights.

The "high church" doctrine means "low Jesus" doctrine. The more people boast about their own church, the less they boast about Jesus Christ and the less they serve Him. So the church may be a form of idolatry.

How many people there are who would follow their denominational program, right or wrong! It may support infidels; it may have people in it who sneer at the deity of Christ and laugh at the virgin birth and mock at the blood, as some do. It may take the songs about the blood out of the denominational hymnals, as some denominations have done. They teach young preachers all the arts and the excuses of the infidels, and some Christians go on sending the Lord's money into that kind of a wicked business! Why? Because the church or the denomination has become to them an idol.

Many a Southern Baptist would not be offended if one denies the virgin birth of Christ. But if one urged people to stop giving to the Co-operative Program, he would be angrily condemned. The truth is that one may go right along and be prominent in the denominational leadership councils and be a regular infidel, just so he is all for the program and says so and raises money for it. That is wicked, but idolatry is always wicked.

Sometimes the idol may be a particular man, and what that man says is swallowed without a thought because he can do no wrong. Some people are that way about Dr. Billy Graham. They know that the Bible says it is wrong to yoke up with unbelievers, but they think that since Billy Graham did it, he probably had some special permission, and so it was all right. Thus the leadership of a man is put above the clear teaching of the Bible. That is idolatry.

Sometimes it is a school from which one graduates, and that school becomes an idol. It can do no wrong. They put the school and its welfare above the plain Word of God.

Yes, religious idolatry is often the most hateful, and there is more persecution and more evil done in the name of religious idolatry than any other kind.

III. Love of Money and Possessions Is Idolatry

Colossians 3:5 says, ". . . covetousness, which is idolatry."

1. The Rich Young Ruler Was an Idolater

We remember the rich young ruler who came to Jesus and said, "Good Master, what good thing shall I do, that I may have eternal life?" He called Jesus a good teacher; that isn't enough. He is God. This rich man didn't ask how to come to get forgiveness; he wanted to get to Heaven by good deeds. But Jesus waived that aside for the moment and drove to the heart of his trouble. He was an idolater. He loved his possessions, so Jesus told him, "If thou wilt be perfect, go and sell that thou hast, and give to the poor, and thou shalt have treasure in heaven: and come and follow me" (Matt. 19:16-21). Oh, giving up your money is not the way to be saved, but until you are willing to put Christ before your money, then you cannot come and trust Him and follow Him. Oh, how money-making and business and career dominate the lives of even born-again Christians.

I was in Siloam Springs, Arkansas, in a conference on revival and soul winning. One morning a fervent preacher preached earnestly about leaving all things that were in the way to follow Jesus. Among those who came forward was a businessman; well dressed, distinguished looking, gray hair, a bright, evidently a prominent and respected personality. He came with choked voice to take my hand and whisper, "It is my business! It is my business! I am giving it up today."

I asked, "What is wrong with your business?"

"There is nothing wrong with the business. It is a good business. It furnishes jobs for many; it makes good things. But I don't need the money. I have plenty to live on. I just love to make money." Then he said, "But I am giving it up today, and the rest of my life I am going to live for Jesus and try to win souls."

Oh, the love of money!

I don't wonder that Jesus said, "Verily I say unto you, That a rich man shall hardly enter into the kingdom of heaven."

2. One May, for Salary or Business, Choose Against God's Best

Dr. Lee Roberson tells of a man who, moving out of Chattanooga to another city, came to plead with Dr. Roberson. "I hope you will pray for my children. There is not a good church where I am going. There is not a good Christian school. My children will be in great temptation. Oh, pray that they will live for God."

Then Dr. Roberson said to the man, "If the situation is as bad as that, why move away from Chattanooga? You have a good job here; your children are in this church and are serving God. Why move away?"

"Because I get $20.00 more a week on the new job," the man said. He was willing to jeopardize his Christian testimony and the Christian lives and influence and happiness of his children for $20.00 more a week!

Oh, I dread the money-making bug! All these years I have fought against it and had to watch myself! It was for this reason that I made a holy vow to God in 1926, that I would never make any requirement of a regular salary. It was for this reason I have begged God from time to time to warn me and speak to me anytime this all-pervasive sin began to take hold of my heart. The love for money is the root of all kinds of evil, the Bible says, and it is a form of idolatry.

A wife and mother will leave her little children unprotected and uncared for to go to a job where she can make more money so the family can have two cars, an expensive vacation, and steak at the table instead of hamburger and macaroni and cheese. A couple will deny themselves the blessing of children in order to have more money to spend. Thus they are idolaters.

IV. Public Opinion Is an Idol
With Many
Oh, how we seek to please people!

1. The Fear of Man Is Idolatry

The Scripture says, "The fear of man bringeth a snare." It was fear of the people that made it so Joseph of Arimathaea, though he was a good man, kept his secret and did not tell anybody that he, a member of the Sanhedrin, had trusted the Lord Jesus (John 19:38). It was the fear of people that made Peter deny Christ when a girl asked him, "Art not thou also one of this man's disciples?" Again, in the midst of the enemies of Christ, he dared not displease them, dared not take on the reproach of Christ. That is a kind of idolatry.

And so in a public restaurant, many fear to bow their heads and thank God for the food lest they should appear to be queer. We learn in Galatians, chapter 2, that even the Apostle Peter was embarrassed to sit down and eat with the new converts because some of the very strict Jewish Christians from Jerusalem were coming down and he knew they would criticise him. And Peter must be rebuked openly by Paul the apostle for trying to please people and dishonoring God.

A good Christian must sometimes walk alone. Sometimes a good Christian like Daniel, the princely boy in a far country who "purposed in his heart that he would not defile himself with the portion of the king's meat, nor with the wine which he drank" (Dan. 1:8), must, no matter what rules the men had made, open the window toward Jerusalem three times a day and pray to God as he had vowed to do.

2. Christian Giving, Praying, to Be Seen of Men, Is Idolatry

In Matthew, chapter 6, Jesus says that in Christian work, this idolatry does always tend to encroach. So He warns plainly that when you give alms, you are not to give alms "to be seen of men." He said hypocrites do that. He said that when you pray, "thou shalt not be as the hypocrites are: for they love to pray standing in the synagogues and in the corners of the streets, that they may be seen of men." He says that when you fast you should not be as the hypocrites are and put on a long countenance that you may appear to men to fast, but that rather your fasting should be a sweet secret between you and God, whom you seek to please. Oh, this business of giving money or having Christian service or public prayers or otherwise trying to make an impression on men when we pretend we are serving God!

So we have organ during prayer to instill a fake "reverence" in carnal-minded people. So we want a funeral hush-hush in the services to please those who prefer the Catholic and Episcopalian method to the New Testament evangelistic informality.

V. One's Family and Loved Ones Are Often Idols

Yes, Jesus did say in Luke 14:26, 27:

"If any man come to me, and hate not his father, and mother, and wife, and children, and brethren, and sisters, yea, and his own life also, he cannot be my disciple. And whosoever doth not bear his cross, and come after me, cannot be my disciple."

1. To Love Father or Mother or Wife or Children Above God Is a Sin

God does not here mean that one should have malice in his heart toward loved ones. It does mean that one's love for Christ should be so far above all his other affections that they are as nothing. They are not even to be considered on a par with one's love for Christ. And to put them before Christ is idolatry.

When I started out to be a preacher, I remember that the

young evangelist with whom I went to lead singing for a season said to me, "I have made a promise to God. As long as He furnishes groceries for my family and clothes and a house to live in, I will go on serving Him. If the time comes that He doesn't provide these things, I will quit preaching."

I am sure he meant well, and I am sure that God did definitely supply his needs. But I quickly answered, "I cannot say that. I plan to preach the Gospel if I have to dig ditches in the day time and preach at night. I plan to preach the Gospel if my family goes hungry and does not have nice clothes like other people have. I don't want to make it so that if God found that I wasn't a very good preacher, He could get me to quit that easy. I am going to preach no matter what happens." I meant it then; I mean it now, I think, just as sincerely.

2. Eli Is a Shocking Example of a Man Who Put His Sons as Idols Between Him and God

When the boy Samuel was living in the Tabernacle and growing up to be a judge, God spoke to him one night and gave him a solemn warning for Eli. God said:

"For I have told him that I will judge his house for ever for the iniquity which he knoweth; because his sons made themselves vile, and he restrained them not."—I Sam. 3:13.

These wicked young men had despised the sacrifices, had determined to take by force whatever they wanted, whether it was according to the rules or not. They committed adultery with the women who came to the door of the Tabernacle. And a prophet of God said to Eli,

"Wherefore kick ye at my sacrifice and at mine offering, which I have commanded in my habitation; and honourest thy sons above me, to make yourselves fat with the chiefest of all the offerings of Israel my people?"

So a curse came on the whole family. The sons died in battle. The ark of God was taken. Eli fell over and his neck was broken and a curse came on his descendants thereafter, because he made idols of his sons.

3. David Also Is an Example of a Father Who Let His Sons Be Idols and Snares

David was "a man after God's own heart," yet David married too many wives, had children he did not discipline.

Amnon, undisciplined, had raped his half-sister Tamar. Absalom, headstrong and independent, murdered Amnon, went his way, seeking to seize the kingdom and kill David. Then later Adonijah, brother of Absalom, set out to seize the kingdom also. God revealed some of the background of all this trouble when He said in I Kings 1:6, "And his father had not displeased him at any time in saying, Why hast thou done so? and he also was a very goodly man; and his mother bare him after Absalom." David sometimes loved his children more than God. They became idols even to this mighty man of God.

4. What a Struggle Abraham Had Over This Business of Leaving His Family for God!

The Word of God came to Abraham to leave Ur of the Chaldees with his kindred. Genesis 12:1 says, "Now the Lord had said unto Abram, Get thee out of thy country, and from thy kindred, and from thy father's house, unto a land that I will shew thee." So Abraham went to Haran but took along his old father and stopped there until his father died. Oh, he could hardly leave the old man, and we suppose the father was not willing to go on into the unknown land of Palestine.

Then Abraham followed the promise into the land of Canaan, but he took Lot, his brother's son, with him. God had told him, "Leave thy kindred." But Lot's father was dead and Lot seemed to need him. Lot was a believer but he was ambitious and somewhat worldly, and so Abraham disobediently took Lot along with him.

At last their possessions grew until there were quarrels among the herdsmen, and Abraham and Lot must separate. Then at long last, when Abraham was alone in the land of promise with Sarah, God gave the son of promise when Abraham was one hundred years old.

But God is not done with these lessons. Oh, will this boy,

given in answer to prayer, be the spoiled darling of an indulgent father? When Isaac was in his teens, the strong word came to Abraham, "Take now thy son, thine only son Isaac, whom thou lovest, and get thee into the land of Moriah; and offer him there for a burnt-offering upon one of the mountains which I will tell thee of" (Gen. 22:2). He was to go to Mount Moriah, three days' journey away, and there he was to take the boy, bearing a pack of wood upon his back, which pictured the sins of mankind, and Isaac picturing the Saviour going to His death. The altar was built and the wood lay thereon, then Abraham bound his beloved son with tears no doubt gushing from Abraham's eyes and lips trembling in trouble of soul, but Abraham lifted high a trembling hand which held the knife, ready to plung it into the heart of his son, his beloved son.

On that journey away from Sarah and to Mount Moriah (where is now Mount Calvary and site of Solomon's Temple), it may be that in the night Abraham looked at the starry heavens and said, "God promised that my seed should be as the stars of heaven for multitudes, and now God has me kill my only son!" Ishmael is not counted; Isaac is the only son—in this sense "the son of the promise" and picturing Christ, God's only begotten Son. I wonder if he did not lift the sand through his fingers one night and, troubled in heart, say, "God, how are my seed to be as the sand of the seashore in multitude if I must kill Isaac as You say?" But God had made the promise; Abraham must leave it to God to fulfill it; and he will go on to kill his son.

But wait! An angel of God stops his hand; God speaks to him and tells him he can use a ram caught in the thicket for a sacrifice instead. But at long last Abraham must come to the point where, not his father, not Lot, his nephew, not the old ancestral home, not Isaac, the beloved son, can come before him and God. Abraham had cured his idolatry.

I wonder how it is in your home?

5. She Gave Up Her Mother

In that conference at Siloam Springs, Arkansas, when the

businessman came by to give up his business, there came also at the invitation time a weeping young woman. She choked and could hardly talk as she whispered in my ear, "It is my mother. It is my mother! I am giving her up today." That seemed a strange thing to say, but she told me the best she could in her sobs that ten years before God had called her to the mission field; He told her she must go to China. She spoke to Mother and Dad but the father said, "No dear. You are the last child at home and we need you. You stay here and take care of us and I will leave this property to you when we are gone, and you will have a good home for a lifetime."

"No," she said, "I must go to the mission field." But her mother then had a heart attack and mocked at her daughter: "You don't love me. You would be willing to leave me here to die, with no one to look after me!"

So, on the pleading and the nagging of her mother, she gave up the dream and the call to the mission field. And those ten years went by with a pain in her heart and sense of guilt; she had not followed the call of God.

Now, weeping, she said, "It may be too late now. Many mission boards won't take one who is thirty years old. But I have promised God now that whatever He wants me to do, I will do it. I will not stay at home with Mother if God wants me somewhere else."

She gave up her mother.

And God wants you to face it. Will you put God before your loved ones?

6. She Gave Up Marriage Plans
for Jesus

One summer I was to speak at Winona Lake Conference ground on a Sunday afternoon, so I drove there hastily from Wheaton, and was in the hotel changing clothes when the telephone rang. It was a pastor from Mishawaka, Indiana, I think, saying, "I must see you." I told him I was dressing to go on the platform in a few moments. "I will come and talk to you while you dress and while you walk to the auditorium."

He said, "You preached last August at the Wheaton Bible Church." Yes, I had.

"You preached on 'Leaving All for Jesus.' " I told him I did not remember what I had preached.

"But I know," he said. "A young woman in my church came home to tell me about it, and she said to me, 'Pastor, we must talk to Jim. We must get Jim converted now.' " So they went to talk to the young man who was engaged to marry this beautiful girl. She said, "Jim, now you must be saved so we can have a Christian home."

But Jim said no. He said, "Now, I am glad that you are a Christian. I want a good, clean girl like you. You will make me a good wife. I am glad that you go to church whenever you want to; sometimes I will go with you. There may come a time when I will be saved, but I don't promise that now. I am going to do what I am going to do. But I am glad to have a Christian wife."

But she told him. "Jim, we must have a home that will please God. I promised to put God first in everything." He told her that she need beg no longer; he would not now become a Christian.

She pulled the engagement ring off her finger, handed it to Jim and said, "Then the wedding is off."

"What is that?"

"I made God a promise. I have put Him first in everything. I cannot marry and have a home where Christ is not first."

The young man was sullen. He said, "Already the invitations are out far and near. Already wedding presents are coming in."

But she said, "They are all from nearby. We can get in a car and take them back. I will tell everybody it was my fault."

So they took the wedding presents back to one home and another and another. Always she boldly said, "I am to blame; it is my fault. But the wedding is off."

He brought her back to the house glum and sullen; he did not even get out to open the car door. As she stepped out of the car and onto the sidewalk, suddenly she collapsed in a heap.

They rushed her to the hospital. They thought she might die, but she recovered.

That pastor said to me, "Brother Rice, something has happened to that girl. She has always had a beautiful voice. But now whenever she sings, everybody cries! There is a strange moving of God in her singing!"

He told me also how she went to sing at a Christian Missionary Alliance Church, and they were so blessed they invited her again and again. The young pastor of this church was so blessed. Once he took her home, and her pastor said to me, "I believe her broken heart will be healed." She determined she would not marry out of the will of Christ, that Christ must be first in everything.

How is it with you, dear reader? Can you honestly say that you are putting Christ first and that nothing can take His place in your life? Oh, today, beware. "Little children, keep yourselves from idols."

We remember that when Jacob was called to go back to Bethel, they not only took off the earrings but took their idols and buried them under an oak; then Jacob went back to Bethel to meet God—the God of the House of God.

I beg you now, bury your idols! I beg you now, turn your heart away from anything that would force itself between you and Christ! Your attention, your love. Never mind if it is the attention of men. Never mind if it is your church or your denomination. Never mind if it is the dearest one on your heart. Make sure that today these be pushed aside that Christ may have first place in everything.

You have read Dr. John R. Rice's sermon, "Keep Yourselves From Idols." In this sermon it has been made clear that the only way to have your sins forgiven and God's promise of a Home in Heaven is by receiving Jesus Christ as your Saviour. Surely you will agree that there is nothing so important as the eternal destiny of your immortal soul. I hope you also see that there is no *one* and no *thing* that should be more important to you than God.

If God has spoken to your heart about your need of a Saviour, right now receive Jesus and trust His promise of eternal salvation. If it is your desire to be saved, and you are willing to trust your eternal soul to Him, then tell Him so by praying this simple prayer: Dear God, I know that I am a sinner and do not deserve salvation and a Home in Heaven. Thank you for loving me in spite of my sin and for Jesus dying on the cross to pay my sin debt. Right now I accept Jesus as my Saviour trusting Him to forgive my sins, to save me, and to give me everlasting life. Thank You for hearing and answering this prayer. Amen.

Dear friend, in Romans 10:13 the Bible says, "For whosoever shall call upon the name of the Lord shall be saved." That means God promised that when you asked Him to save you He did. Now on the basis of God's Word you see that you are saved and have a Home in Heaven. This is wonderful, and I would like to rejoice with you and pray for you. Also I have some free literature to send you if you will write and let me know of your decision.

Decision Form

Dr. Shelton Smith
Sword of the Lord Foundation
P. O. Box 1099
Murfreesboro, TN 37133

Dear Dr. Smith:
After having read Dr. John R. Rice's sermon, "Keep Yourselves from Idols," I have seen my need of Jesus as my Saviour and have by faith received Him. Please send me the helpful free literature that will encourage me and help me as I begin the Christian life.

Name_____

Address_____

_____

City_____ State _____ Zip_____

CHAPTER X

You Are Called to Be a Fisher for Men

"Let's go fishing," Dad said. It was about 1911, near the little cow town of Dundee in West Texas. Our grain was already cut with a binder, chopped in the field and the thresher had come, the oats had been stored for feed in the winter, the wheat had been sold. No work was pressing, and Dad said to me, "Let's go fishing." We hitched the big black horse Prince to the sturdy buggy and drove out seven or eight miles to the Little Wichita River. We took along a frying pan, some meal to roll the fish in that we would catch and fry, some bread, and some bacon, in case we didn't catch any fish! Yes, and some potatoes. We had along a shotgun, for we must get some bait—a cottontail rabbit or a crow.

How pleasant it was beside the deep pools where the river was just barely flowing. Trees shaded all about. We caught catfish and sometimes perch, and cooked them over an open fire. Then we sat around the campfire and Dad told stories of his cowboy days, when there was not a fence between Fort Worth and Denver, about 1877-78. He told about the open range and Indians and cattle drives to the North.

We had thanks over our meal, and after awhile, laid out our bedrolls and slept under the stars. And as I went to sleep or waked in the night, I could hear old Prince, hobbled but never straying far from the camp and us, cropping the grass about us.

On such trips we would go home the next day hoping to have some fish for the homefolks after having a fine refreshing in the midst of a summer's work.

Sometimes we would get neighbors and take a farm wagon of folks and perhaps the buggy, and a big seine and go north to the Big Wichita River. Then it was permissible to use the seine net. With my older brother Jesse and my younger brother George and Dad and sometimes a neighbor man, we would catch lots of fish. Once Dad suggested we gather the seine around an old tree that had fallen into the river. In that deep hole he would dive down. Once he found next to the bank a big catfish. He got a hand in his gills and an arm around his tail and, carefully avoiding the poisonous fins, brought the catfish to the surface. It splashed and pulled Dad under the water, but he held on and we got Dad and the fish in the net. I suppose the fish weighed fifteen or twenty pounds!

Sometimes we would find a low bank undercut by the current, and creeping softly along, in the water would feel under the bank until we would touch a channel catfish. We would softly feel along until we could get a hand in his gills, then hold him by the gills and bring him out.

Of course, we would have a big fish fry at noon, and cornbread or johnnycakes, and perhaps some canned fruit from home. Then in the afternoon we would take a little rest and then everybody, fully clothed, would swim and play in the river.

Going fishing, then, has a good sound to those who have enjoyed such vacations.

Once Jesus came along by the Sea of Galilee, and wanted to preach to the people. He asked permission to sit in a boat shoved out a little way from the shore, then He preached to the multitudes. He then turned to the disciples and, in effect, said, "Let us go fishing." The story is told in Luke 5:1-11. But this much of it we find in Mark's story:

"Now as he walked by the sea of Galilee, he saw Simon and Andrew his brother casting a net into the sea: for they were fishers. And Jesus said unto them, Come ye after me, and I will make you to become fishers of men. And straightway they forsook their nets, and followed him. And when he had gone a little farther thence, he saw James the son of Zebedee, and John his brother, who also were in the ship mending their nets. And straightway he called them: and they left their father Zebedee in the ship with the hired servants, and went after him."—Mark 1:16-20.

Then Jesus called these fishermen to a far greater task. Instead of fishing for fish, they were to fish for men! They were to be His soul-winning disciples! In Matthew 4:19 He said, "Follow me, and I will make you fishers of men." So here in Mark 1:17 He says, "Come ye after me, and I will make you to become fishers of men."

I. Called to Follow Jesus in the Great Adventure!

I take it that these men were already saved. In John, chapter 1, we learn how Andrew first saw Jesus, went home with Him, then went and found his brother Simon and brought him to Jesus. So this is not just a call to be saved. This is a call to be a disciple, a soul winner, to be a special worker for the Lord.

You see, it costs more to be a disciple than just to be a Christian. Anyone can be saved. One who comes to Christ is never cast out, Jesus said in John 6:37. "Whosoever shall call upon the name of the Lord shall be saved," we learn in Romans 10:13. Oh, without any merit or work or deservings, a poor sinner can come to Christ, trust Him and be saved. So the publican in the Temple could pray, "God be merciful to me a sinner," and go home justified, saved.

But here we learn what it costs to follow Jesus after we have been converted, after we are God's children, and after we know our sins are forgiven and we have everlasting life.

1. God's Call Is for Total Surrender to Jesus as Lord and Master

What a picture that is when one is baptized! One who has trusted Christ and has a new heart now follows Jesus down into the watery grave. He counts the old sinner already dead: now symbolically the old sinner and the old life are buried. Then he is raised up "to walk in newness of life." That means that he believes Christ rose from the dead. It also means that the Christian expects one day to be raised from the dead or marvelously changed when Jesus comes. Still it means more: The Christian now says, "I am going to live a new life. I belong to God. Christ lives in me and I live for Christ!"

Not every Christian goes on to make the Lord Jesus the Master of his life, as he should. Some of the gospel seed sown will fall among thorns and the cares of this world and the deceitfulness of riches may choke the Word so that it brings no fruit to perfection. The seed sprouted, the change has been made in the heart of one, but his life may not be as devoted to Christ as it should be. Some born-again people still smoke cigarettes. Some born-again people do not read the Bible daily. Yes, some born-again people never have a daily time of family prayer and Bible reading, never win a soul. You see, this matter of following Jesus means surrendering one's life into His hands now that He is the Saviour.

In the American Revolution some men followed Washington when they did not get enough to eat, when there were not enough clothes, when their bare feet left blood marks in the snow of Valley Forge. They followed at great cost. So must have men fought with Garibaldi as he led in unifying Italy. So a great military leader has invited people to come through blood, sweat and tears! Oh, if these fishermen follow Jesus, it will mean a change in their lives. They are not now invited simply to be saved, but to be fishers of men.

2. To Follow Jesus May Mean Forsaking Many Things Which Are Dear

Here Peter and Andrew, James and John, had to give up their livelihood. They left their nets and boats. They gave up their income. And they were to go wherever Jesus said.

Now it is not wrong to fish for a living, to farm for a living, to run a filling station, to hold an office job, to be a physician or a lawyer or a teacher or an engineer. But sometimes one must give up good things for the best if he would follow Jesus.

I preached in Augusta, Georgia, in a revival. One day I had a luncheon with twenty-three pastors. I spoke to them on leaving all for Jesus. A pastor of the Presbyterian church where once the father of President Woodrow Wilson had been pastor, a graduate of Princeton University and Princeton Seminary, a gifted man, called me aside and said: "Do you know what I gave up today? I gave up golf."

"But what is wrong with golf? Why must you give that up?"

"Golf is not wrong in itself," he said, "but I have become too good at it. I live down here close to the tradition of Bobby Jones, the great golfer. The professionals come here regularly, and I have been playing golf so much and so well, I often beat the professionals. Golf has become a great part of my life. So today I told God I was giving up golf. I may play again sometimes, and I may not—I don't care. I am going to put soul winning and the work of my ministry first from now on!

In Siloam Springs, Arkansas, after a sermon on the cost of discipleship, many came forward to take my hand and tell what decisions they had made for God. A distinguished-looking businessman, nicely dressed, evidently an executive, came forward. He was so moved he could hardly speak. He whispered to me, "I am giving up my business."

I asked him, "What is wrong with your business?"

"There is nothing wrong with the business. It is a good business. It gives work to a lot of people. It is a useful business and makes things people need. But, I don't need the money. I just like to make money! Now I am giving up my business to work for God and to win souls."

There is no way to follow Jesus unless you say good-by to some other things.

Remember that in Hebrews 12 Christians are invited to "run . . . the race" and "let us lay aside every weight, and the sin which doth so easily beset us." The sin of unbelief and other sins may hinder. Also there are some weights that are not themselves wrong, but they ought not take too much time or thought for a Christian. Oh, we must lay aside many things for Christ if He becomes the Lord of our lives, and if we are to be soul winners.

3. To Fish for Men and to Be a Disciple Means Forsaking Loved Ones

We notice that when Jesus called James and John "they left their father Zebedee in the ship with the hired servants, and went after him." Did they love their father? Oh yes! Perhaps he was getting old. Perhaps he said, "James, you know you can't depend on hired help these days. What am I going to do without you boys?" Or perhaps he said, "John, you are your mother's favorite. What will she think if you don't help us in this little business but go off and leave us?"

They had to say good-by to people they loved.

Jesus said in Luke 14:26, 27: "If any man come to me, and hate not his father, and mother, and wife, and children, and brethren, and sisters, yea, and his own life also, he cannot be my disciple. And whosoever doth not bear his cross, and come after me, cannot be my disciple."

Hate father and mother? The word is used in the sense of rejecting instead of holding on to. That is the sense in which God said, "Jacob have I loved, but Esau have I hated." God rejected Esau as the head of the nation Israel he was establishing. It did not mean He did not love Esau or that Esau was not saved. So, when you are going to compare father and mother with the Lord Jesus, you must choose the Lord Jesus and reject your father and mother. So with wife and children and brothers and sisters and your own life also. Nothing must stand in the way of your putting Jesus first. To be a disciple of Jesus means forsaking those we love.

I have been a preacher fifty-two years. More than thirty years of that time I have been away from my wife and children.

When I started out as a young evangelist, I left my wife with one baby, and another on the way, in a tiny, two-room apartment on Seminary Hill, Fort Worth, Texas. She had no telephone. I could leave almost no money at home for an emergency or extra food. I was gone for a two-weeks' revival campaign and my heart trembled a bit. What would my wife do if there were sickness of either her or the baby? She would have little money for food or medicine or anything else she needed. She had no car, no telephone to call a taxi. I saw then I must get this matter settled.

That afternoon I walked away from the home where I was staying, down a country road to a schoolhouse, went inside and laid the matter out before the Lord. If I were to serve Him, I must have peace about my family; I must have assurance He would care for them. I didn't leave until I got it settled.

From that time to now, by God's great mercy He has given me sweet peace about this lonely road I have traveled and about being away from home and loved ones. There is sorrow, but it is for Jesus. Oh, one must choose Jesus before all else in the world! No one can be a good soul winner unless soul winning is first. If you want to go fishing with Jesus for lost souls, then Christ must be the Master, and His work must come before all your own comfort or your loved ones or your plans.

4. To Follow Jesus Means to Take Him as a Pattern, to Strive to Be Like Him

In I Peter 2:21 is this wonderful verse: "For even hereunto were ye called: because Christ also suffered for us, leaving us an example, that ye should follow his steps." We are to follow in the steps of Jesus and that may mean suffering.

So in Philippians 2:5-8, we have the same kind of command:

"Let this mind be in you, which was also in Christ Jesus; Who, being in the form of God, thought it not robbery to be equal with God: But made himself of no reputation, and took upon him the form of a servant, and was made in the likeness of men: and being found in fashion as a man, he humbled himself, and became obedient unto death, even the death of the cross."

We are to be like Jesus and let His attitude and His mind be our mind and attitude. We are to give up whatever reputation and wealth and approval of men we have sought, and humble ourselves to follow Jesus for this blessed work.

Jesus told His disciples that ". . . the Son of man must suffer many things, and be rejected of the elders and chief priests and scribes, and be slain, and be raised the third day. And he said to them all, If any man will come after me, let him deny himself, and take up his cross daily, and follow me" (Luke 9:22, 23). So this matter of being soul winners, following Jesus, means day by day to deny self, yes, and offer self for crucifixion again. Let us face it. The Lord Jesus who died on a cross for us wants us to join in His soul-winning passion and labor and so to be willing as He was willing to offer ourselves, for whatever death to self and death to our plans it takes. Paul said, "I die daily." So we should daily "put off the old man" and reckon ourselves to be dead to sin and follow Jesus.

5. Oh, if We Follow Jesus, We Can Trust Him to Care for Us and Our Own

This passage in Mark is very sweet. In verses 16 to 20 we find how these disciples were called to follow Jesus and then we read in the same chapter, verses 29 to 31:

"And forthwith, when they were come out of the synagogue, they entered into the house of Simon and Andrew, with James and John. But Simon's wife's mother lay sick of a fever, and anon they tell him of her. And he came and took her by the hand, and lifted her up; and immediately the fever left her, and she ministered unto them."

I suppose that Simon and Andrew lived in the same house. We suppose that James and John simply came with Jesus this time. But Simon's mother-in-law was sick with a fever when the dear Lord Jesus took her by the hands and lifted her up, and the fever left her.

I think that now Peter, James, John and Andrew would feel, "The Lord will take care of us and our loved ones. We may not have the money to go to the most expensive doctors or hospitals, but we do have Jesus." Maybe they thought, "If He wants me to go with Him and serve Him, then He is able to care for me and He will." Oh, God takes care of His own!

I write this now at 78 years of age. My wife and I often mention what gloriously little we have spent for doctors or hospitals! We are healthy, we digest our food, we rest well at night, we have few aches and pains, we are strong for the Lord's work. How wonderfully He has cared for us!

In 1926 I made a little trade with God. I said, "Lord, You look after my business and I will look after Yours." I set out to never have a regular salary. I do not think salaries are wrong, but I wanted to leave my support wholly in the hands of God. I gave up my life insurance. That is not commanded; I did it voluntarily and as a matter of faith. Now through these years He has taken care of me and mine so wonderfully well, and I think I know somewhat how Peter and James and John must have felt when Jesus healed the sick woman in the home: God takes care of us. C. D. Martin's song says,

> **Be not dismayed whate'er betide,**
> **God will take care of you;**
> **Beneath His wings of love abide,**
> **God will take care of you.**
>
> **Thro' days of toil when heart doth fail,**
> **God will take care of you;**
> **When dangers fierce your path assail,**
> **God will take care of you.**
>
> **All you may need He will provide,**
> **God will take care of you;**
> **Nothing you ask will be denied,**
> **God will take care of you.**
>
> **No matter what may be the test,**
> **God will take care of you;**
> **Lean, weary one, upon His breast,**
> **God will take care of you.**
>
> **God will take care of you,**
> **Thro' every day, o'er all the way;**
> **He will take care of you,**
> **God will take care of you.**

God WILL take care of you. Now we have the sweet promise of Hebrews 13: 5, 6:

"Let your conversation be without covetousness; and be content with such things as ye have: for he hath said, I will never leave thee, nor forsake thee. So that we may boldly say, The Lord is my helper, and I will not fear what man shall do unto me."

Those who follow Jesus may trust Him. He takes care of His own and our loved ones as we follow Him and rely upon Him.

II. Christ Promises to Make Soul Winners

Isn't that a sweet promise? "Come ye after me, and I will make you to become fishers of men." The Lord Jesus takes the responsibility.

I knew a man who was hired to sell bonds for a tremendous project, to get out many millions of dollars' worth of bonds. He and other men were trained for two weeks. They stayed in a hotel day and night, not going outside. They learned not only about bonds but the principles of selling; other kinds of arguments; the answers to questions. Always they were told that they could do it. He came out of that ready to sell these bonds with only a few well-trained men to do it, and he succeeded. The company guaranteed the job and taught him how to do it.

When a football coach enlists a bunch of men, he sets out to make them into a football team. That takes work and practice They must learn blocking and tackling. They must learn about toughness and speed. They must learn the signals and learn to cooperate with the plays. But in that case a man must have a certain aptitude, certain size and reflexes and speed. A coach doesn't make a football star out of just anybody.

But the Lord takes the most ordinary Christian and makes him into a soul winner. He takes all the responsibility for it You just follow Jesus, and He will make you into a fisher of men, He said.

1. The Lord Furnishes the Tackle and Bait

You see, you do not have to be a great philosopher nor a trained theologian to be a soul winner. The Gospel is very simple. Here it is in the Bible—". . . how that Christ died for our sins according to the scriptures; And that he was buried, and that he rose again the third day according to the scriptures" (I Cor. 15: 3, 4). How simple it is again in John 3:16. God loves poor, lost sinners. They need not perish. Jesus died for them and if one will personally turn to Christ and trust in Him, he can be born again and have everlasting life.

Paul said, "For I am not ashamed of the gospel of Christ: for it is the power of God unto salvation . . ." (Rom. 1:16). It isn't brilliant speaking but the Word of God and the power of God on any humble believer who follows Jesus that makes him a soul winner.

Sometimes the greatest preachers, the most eloquent, those even with the most knowledge of the Bible, are not the greatest soul winners. You see, soul winning is not some matter for learned experts only. It is for anybody who loves the Lord Jesus enough to follow Him and let the Lord make him into a fisher of men.

2. Christ Also Furnishes the Detailed Leadership of How and When in Soul Winning

It is a blessed truth that when a Christian sets out to follow Jesus, he can have the power of the Holy Spirit and daily leading of the Spirit of God. We read in Acts 8:26, "And the angel of the Lord spake unto Philip, saying, Arise, and go toward the south unto the way that goeth down from Jerusalem unto Gaza, which is desert." The "angel of the Lord" is a term used in the Bible meaning simply a messenger. Perhaps the "angels" of the seven churches in Revelation, chapters 2 and 3, simply meant pastors. So, here God's messengers, through the Spirit of God, told Philip where to go. The Ethiopian eunuch was there in his chariot. "The Spirit said unto Philip, Go near, and join thyself to this chariot." Philip ran to obey. There was the man reading in Isaiah 53, the sweetest part of the Old Testament on the atoning sacrifice of Jesus our Saviour. Soon the eunuch learned how to get saved and he trusted the Lord and was baptized. Then, ". . . the Spirit of the Lord caught away Philip . . ." (vs. 39). Isn't that good leading?

Then we learn in Acts, chapter 9, how the Spirit of the Lord led Ananias to Saul, the great persecutor who is now saved and praying for light and power. We learn in Acts, chapter 10, how God led Peter to go to Cornelius when he never would have thought he would preach to a Gentile. In Acts, chapter 16, we see how the Spirit of God led the Apostle Paul and his companions not to preach in this place or that but to go over into Macedonia in Europe. Acts 16:6-11 says:

"Now when they had gone throughout Phrygia and the region of Galatia, and were forbidden of the Holy Ghost to preach the word in Asia, After they were come to Mysia, they assayed to go into Bithynia: but the Spirit suffered them not. And they passing by Mysia came down to Troas. And a vision appeared to Paul in the night; There stood a man of Macedonia, and prayed him, saying, Come over into Macedonia, and help us. And after he had seen the vision, immediately we endeavoured to go into Macedonia, assuredly gathering that the Lord had called us for to preach the gospel unto them. Therefore loosing from Troas, we came with a straight course to Samothracia, and the next day to Neapolis."

The Lord Jesus provides the leadership for the soul winner. Oh, let us listen to the still, small voice and let us wait now for His guidance—just how to do it, where to go, whom to see. How often He has led me, giving the very words that were needed. You see, if the Lord is going to guarantee you can be a soul winner, you must have daily leading, which He gives.

3. But if Christ Is to Make Us Soul Winners, We Must Have Holy Spirit Power

The Lord Jesus taught these same apostles very clearly, ". . . but tarry ye in the city of Jerusalem, until ye be endued with power from on high" (Luke 24:49). He taught them, "But ye shall receive power, after that the Holy Ghost is come upon you: and ye shall be witnesses unto me both in Jerusalem, and in all Judaea, and in Samaria, and unto the uttermost part of the earth" (Acts 1:8). As He called them to win souls, so He calls us. As He taught them to have power, He teaches us. D. L. Moody said, "It would be foolish to try to do the work of God without the power of God." Oh, and we have learned that these men had the mighty enduement of God upon them and they won many.

4. If These Disciples Follow Jesus and Become Soul
Winners, They Will Also See the Mighty
Working of His Power

It is true, a Christian needs the power of the Holy Spirit to win souls. But Peter and Andrew and James and John saw many marvelous works of Christ as they followed Him and became soul winners. I take this first chapter of Mark as addressed to me, then He says to me, "Come ye after me, and I will make you to become fishers of men." If that part of the chapter is for me, is not the rest of it also for me? Immediately hereafter He raised Peter's wife's mother who was sick of a fever. And then verses 32 to 34 tell us:

"And at even, when the sun did set, they brought unto him all that were diseased, and them that were possessed with devils. And all the city was gathered together at the door. And he healed many that were sick of divers diseases, and cast out many devils; and suffered not the devils to speak, because they knew him."

He had already cast out devils in Capernaum and elsewhere. Now surely the disciples see many wonderful works from the hands of Christ.

Do you think that we ought to expect to go without the power of God for physical ills?

Over a year ago the doctors, after operations on Dr. Lee Roberson's throat, came to the conclusion that he could never preach again. Oh, what a blow to a dedicated, mighty, soul-winning preacher! He told me, "I would rather die than not preach again."

But I was greatly impressed, as I thought and prayed about it, with a verse in Acts 4:29, 30, when the disciples, threatened by the Sanhedrin and chief priests, prayed, "And now, Lord, behold their threatenings: and grant unto thy servants, that with all boldness they may speak thy word, By stretching forth thine hand to heal; and that signs and wonders may be done by the name of thy holy child Jesus."

I said in my prayers again and again to God, "I want to see

those signs and wonders too." And many Christians prayed, and God wonderfully restored Dr. Roberson. Now for some months he has been preaching in all of his own services and elsewhere with mighty power and tenderness.

Oh, we need signs and wonders too. If I preach the Gospel like Peter and James and John did, why shouldn't I see that kind of results too? I think the Lord Jesus did not heal everyone, nor are we promised that all will be healed, but many could be.

I had a letter this week from a man and his wife who, some eighteen or twenty months ago asked me to pray that God would give them a baby. They were so anxious and it seemed that they could not have a child. I prayed. Now the sweet letter comes praising God for the baby God gave and asking me to pray that they may have another! I believe they will. I could tell of a dozen different cases where people have seemed unable to have children who have been married for years, but they, in answer to my prayers and theirs, were wonderfully given a child. Why should God do that for Zacharias and Elisabeth and not for us today? Why should He do that for Hannah and give her the Prophet Samuel, and not do it for hungry hearts today?

Yes, God raised Peter's wife's mother. I remember when He raised my father after doctors had said he couldn't possibly live until morning. The next day my father got out of bed perfectly healed, and went on to serve God. I can remember when our daughter Grace had diphtheria, with a fever of 105, when Mrs. Rice and I knelt by the bed and prayed, the fever left that afternoon and the next morning the doctors and nurses could find no evidence of diphtheria, so the quarantine card was taken down.

I remember when Mrs. Jewel Duncan, wasting away with tuberculosis after two years in a state hospital in Kerrville, Texas, had been sent home to die. That was before sulfa drugs, penicillin and other antibiotic drugs. I prayed for her. Following the command of James 5:13-16, I put a bit of oil upon her forehead as a token that we were relying upon the Spirit of God. I went on my way. In two weeks she was up doing all of her own housework and when I saw her three months later, she had gained from 90 to 140 pounds, and was the picture of health. I have known of her work more than thirty years after that.

Oh, if we are going to believe the Bible, let's take the blessing and the power of it, too, as well as the Gospel of it. It is a wonderful thing to follow Jesus if we can have Him with us, have His power and have His blessing.

III. And Now Catching Men for Christ

What a wonderful thing it is to fish for men! Think what a blessing it is that God gives us a part in making black hearts white, in making children of Hell into children of God, in snatching people out of the hands of Satan and pulling them out of the fire and so giving them everlasting life. I have wondered often, and I have even trembled in my heart, at the promise Jesus gave the disciples in John 20:21-23:

"Then said Jesus to them again, Peace be unto you: as my Father hath sent me, even so send I you. And when he had said this, he breathed on them, and saith unto them, Receive ye the Holy Ghost: Whose soever sins ye remit, they are remitted unto them; and whose soever sins ye retain, they are retained."

I have the authority from God to tell a man how he may have his sins remitted and assure him it is done when he trusts the Lord. I have authority to tell a man he is doomed and going to Hell when he refuses to take Christ as Saviour.

1. Success and Failure, Winning Some and Losing Some

We remember when Jesus told the parable of the sower and of how some seed fell by the wayside and the birds took it away. So Satan takes the Gospel out of the hearts of the careless and indifferent. We learn that some seed fell on stony ground and so those with hard hearts sometimes will not heed but will deliberately and persistently reject the Gospel and the sweet invitation. Even sometimes the Gospel falls among thorns and so brings no fruit to perfection, though it springs up, and some are saved. Ah, but praise God, sometimes the Gospel brings forth "some an hundredfold, some sixtyfold, some thirty-fold." And always there is the certain promise that we can win some. The promise of Psalm 126, verses 5 and 6, is this:

"They that sow in tears shall reap in joy. He that goeth forth and weepeth, bearing precious seed, shall doubtless come again with rejoicing, bringing his sheaves with him."

Jesus said, "A certain man made a great supper and bade many," and sent his servant to invite them. Oh, what trials that servant had! Those invited all began to make excuses. One must see his land; another must yoke up his oxen; another has a bride. So the servant must go into the streets of the city and get the poor and the maimed and the halt and the blind and out in the country, quickly, if he fills the house for the big supper.

So some will make excuses, and others will promise to come and will not, but always there are some we can win. "They that sow in tears shall reap in joy." And we are exhorted, "And let us not be weary in well doing: for in due season we shall reap, if we faint not" (Gal. 6:9). Always there is somebody you can win. And if you can't win at one house, let us go to another. If sometimes it is out of season we are still to preach the Word for it will sometimes be in season.

2. Many Are Won Person to Person; Others in Multitudes

Once Simon Peter told Jesus that the tax collector wanted taxes. Peter was instructed to cast a hook into the Sea of Galilee and the first fish that came up would have a coin in its mouth to pay taxes. So sometimes we can catch people one at a time. That is the best way and the main way people are won to Christ. In the parable of the great supper in Luke 14, it is obvious that person to person is the main way. And the Great Commission is given in Mark 16:15, "Go ye into all the world, and preach the gospel to every creature." The main way is not preaching to the multitudes but person to person.

We learned how the church at Jerusalem won so many souls.

"And daily in the temple, and in every house, they ceased not to teach and preach Jesus Christ" (Acts 5:42).

Yes, and Paul the apostle told the elders of Ephesus, when he met with them at Miletus, "I . . . have taught you publicly, and from house to house" and then said, "Remember, that by the space of three years I ceased not to warn every one night and day with tears" (Acts 20:20, 31). Oh, many can be won personally, and everyone can win some that way.

But we ought also to understand that God is not satisfied with a few. God wants multitudes saved. When He called these men to be fishers of men, Luke 5:4-10 tells us:

"Now when he had left speaking, he said unto Simon, Launch out into the deep, and let down your nets for a draught. And Simon answering said unto him, Master, we have toiled all the night, and have taken nothing: nevertheless at thy word I will let down the net. And when they had this done, they inclosed a great multitude of fishes: and their net brake. And they beckoned unto their partners, which were in the other ship, that they should come and help them. And they came, and filled both the ships, so that they began to sink. When Simon Peter saw it, he fell down at Jesus' knees, saying, Depart from me; for I am a sinful man, O Lord. For he was astonished, and all that were with him, at the draught of the fishes which they had taken: And so was also James, and John, the sons of Zebedee, which were partners with Simon. And Jesus said unto Simon, Fear not; from henceforth thou shalt catch men."

They let down their nets under the leading of the Lord Jesus and where He said. Suddenly they had "a great multitude of fishes." They had to call for another ship to come and they "filled both the ships, so that they began to sink." Note the connection. Peter was astonished and felt how guilty he was in the view of this marvel, this miraculous catch of fish, but Jesus told him, "Fear not; from henceforth thou shalt catch men."

Again let me say, all this is the Word of God. Here, along with calling them to be soul winners, there came a call to see marvelous results. Don't let anybody think that God is content for most of the people to go to Hell. Neither should you ever be content that way. He wants us to catch many.

So in Jerusalem they had three thousand saved in a day. Then the number of converts was about five thousand. Then, later, that multitudes, both of men and women, were wonderfully saved. That is the kind of New Testament results we ought to have.

I hear slighting remarks by those in churches who win few souls. They criticise the people who go out in buses and bring in multitudes. They criticise anybody who gives a child bubble gum or an apple or hot dog to get him to ride the bus and come to Sunday school to hear the Gospel. Oh, but if we really meant business like Jesus taught these disciples to mean business, we would go out and compel them to come in and we would see multitudes saved.

So, that is Bible Christianity and we have the right to claim that. If this part of the Bible is for us, with the call, then the blessings He pictures here are also for us. I rejoice that many churches are now baptizing many converts. In 1966 and 1967, I urged many churches to set a goal to win to Christ and to baptize at least two hundred converts and many churches have done beyond that and we rejoice. God wants to save multitudes and so when people want to be fishers of men, let's expect, and hope and pray and cry to get multitudes saved.

IV. Christ Is Calling Us, Also, to Be Fishers of Men

I do not believe that God calls only a few people to follow Him. I think He wants every Christian to follow closely, to be a disciple, to pay whatever price is necessary to please God. I do not believe that anybody ought to be content for people near them to go to Hell when Christ died for them and when He came into the world to save sinners. We are bought with a price. All authority is given unto Jesus and He has a right to tell us what to do and He wants us, too, to take up our cross and follow Jesus and we, too, can be soul winners.

Would you say that you are trying to follow Jesus? Then He

will make you a fisher of men if you mean it. Are you willing to pay the price like these men paid to leave the ship, the nets, their father, their loved ones, to win souls? Then you can be a fisher of men. I do not know whether God will require you to give up your business. I know that you ought to be willing to do so. I know that you ought to say that Christ is to have the first place in your life. You are to follow Him and do His will above everything else. Oh, that all of us may be fishers of men.

Not to win souls shows a lack of love for Jesus. He said, "If ye love me, keep my commandments." And surely if you don't keep His command about going out to get the Gospel to every creature, then you don't love Him as you ought.

I beg you now. Take it to heart and set out to live a life of soul winning. And may God give you the blessing day by day and marvelous fruit in Heaven.

What a wonderful payday it will be in Heaven for the soul winners. "And they that be wise shall shine as the brightness of the firmament; and they that turn many to righteousness as the stars for ever and ever" (Dan. 12:3). May the dear Lord speak to a thousand hearts as they read this and with compelling insistence, "Come ye after me, and I will make you to become fishers of men."

CHAPTER XI

Facts About Personal Soul Winning

Every Christian is commanded to win souls. We are to obey the Great Commission to "go ye into all the world, and preach the gospel to every creature" (Mark 16:15). We are to be like the Christians at Jerusalem. Of them we are told: "And daily in the temple, and in every house, they ceased not to teach and preach Jesus Christ."

I. It Is the Way Most Are Won

A famous preacher, Dr. Charles Gallaudet Trumbell, said he had preached for years to great congregations, for 20 years had written weekly to and edited a religious paper which had some of the time a circulation of 100,000 copies, and was the author of 30 books, but that in this time he had won more people to Christ in private conversation than in sermon, or print, as far as he knew. The late Dr. A. C. Dixon said the same thing. Some preachers think that the public expounding of the Word to crowds is the main thing. Not so. Preaching the Gospel is the main thing, and every Christian can do that with one hearer. Great preachers must be great personal soul winners. And those who are saved in public service without private help are few.

II. Every Christian Can Do It

Yes, every Christian can win souls if he will pay the price. The Bible does not leave the preaching to preachers. Deacons also preached in public. John 15 is to every Christian. Matthew 28:19, 20 is to all. It doesn't take worldly wisdom, nor gift of speech, nor special training. It just takes a broken heart and Holy Spirit power, thank God. It can be done anywhere. I have seen people saved in church, at home, by a well, two in an orchard, and at least 20 by the roadside, some in my car, one on an interurban car, several in hospitals, 50 in jails, one walking down Main Street in Fort Worth, one on top of a barn, one Methodist at baptizing, even. I have seen them saved in a crowd or alone. Mothers, fathers, brothers, sisters, sweethearts, teachers and rank strangers can win them. Sometimes just tears will decide it. More often a verse of Scripture. Many, many times just the touch of a hand turns a man to Christ. All can win souls.

III. It Costs Something

A woman once said to an evangelist, "Oh, I would give the world if I could win souls as you do!"

"That's just what it cost me," answered the soul winner.

Soul winning costs something. It cannot be done best and most without deep knowledge of God's Word and experience. It cannot be done at all without surrender to God and Holy Spirit leadership. It costs time, tears, labor, and sacrifice to become an artist, and soul winning is the finest of arts. Thank God, this is the one artistic possibility born in us all, but at the second birth.

Great soul winners are men of burdened hearts, single purpose, secret vigil, and unreserved surrender. Oh, it costs! It cost Jesus Bethlehem and Gethsemane and Calvary—betrayal and blood, torture and tears. It costs, but thank God, it pays more than it costs.

IV. It Is Contagious

One example is worth a thousand arguments. Let a fellow but try this blessed business of winning souls, and others see that people want to be saved, see that it is not natural ability, but Holy Spirit leadership, and humble surrender to God that gets results, and they will try it. The way to learn to preach is to preach, and the way to learn to win souls it to get at it. How preachers should set the holy example of personal approach to individuals! How we should hold up the personal work of Jesus and of Paul, His great apostle! How we should pray for an irresistible epidemic of individuals seeking individuals, like that which modern times has seen in Wales and Korea, and that in Russia since the beginning of the war. It will take examples, examples from the ministry especially, but also from the ranks of businessmen, women, and young people to start a revival of personal seeking and winning the lost in private and in public services outside the pulpit. Soul winning is contagious.

V. It Will Keep the Christian Right

The monks who spent their days in prayer and self-affliction were not near to God's heart and plan. A preacher who preaches to crowds and lives in pleasant places among generous and kindly people, is often not right with God, nor happy, nor victorious. I know; I have been there. But the man who has had the continuous evidence of God's blessing on his ministry in personally winning the lost, may be sure he is on the right track. How often I have tried to preach when words were hollow, the sky was brass, and weighty words went from a cold heart to colder ears. How often the Book had no message, and there was no joy in prayer. How often the weight of a service was breaking my heart and I had no victory for the sermon. Then I have slipped away to a neighbor or more often among boys and girls, privately sought the appointed one with the hungry heart, and told again the sweet story that lived again in my heart with the telling, saw tears flow, heard the confession, felt the angels rejoicing again. Then I have gone again to public ministry and found that the Holy One had taken an ember from dead ashes in my heart, lighted a coal from the Book of God and fanned it with His Heavenly Presence to a holy, blessed flame.

O brethren, personal, earnest heartbroken seeking of the lost by us preachers, not as preachers but as Christians, will fix our ministry, will fix our temptations, will fix our prayers, as nothing else will, because God will see to it that we can win souls only in proportion as we are right. Soul winning both gains and proves the abiding Holy Spirit.

Young Christian, what about worldly amusements? Is it hard to give them up? Soul winning will take away their charm.

Jesus said, "Every branch that beareth fruit, he purgeth it that it may bring forth more fruit." Do you have trouble remembering prayer? Get a sinning, helpless, hopeless, hungry lost world on your heart, and go fishing for men with tears, and you cannot help praying. Soul winning will keep the Christian right.

VI. It Is the Highest Joy

"They that sow in tears shall reap in joy." A Christian's best joy does not come when he is saved, but when he helps someone else to the Saviour. The soul winner has the joy of God's favor, of the saved one's gratitude, and Holy Spirit abiding. Clothes wear out, money disappears, land doesn't go to Heaven, a night of pleasure is gone in the morning, but souls won will be in Heaven to meet and shine "as the stars for ever and ever" (Dan. 12:3).

Christians, the personal seeking, wooing, winning of Christ's lost sheep is God's balm of Gilead to restless, worrying, unhappy hearts. To win souls is the greatest glory to Jesus, the greatest gain in Heaven, the greatest growth to the winner, and the highest joy on earth.

Why not right now, before you lay this book down, open your heart and ask God to make you a compassionate winner of lost men. Nothing else on earth pays in such coin.

CHAPTER XII

"Power From on High"

"Thus it is written, and thus it behoved Christ to suffer, and to rise from the dead the third day: And that repentance and remission of sins should be preached in his name among all nations, beginning at Jerusalem. And ye are witnesses of these things. And, behold, I send the promise of my Father upon you: but tarry ye in the city of Jerusalem, until ye be endued with power from on high."—Luke 24:46-49.

D. L. Moody said, "It is foolish to try to do the work of God without the power of God." Thus when one starts out to win souls, he must seek to have a holy enduement come upon him from God. One needs the power of the Holy Spirit to help him witness for Christ, help him win souls. What we need is not talking in tongues, not a "second work of grace." We simply need to be endued with power from on High. Then, dear Christian, learn now about this power of God.

Here the Word of God has for us something that we need. Jesus has been raised from the dead, and had been forty days among the disciples. He is about to go away, and gives the apostles the Great Commission.

And then Jesus led them out to the Mount of Olives and went to Heaven, visibly, before them.

The Lord Jesus is telling them what to do: 'You are to carry the Gospel,' He said. "Thus it is written, and thus it behoved Christ to suffer, and to rise from the dead the third day: And that repentance and remission of sins should be preached in his name among all nations, beginning at Jerusalem. And ye are witnesses of these things. And, behold, I send the promise of my

Father upon you: but tarry ye in the city of Jerusalem, until ye be endued with power from on high."

The Great Commission Repeated Five Times

This is one of five times that Jesus gave the Great Commission that is recorded in those forty days after He rose from the dead. He may have mentioned it twenty times or fifty times, but these five different times are recorded. This is one of them. Another is in Matthew 28:19, 20: "Go ye therefore, and teach all nations, baptizing them in the name of the Father, and of the Son, and of the Holy Ghost: Teaching them to observe all things whatsoever I have commanded you: and, lo, I am with you alway, even unto the end of the world," so said Jesus.

The Great Commission is given again in Mark 16:15, 16: "Go ye into all the world, and preach the gospel to every creature. He that believeth and is baptized shall be saved; but he that believeth not shall be damned."

It is given again in John 20:21 when Jesus was risen from the dead and came and breathed on His disciples and said, ". . . as my Father hath sent me, even so send I you."

And then it is given in Acts 1:8, "But ye shall receive power, after that the Holy Ghost is come upon you: and ye shall be witnesses unto me both in Jerusalem, and in all Judaea, and in Samaria, and unto the uttermost part of the earth."

According to the Scriptures, this was the most important thing Jesus could tell the disciples: "You are to go and win souls."

Now notice that the Great Commission is basic to any understanding about Holy Spirit power. Anywhere the Lord talks about enduement of power, it is in connection with carrying out the Great Commission. He didn't say, "Do you want to feel light as a feather? Then be filled with the Spirit." "Do you want to talk in tongues? Then be filled with the Spirit." He didn't mean that. "Do you want to have some sign to prove to everybody you have what they don't have?" He didn't say that. No, 'You are to go and preach the Gospel, that repentance and remission of sins should be preached in his name among all nations, beginning at Jerusalem.'

Oh, but He said, 'Tarry . . . until ye be endued with power from on high. You are witnesses. You are supposed to tell it, but tarry until ye be endued with power from on high.'

Pentecost Must Mean Soul-Winning Power

So here we have the basic fact that everybody must consider. If you want to talk about Pentecost and the fullness of the Spirit, remember what God had in mind is power to carry the Gospel everywhere.

In the first place, this is what Jesus came into the world for. First Timothy 1:15 (I never get tired of saying it): "This is a faithful saying, and worthy of all acceptation, that Christ Jesus came into the world to save sinners; of whom I am chief." Jesus came to save sinners. He said, "For the Son of man is come to seek and to save that which was lost" (Luke 19:10).

He said, "I came not to call the righteous, but sinners to repentance" (Luke 5:32). The purpose of Jesus' coming to earth —His incarnation, His sufferings at Calvary, His resurrection— the whole business is summed up in this: He wanted us to take the Gospel and save sinners.

So, don't anybody come to me talking about the fullness of the Spirit unless you mean what God means—power to win souls, power to witness for Jesus. Jesus says—here is a command—that repentance and remission of sins be preached in His name among all nations, beginning at Jerusalem. And you are the witnesses to do it. Oh, but He said, 'You must wait until you are endued with power from on High; tarry . . . until ye be endued with power.' So they did.

Never, never does God mention this matter of Holy Spirit power without implying or stating that He is referring to power to get souls saved—the Great Commission. For example, in Luke 11:13 in the parable of bread for children, He said, ". . . How much more shall your heavenly Father give the Holy Spirit to them that ask him?"

He is talking about the parable of getting bread for a friend who has come to you, and asks for three loaves—that is a Christian begging God for bread for sinners. That is the Great Commission.

And, again, it is at Pentecost, in Acts 1:8, "Ye shall receive power, after that the Holy Ghost is come upon you: and ye shall be witnesses unto me. . . ."

In Acts 4:31—"And when they had prayed, the place was shaken where they were assembled together; and they were all filled with the Holy Ghost, and they spake the word of God with boldness." That is what it is about.

And so in Acts 2, Peter stood up and said, "This is that which was spoken by the prophet Joel; And it shall come to pass in the last days, saith God, I will pour out of my Spirit upon all flesh: and your sons and your daughters shall prophesy, and your young men shall see visions, and your old men shall dream dreams: And on my servants and on my handmaidens I will pour out in those days of my Spirit; and they shall prophesy. . . ." And he ended that quotation from Joel saying, "And . . . whosoever shall call on the name of the Lord shall be saved."

The Important Thing Is Not Fire, Nor Earthquake, Nor Tongues, but Soul-Winning Power!

You see, the fullness of the Spirit is given to get people saved. It is not given to make you feel good; it is not given to give you a sign and proof; it is given to win souls. "Tarry . . . until ye be endued with power from on high."

Here before Pentecost Jesus defines what we call the Pentecostal experience. I do not mean there is some particular way you must feel. I do not mean you must have certain outward signs, but what they got at Pentecost is here clearly defined. What is it? It is "power from on high."

In this passage where Jesus commanded it, and in a similar passage as quoted in the first chapter of Acts, again preceding Pentecost, He didn't even discuss the matter of tongues of fire; yet at Pentecost, the Scripture says, "There appeared unto them cloven tongues like as of fire, and it sat upon each of them" (Acts 2:3). Why didn't God mention it? In the first place, that will vary; it won't be true in every case. It isn't promised; it is not necessary. It was useful then. So outward and incidental manifestations are not discussed.

And did you notice here in Acts 4:31, "the place was shaken where they were assembled together," and they prayed and the Holy Spirit came on them? Does that mean that we should have an earthquake each time? No, that isn't mentioned ahead of time, and it is not a requirement.

Now does Jesus say, "When the Holy Spirit comes upon you, everybody will talk in tongues"? No, He didn't say that and nobody else has a right to say it. That was a matter of a local situation. Here were Jews from many countries, speaking some sixteen different languages, and God gave these Jews power to witness to them in their own language in which they were born. But the matter of foreign languages is not mentioned in this Commission, because that is incidental.

It doesn't matter to God. You can have power to preach to people who understand English, in English. You can have power to talk in German to people who understand German. You can have power to talk to people in the Congo when you learn their native language and use that. But God is not talking about the collateral matters; He is talking about the power to win souls. You can have that.

Now people may feel different. Some may weep, and some may rejoice. The incidents that surround the matter of the fullness of the Spirit may be different; but always there is one purpose that never varies, "Ye shall receive power, after that the Holy Ghost is come upon you: and ye shall be witnesses unto me." Jesus said, "Tarry . . . until ye be endued with power from on high."

So, then, here is defined the Pentecostal matter: "power from on high." God can use other incidental matters. He doesn't always do so, He doesn't promise it, but He does say here, "power from on high."

The tongues were needed for people who only thus could hear the Gospel in their own language; not for some sign, not just to please this fleshly, carnal appetite or feeling, or to show you have something better than other people. No, no! The power of God was given to win souls. And that is the key of Pentecost. That is what the Lord talks about in Acts 1:8: "But ye shall receive power, after that the Holy Ghost is come upon you: and ye shall be witnesses unto me. . . ."

Now, do not confuse the fullness of the Spirit with certain gifts of the Spirit. There is the gift of healing. That doesn't often occur but it has sometimes in times past; it may do so again. It may be again someone may be given the power to talk in the language of some sinner so he can understand in his own language in which he was born, just as it happened at Pentecost. That won't often be necessary—certainly not generally so. I say, the gifts of the Spirit are different, but the fullness of the Spirit they tarried for is to witness for Jesus and win souls, or prophesy. That means witnessing in the power of the Spirit.

The Apostles Were Commanded to Tarry and Pray for Power

Now, then, they were to tarry. You say, "Well, does it mean pray?"

I was in a great congregation in Fort Worth, Texas, and one preacher spoke up and said, "Yes, they tarried, but where do you get the idea they prayed?"

I get it from Acts 1:14—"These all continued with one accord in prayer and supplication, with the women, and Mary the mother of Jesus, and with his brethren."

They continued in prayer. And Jesus had said, "When the bridegroom shall be taken from them . . . then shall [my disciples] . . . fast" (Matt. 9:15). So I think they did fast and they did pray.

Oh, then, we need to wait on the Lord.

You say, "Wait on the Lord? Is that necessary?" Yes, it is taught many times in the Bible.

In Luke 11:8, "I say unto you, Though he will not rise and give him, because he is his friend, yet because of his importunity. . . ."

In Isaiah 40:29-31: "He giveth power to the faint; and to them that have no might he increaseth strength. Even the youths shall faint and be weary, and the young men shall utterly fall: But they that wait upon the Lord shall renew their strength;

they shall mount up with wings as eagles; they shall run, and not be weary; and they shall walk, and not faint."

Ah, the mighty power of God, the waiting on God! They did at Pentecost. D. L. Moody cried to God. And much of two years he had a little power, but one day the floodtide came as he walked in that little canyon-like street, Wall Street, in New York. You can have the power of God, too. Turn to Him today and have the power to witness for Jesus.

CHAPTER XIII

Holy Spirit Enduement Always Available

The Enduement of Power Which God Gave
Christians at Pentecost When They
Were "Filled With the Spirit" Was
Repeated in Acts 4:31 and Should
Be Repeated in the Life of
Every Christian

"And when they had prayed, the place was shaken where they were assembled together; and they were all filled with the Holy Ghost, and they spake the word of God with boldness."— Acts 4:31.

Two great hindrances tend to keep Christians from having New Testament power and blessing and fruitfulness. One is the emphasis on incidentals and so missing the main thrust of Bible teaching that Christians need to be filled with the Holy Spirit for soul winning. Instead of this mighty enduement of power some would teach you to seek to speak in the jabber of unknown tongues that cannot save anybody and let the people around you go on lost while you "enjoy" what you think is some very distinctive evidence of your spirituality that you talk in tongues. Or you may be taught that what you need is simply some kind of special sanctification, a special work of grace wherein the old carnal nature is burned out and you don't sin any more. But this false emphasis leaves you without the mighty power of God.

The other great hindrance is that people have a tendency to say that the day of miracles is past, that the great blessings of Pentecost in the book of Acts were for another age, now we no more have apostles on earth, God does not now generally

212

work miracles, and we cannot now expect, so some people say, the mighty working of God in saving multitudes which Bible Christians saw. Oh, they are wrong.

Christians can have the power of the Holy Spirit and this Holy Spirit enduement of power for soul winning and witnessing is always available.

I beg you to go into a careful Bible study on this question and know that Pentecostal power and joy is for all of God's Christians again and again all of our days if we but seek this power of God for His work.

In Acts, chapter 4, we find how Peter and John after healing the lame man at the gate of the Temple by the power of God in chapter 3 and addressing a great multitude that assembled after that, saw many people saved. But Peter and John were arrested and kept in jail overnight, came before the Sanhedrin and were commanded to preach no more in the name of Jesus. They insisted, ". . . Whether it be right in the sight of God to hearken unto you more than unto God, judge ye. For we cannot but speak the things which we have seen and heard" (Acts 4:19, 20).

So Peter and John came back to their company and reported the whole matter. Then we read the following account of how they prayed and were filled with the Holy Spirit:

"And when they heard that, they lifted up their voice to God with one accord, and said, Lord, thou art God, which hast made heaven, and earth, and the sea, and all that in them is: Who by the mouth of thy servant David hast said, Why did the heathen rage, and the people imagine vain things? The kings of the earth stood up, and the rulers were gathered together against the Lord, and against his Christ. For of a truth against thy holy child Jesus, whom thou hast anointed, both Herod, and Pontius Pilate, with the Gentiles, and the people of Israel, were gathered together, For to do whatsoever thy hand and thy counsel determined before to be done. And now, Lord, behold their threatenings: and grant unto thy servants, that with all boldness they speak thy word, By stretching forth thine hand to heal; and that signs and wonders may be done by the name of thy holy child Jesus. And when they had prayed, the place was shaken

*where they were assembled together; and they were all filled
with the Holy Ghost, and they spake the word of God with
boldness."*—Acts 4:24-31.

This is the aftermath of Pentecost. Before Jesus went away
He commanded the disciples to tarry in Jerusalem until they
be endued with power from on High, then they were to carry
out the Great Commission, preaching the Gospel to every creature possible. After ten days of prayer and, we suppose, fasting,
in the Upper Room, the power of God wonderfully came on
them at Pentecost. So in Acts 2:4 we are told, "And they were
all filled with the Holy Ghost" and began to speak to the
people assembled there, people from sixteen different countries.
God gave some of them the power to speak to them in their own
languages in which they were born. What a marvelous result
there was! What repenting! Some three thousand souls were
added to them and baptized that day.

That wonderful enduement of power (as it is defined by the
Lord Jesus in Luke 24:46-49), was given several names. The
disciples were to be "Baptized with the Holy Ghost," Jesus
said (Acts 1:4, 5). That is, they were to be overwhelmed,
covered, submerged, in the power of the Holy Spirit. It was "the
gift of the Holy Ghost," as Peter told the people (Acts 2:38).
This was a fulfillment of the promise, "And it shall come to
pass in the last days, saith God, I will pour out of my Spirit
upon all flesh," prophesied in Joel and quoted by Peter in
Acts 2:17, 18. And when this blessing came, it is said that "they
were all filled with the Holy Ghost." But in Acts 1:8 Jesus had
said, "But ye shall receive power, after that the Holy Ghost is
come upon you: and ye shall be witnesses unto me. . . ." So if
one has in mind that Jesus is talking about a special enduement
of power to carry out the Great Commission and witness and
win souls, and if one is not misled by all the talk about the
origin of the church or sanctification or talking in tongues, then
it will be easy to see that the Lord simply uses several ways to
describe that enduement of power for witnessing and winning
souls.

I. Here We See Pentecost
Repeated

A note in the Scofield Reference Bible says, "One baptism, many fillings." But the Bible does not say that. Many Bible teachers, particularly Plymouth Brethren and those who followed them and the Scofield Bible, say, "Pentecost can never be repeated." They say that because they have misinterpreted what happened at Pentecost. They are not impressed that the fullness of the Spirit or the baptism of the Spirit was simply an enduement of power from on High to witness. They prefer to make it a dispensational matter.

Here, they think, was the origin of the church, or here, many think, was the beginning of a new age or dispensation of God's dealings with men. Some make that statement because they are retreating from the tongues heresy. They would like to say that one time they did have a great ecstasy, speaking without rhyme or reason in some unknown heavenly language, but that now that has passed away. But that *was not* the meaning of tongues at Pentecost, and it *was* an enduement of power from on High. And the Bible never discusses the origin of the church. The simple fact is that that church, the body of Christ, will include all who are called out at the rapture and assembled in Heaven, that "general assembly and church of the firstborn, which are written in heaven" (Heb. 12:23), and it did not start at Pentecost.

1. The Same Identical Statement Is Given
in Acts 2:4 and Acts 4:31

At Pentecost, after they had waited and prayed for an enduement of power from on High, we read in Acts 2:4, *"And they were all filled with the Holy Ghost."* And we read how they witnessed for God and three thousand people were saved when this enduement of power came upon them.

But as the disciples witnessed and preached and a great persecution arose, again they needed to unite in earnest prayer, and so they did. They prayed, "Lord, behold their threatenings: and grant unto thy servants, that with all boldness they may speak thy word, By stretching forth thine hand to heal; and that signs and wonders may be done by the name of thy holy child Jesus. And when they had prayed, the place was shaken where they were assembled together; and they were all filled with the Holy Ghost, and they spake the word of God with boldness" (Acts 4:29-31).

Note here two statements exactly the same: in Acts 2:4, "AND THEY WERE ALL FILLED WITH THE HOLY GHOST." Now in Acts 4:31 note again the same statement, word for word, "AND THEY WERE ALL FILLED WITH THE HOLY GHOST." It is obvious that here Pentecost was repeated. The disciples again were "endued with power from on high" and witnessed to win souls. In each case they prayed for power and got it. In each case the enduement of power was followed with great witnessing. Here in Acts 4:33, "with great power gave the apostles witness of the resurrection." Following Pentecost, "they that gladly received his word were baptized: and the same day there were added unto them about three thousand souls" (Acts 2:41). But here at the second Pentecost, the second enduement of power, the second time "and they were all filled with the Holy Ghost." We read in Acts 5:14, "And believers were the more added to the Lord, multitudes both of men and women."

There were incidental miracles and conditions that varied around the day of Pentecost and what happened later in Acts 4:31. In one case there was the sound of a rushing mighty wind and tongues of fire sitting on the people. In the other case, "the place was shaken" with an earthquake. In one case, since Jerusalem was filled with Jews "out of every nation under heaven" for the Passover season, it was necessary for some of them to preach the Gospel to them 'in their own tongue in which they were born.' In the other case, as far as we know, all present could understand the Aramaic language and so they witnessed to them in their own tongue.

But those variations were incidental compared to the main thing. The main thing was that in each case they were "endued with power from on high" to witness for Christ. In each case they prayed to God for that power, and He answered. In each case they witnessed with great boldness and power and many were saved.

When God says in one place, "And they were all filled with the Holy Ghost," and then in the next place when He says again, "And they were all filled with the Holy Ghost," it is only fair to assume that God meant the same thing when He said the same thing. The people a second time had a Pentecostal blessing. It was a second Pentecost if you mean what God was emphasizing, the power of the Holy Spirit to witness for Him.

2. The Scriptural Explanation of What Happened at Pentecost Referred to a Period of Time—Not One Day but "the Last Days"

Peter explained what was happening at Pentecost. In Acts 2:14-21, we read:

"But Peter, standing up with the eleven, lifted up his voice, and said unto them, Ye men of Judaea, and all ye that dwell at Jerusalem, be this known unto you, and hearken to my words: For these are not drunken, as ye suppose, seeing it is but the third hour of the day. But this is that which was spoken by the prophet Joel;

"And it shall come to pass in the last days, saith God, I will pour out of my Spirit upon all flesh: and your sons and your daughters shall prophesy, and your young men shall see vision, and your old men shall dream dreams: And on my servants and on my handmaidens I will pour out in those days of my Spirit; and they shall prophesy: And I will shew wonders in heaven above, and signs in the earth beneath; blood, and fire, and vapour of smoke: The sun shall be turned into darkness, and the moon into blood, before that great and notable day of the Lord come: And it shall come to pass, that whosoever shall call on the name of the Lord shall be saved."

So, quoting from Joel 2:28-32, Peter says that here is happening exactly what was promised then. It is now "the last days" and the term is for the whole New Testament age. Verse 20 tells us that includes Pentecost and right on down until "that great and notable day of the Lord" when Christ returns to reign on the earth. This period of time is called "the last days."

Note carefully that it is not a day but a series of days—plural. The promise was good for the day of Pentecost. It was exactly the same promise for the next day and the next and the next—right on down through the years, through this whole New Testament age. And in Acts 2:19 and 20, quoting from Joel, we know that it will include even those plagues of the tribulation time until the return of Christ in glory. So the promise is not just to Pentecost but to all these days. To think that it was exclusively for one day misses the point of God's own explanation of Pentecost. The pouring out of the Spirit, the witnessing in the power of God, prophesying, are for this whole New Testament age, on exactly the same basis.

For other Scriptures showing that "the last days" refer to this whole New Testament age, see Hebrews 1:1, 2; I John 2:18; II Timothy 3:1-8. And note that the present tense is used, and Timothy was commanded to turn away from such. The "last days" is this whole New Testament age.

3. In Acts 2:38 and 39 We Are Plainly Promised That the Same "Gift of the Holy Ghost" Which They Had Is Available for Everybody God Ever Calls to Be Saved

When Peter was preaching at Pentecost to these people about the marvelous signs, the cyclonic winds, the tongues of fire on the people, the power of some to witness in the language of all who were present, they wondered what it was; so Peter explained in Acts 2:32, 33:

"This Jesus hath God raised up, whereof we all are witnesses. Therefore being by the right hand of God exalted, and having received of the Father the promise of the Holy Ghost, he hath shed forth this, which ye now see and hear."

And now these convicted hearers want the same blessing, not only salvation but the gift of the Holy Ghost which they see obviously manifested here in the powerful witnessing of these Christians. So we read verses 37 to 39:

"Now when they heard this, they were pricked in their heart, and said unto Peter and to the rest of the apostles, Men and brethren, what shall we do? Then Peter said unto them, Repent, and be baptized every one of you in the name of Jesus Christ for the remission of sins, and ye shall receive the gift of the Holy Ghost. For the promise is unto you, and to your children, and to all that are afar off, even as many as the Lord our God shall call."

Here is asked, "What shall we do?" Not just to be saved but how to have the power of the Holy Spirit, too. So Peter told them they should repent and thus they would be saved. Then they should be baptized "for" or, more literally, "with reference to," the remission of sins received when they repented, and "ye shall receive the gift of the Holy Ghost." But that promise of the same gift of the Holy Ghost these apostles and others had is promised to more—"For the promise is unto you, and to your children, and to all that are afar off, even as many as the Lord our God shall call."

Doesn't that clearly say that the gift of the Holy Ghost, which they here saw in these Pentecostal Christians and wanted for themselves, was for them and for their children and for all who were afar off who should be saved everywhere? Doesn't that mean that the promise of Holy Spirit enduement of power like at Pentecost, the same enduement of power these people had, is to be available wherever the Gospel is preached and people are saved? It is as extensive as the Great Commission itself. The command for Christians to take the Gospel to all the world is for every Christian, in all generations, and so likewise the promise of Holy Spirit power for witnessing is given to all. If one is to speak in the power of God he must have enduement of power; so the promise is to all who are saved.

Surely any honest Christian considering this must consider that he, too, can have a Pentecost. He, too, may have the power of God to witness.

Remember, I am not saying that the incidentals surrounding must be the same. I am saying that what God plainly promised was an enduement of power from on High for Pentecost, and it came and He makes to us exactly the same promise He made to them.

4. In Ephesians 5:18 Christians Now Are Commanded to Be "Filled With the Spirit"

There are a number of terms used about this enduement of power from on High. In Acts 1:5 Jesus used the figure of speech, "Ye shall be *baptized* with the Holy Ghost." This enduement is called "the gift of the Holy Ghost," "the pouring out of the Holy Ghost," and "the coming of the Holy Ghost upon them." But the term most often used in the book of Acts is the one primarily used in Acts 2:4, "And they were all *filled* with the Holy Ghost." It is used again in Acts 4:31, "And they were all *filled* with the Holy Ghost."

The same term is used in a command to all of us in Ephesians 5:18, "And be not drunk with wine, wherein is excess; but be *filled* with the Spirit." Remember that the terms "Holy Spirit" and "Holy Ghost" refer not only to the same Person but are translations of the same Greek terms. Here we are commanded to be filled with the Spirit just as they at Pentecost were filled with the Spirit. So Pentecost is for everybody.

It is clear that God never intended that all the same emotions and incidental surroundings should be just alike with everybody. Some laugh when they get saved and some cry. Some are very quiet, some are exuberant, some have perfect assurance from that moment, while others are hesitant and doubtful before they have assurance. But people who trust Christ are saved, and salvation is the essential thing. Thus when people are filled with the Holy Ghost, the incidental, outward circumstances may vary.

But certain things are always alike. For one, it is an enduement of power from on High given for witnessing, prophesying, winning souls. Second, this power is given in answer to pleading prayer, as it was given at Pentecost following Acts 1:14 and after these who prayed in Acts 4:31.

Note carefully that although many times we find that people in the Bible were filled with the Holy Ghost, or filled with the Spirit, only in the one case at Pentecost was there an occasion to speak to people in their own languages in which they were born, foreign languages. So the tongues do not appear anywhere else, for there was no need for them.

When John the Baptist was filled with the Holy Ghost (Luke 1:15), he never talked in tongues. When Jesus was filled with the Holy Ghost and anointed for His ministry (Luke 3:21, 22), He did not talk with tongues. Paul the apostle was filled with the Holy Spirit (Acts 9:17), but there is no record of his talking in any foreign language. So speaking in tongues is not the evidence of the fullness of the Holy Spirit, not even the "initial" evidence, as some claim. And a jabber that nobody can understand is not like the Bible gift at Pentecost in any case.

But praise the Lord the enduement of power from on High, the fullness of the Holy Spirit, is promised to every Christian. Everybody can have a Pentecost.

II. To Be Filled With the Spirit Means a Special Enduement for Soul Winners

It is strange that so many who teach and preach about Pentecost miss the point that God has made so clear for honest seekers.

1. It Was the Enduement of Power They Were Promised

In Luke 24:46-49 Jesus made that plain:

"And said unto them, Thus it is written, and thus it behoved Christ to suffer, and to rise from the dead the third day: And that repentance and remission of sins should be preached in his name among all nations, beginning at Jerusalem. And ye are witnesses of these things. And, behold, I send the promise of my Father upon you: but tarry ye in the city of Jerusalem until ye be endued with power from on high."

They were to preach the Gospel to all nations, but first they must be endued with power from on High for that witnessing, He said. Always in the Bible the fullness of the Spirit is a simple matter of being given divine help and power to carry out the Great Commission which He has given.

So it was in Acts 1:8. There Jesus said, "But ye shall receive power, after that the Holy Ghost is come upon you: and ye shall be witnesses unto me both in Jerusalem, and in all Judaea, and in Samaria, and unto the uttermost part of the earth."

What will happen when the Holy Spirit would come on people? They would be witnesses for Jesus, they would go out as soul winners.

2. The Fullness of the Spirit on Bible Christians Made Them Soul Winners

When the angel told Zacharias he was to have a son, John the Baptist, to be a forerunner of Jesus, he gave this promise:

"He shall be filled with the Holy Ghost, even from his mother's womb. And many of the children of Israel shall he turn to the Lord their God. And he shall go before him in the spirit and power of Elias."—Luke 1:15-17.

The fullness of the Spirit is to get people saved.

Another case giving the same evidence is that of Barnabas. We are told about him in Acts 11:24: "For he was a good man, and full of the Holy Ghost and of faith: and much people was added unto the Lord." What happens when one is filled with the Holy Ghost and faith? Many people get saved. Holy Spirit enduement is given to win souls.

The Apostle Paul was converted on the road to Damascus. He met Jesus and surrendered to Him as Lord. And when Ananias came to meet him he called him "Brother Saul." Read Acts 9:17:

"And Ananias went his way, and entered into the house; and putting his hands on him said, Brother Saul, the Lord, even Jesus, that appeared unto thee in the way as thou camest, hath sent me, that thou mightest receive thy sight, and be filled with the Holy Ghost."

And what did Paul do when he was filled with the Holy Ghost? He received his sight, he arose and was baptized, he ate after fasting three days and nights, and then we read, "And straightway he preached Christ in the synagogues, that he is the Son of God" (Acts 9:20). What people have the enduement of power for is to witness for Jesus and get people saved. So

Paul did. It seems to me an amazing thing that anyone can read about Pentecost and not be exalted beyond measure that here the power of God was on the witnessing so that three thousand people were saved!

Acts 2:4 says, "And they were all filled with the Holy Ghost, and began to speak. . . ." Verse 41 says, "Then they that gladly received his word were baptized: and the same day there were added unto them about three thousand souls." When you talk about Pentecost, why not talk about what God is talking about? Why not be concerned with what the Lord is most concerned about? Why would men prefer to talk about "the origin of the church" or "a new dispensation" or "sanctification" or "speaking in tongues" and ignore the wonderful truth that three thousand people wonderfully trusted Christ, claimed Him openly and were baptized on that glorious day! Something is bad wrong with the heart attitude of people who are interested in Pentecost and not especially interested in those three thousand souls who were the direct result of the fullness of the Spirit and the witnessing in the power of the Spirit.

3. But the Same Soul-Winning Power Came Again on the Same Disciples in Acts 4:31

The same kind of results happened when the disciples again prayed and again were mightily filled with the Spirit. In Acts 4:31 we read, "And when they had prayed, the place was shaken where they were assembled together; and they were all filled with the Holy Ghost, and they spake the word of God with boldness." Verse 33 says, "And with great power gave the apostles witness of the resurrection of the Lord Jesus: and great grace was upon them all."

(Then there is parenthetically the story of Barnabas who sold land and brought the money and laid it at the apostles' feet: and of Ananias and Sapphira lying to the Holy Ghost and being killed by the wrath of God.)

But verse 14 of Acts 5 continues, "And believers were the more added to the Lord, multitudes both of men and women." Surely the spiritual mind is impressed that the fullness of the Spirit was given for soul-winning power and always when people sought and found the fullness of God's Spirit they witnessed, they prophesied, that is, they won souls for Christ.

III. What Happened in the Climate and Context of Holy Spirit Power?

There are some sweet evidences and results that accompany the outpouring of God's Holy Spirit power in saving souls. The end and aim of the enduement of power, of course, is to win souls. It would be a great mistake to set out to grow corn just for the fodder. The fodder is a rather incidental by-product after you gather the main crop, the corn itself. So people miss the aim of God's plan when they set out to seek the Holy Spirit just to make them happy or to help in some other way, or even to seek the fruits of the Spirit without seeking the one main thing that God speaks about in connection with Pentecost and the fullness of the Spirit. Yet it is sweetly true that in the climate and context of a time of Holy Spirit power and witnessing, God's presence is manifested in many details.

1. The Holy Spirit Enduement Gives Boldness in Witnessing

One inevitable secondary result of the fullness of the Spirit is the boldness in proclaiming the Gospel, in witnessing for Jesus. And so the disciples prayed for that boldness in this connection. In Acts 4:29 they said, "And now, Lord, behold their threatenings: and grant unto thy servants, that with all boldness they may speak thy word." So when they prayed, Holy Spirit power came upon them again, and these men whose lives were threatened if they should continue preaching the Gospel, went on preaching with boldness and great power.

If one goes back and reviews the preaching of Peter at Pentecost, openly blaming these people and their rulers for murdering Jesus, demanding that they repent, one sees that boldness properly goes with the enduement of power.

This boldness is indicated also in the way Peter faced Ananias and Sapphira, and evidently at Peter's demand God struck both of them dead because they had "lied to the Holy Ghost," making false claims about their liberality.

Oh, that upon God's preachers today there would come boldness to preach the Word so they would not be afraid of the anger of people, not be afraid of losing their crowd, not be afraid of their positions! How boldly Paul preached the Gospel while fleeing for his life, barely escaping over the wall at Damascus, being stoned and left for dead at Lystra, jailed at Philippi, narrowly escaping death under the sentence of the Sanhedrin at Jerusalem, then long imprisonment for two years at Caesarea and other years at Rome, and finally beheaded. Bible Christians, filled with the Holy Spirit, had the boldness of God upon them.

In a citywide campaign in Seattle, Washington, I met with a group of sponsoring pastors when the first week drew to a close and I was announcing the sermons for the second week. The pastors were uneasy. One pastor said, "Brother Rice, if you preach sermons like you are announcing now, you are going to make a lot of people angry." I told them, "Yes, unless God has forsaken me on that matter and does not help me to preach as plainly as I should, we will make people angry." The right kind of preaching in the power of God challenges Satan, arouses opposition and persecution, yet is blessed wonderfully in soul-saving results.

2. Witnessing in Spirit's Power, Getting People Saved Results in Great Joy

The fullness of the Spirit on the testimonies and witnessing of Christians gets people saved and thus, of course, leads to great joy. The promise of Psalm 126:5 is, "They that sow in tears shall reap in joy." Dr. L. R. Scarborough in Southwestern Seminary used to tell us, "No sowing, no reaping; no weeping, no rejoicing." And the next verse in Psalm 126 says, "He that goeth forth and weepeth, bearing precious seed, shall doubtless come again rejoicing, bringing his sheaves with him." Rejoicing follows bringing in the sheaves, and it ought to.

Following Pentecost we learn that the Christians "did eat their meat with gladness and singleness of heart, Praising God" (Acts 2:46, 47). And so, likewise, following the second great anointing or the second recurring Pentecost in Acts 4:31, we find a kind of joy underneath all the wonderful things that happened. Those who believed were "of one heart and of one soul." They didn't care about their possessions, "and with great power gave the apostles witness of the resurrection of the Lord Jesus: and great grace was upon them all." People were saved and many sick were healed.

In Acts, chapter 8, we find that Philip the deacon went down to the city of Samaria and preached the Gospel. He had a multitude of people saved, devils were cast out, and the sick were healed, "And there was great joy in that city" (Acts 8:8).

We often quote Ephesians 5:18 and the command, "And be not drunk with wine, wherein is excess; but be filled with the Spirit"; but it is not sensible to stop there; that is not even the end of a sentence. After the semicolon, that sentence continues that these who are filled with the Spirit should be "speaking to yourselves in psalms and hymns and spiritual songs, singing and making melody in your heart to the Lord; Giving thanks always for all things unto God and the Father in the name of our Lord Jesus Christ" (Eph. 5:19, 20). Yes, to be filled with the Spirit means to sing with psalms and hymns and make melody in your heart to the Lord. Joy is part of the context, part of the climate of the soul-winning power.

That is indicated also in the parable of the shepherd who, when he found the lost sheep, laid it on his shoulder rejoicing and coming home called his friends and neighbors saying, "Rejoice with me; for I have found my sheep which was lost." The joy in Heaven is a proper reverberation, a great magnified echo of the joy on earth when a soul is saved.

That means that soul-winning Christians are happier than those who do not win souls. And I think that the joy of a Christian who wins souls makes him digest his food better, makes him sleep better, makes him live longer.

3. Soul Winners Live in a Climate of Love and Christian Fellowship

It is not surprising that five times in the first five chapters of Acts we are told that the Christians were "of one accord." We are told that people did not count their possessions as their own but divided them severally to all men as they had need. Good Christians wept together over sinners and joined together in nights of prayer or days of fasting or house-to-house visitation for soul winning, and these same Christians found a sweet fellowship and joy.

4. Along With the Blessed Reviving, the Power of God, Come Many Wonderful Answers to Prayer

I am certain in my own mind that the scarcity of miracles today is largely because there are so few people, so few congregations, where soul winning becomes a holy obsession, the one great aim, the one great activity, the all-encompassing prepossession and obsession of the people!

I am not surprised that at Pentecost, since there were people who needed to hear the Gospel and there was no other way to reach them, God gave power to some to speak to these strangers from other countries "in our own tongue, wherein we were born." I think probably we should not be expecting the cyclonic wind and the tongues like as of fire that sat on people at Pentecost, nor the great shaking earthquake that came in Acts 4:31, but I am not surprised when I read about them. They fit in well when God has manifested Himself in wonderful soul-saving power. It seems altogether fitting that when Peter and John went to the Temple and there was a lame man forty years old who had never walked a step, that in the midst of the fires of mighty revival, with multitudes being saved and preaching in spite of all the threatening and dangers, Peter and John felt boldness to heal the lame man.

Since Peter and the others were so bold and the power of God surrounded them, baptized them, immersed them, covered them, I feel it perfectly fitting that we read in Acts 5:15, 16: "Insomuch that they brought forth the sick into the streets, and laid them on beds and couches, that at the least the shadow of Peter passing by might overshadow some of them. There came also a multitude out of the cities round about unto Jerusalem, bringing sick folks, and them which were vexed with unclean spirits: and they were healed every one."

Why the argument about miracles? Getting people saved is

more important than healing of the body. And yet, we cannot avoid the clear implication of Scripture that God in great times of revival and blessing did often heal the sick, did often stretch out His hand in a wonderful way.

In fact, that is what the disciples asked for when they prayed in Acts 4:29, 30, "And now, Lord, behold their threatenings: and grant unto thy servants, that with all boldness they may speak thy word, By stretching forth thine hand to heal; and that signs and wonders may be done by the name of thy holy child Jesus."

They wanted boldness to preach the Gospel, but if they would have the boldness they ought to have, God must show His power. They asked that God give them boldness "by stretching forth thine hand to heal; and that signs and wonders may be done by the name of thy holy child Jesus." And so it followed that not only was the place shaken as they were filled with the Holy Spirit, but wonderful healings followed.

It is true that God heals usually by medicine, by diet, by exercises and specific remedies. Yes, God usually uses means to heal His people. He also uses human instruments in getting people saved. But in the matter of healing of body, God does not limit Himself to ordinary means. He can heal people when doctors say it is impossible. He can heal people when no medicine, no surgery, can.

I saw my father raised up in one day when the doctor said he could not live till morning. I saw my five-year-old daughter Grace, with diphtheria, healed in a few hours. The nurse could find no evidence of diphtheria and they tore down the quarantine sign on our home. I once felt led to pray for a woman with TB, brought home to die after two years in the State Sanitarium for tubercular patients run by the state of Texas. This was before the days of antibiotic drugs. The home was tentatively sold, the two boys were given to relatives. I put a bit of oil upon the forehead of this woman whom the doctors had said could not survive one more hemorrhage. I told her that I had no special power but that it was always right to pray. She promised me and God that if He would heal her, she would tell it and would live for Him. She earnestly searched her heart to find if there were some sin she ought to confess. I prayed for her as she requested and went away.

Three months later I found that she seemed to have been immediately healed and in two weeks after I prayed with and for her, she was up and doing her own housework! Then I saw her two years later, then heard from her twenty-two years later, then again after ten years or more. After more than thirty years this woman, who had been miraculously, wonderfully healed contrary to all the doctors and all human reason, had not had any recurrence at all of the dreaded disease.

I have seen God send rain in time of great drouth. After prayer, I have seen Him stop rain at once when it threatened a great outdoor service. I say that in a climate of great soul-winning power God often heals the sick, He often controls the elements, He often does that which is otherwise humanly impossible in material matters. What a wonderful climate it is in the midst of great revival and soul-winning power!

IV. This Enduement of Power Comes Only in Answer to Persistent Prayer

How did these Christians at Jerusalem receive again an enduement of power for witnessing and bold speaking and soul winning? The answer is given in Acts 4:31, "And when they had prayed, the place was shaken where they were assembled together; and they were all filled with the Holy Ghost, and they spake the word of God with boldness." It came "when they had prayed."

And that is how they received enduement of power for witnessing before at Pentecost. We read in Acts 1:14 about the twelve apostles, "These all continued with one accord in prayer and supplication, with the women, and Mary the mother of Jesus, and with his brethren." The power at Pentecost came as a special enduement for witnessing, and it came in answer to persistent prayer in that Upper Room as they waited on God. We think they probably fasted also, for Jesus had said, ". . . when the bridegroom shall be taken from them, then shall they fast" (Matt. 9:15).

Now, in Acts 4:31 they prayed again. This time they did not

need to wait and cry to God for ten days. And evidently the teaching is that we should pray continually for a continual fullness of the Holy Spirit.

1. Jesus Promised Holy Spirit Power
"to Them That Ask Him"

Does the Bible clearly teach that this fullness of the Spirit comes only in answer to persistent prayer? Yes, it certainly does. In Luke 11:13 Jesus said, "If ye then, being evil, know how to give good gifts unto your children: how much more shall your heavenly Father give the Holy Spirit to them that ask him?" You must read the context to understand that here God is not speaking about the indwelling of the Spirit, the Holy Spirit living within the Christian's body. That is the blessed state of every born-again Christian since Jesus rose from the dead. Before His resurrection, Jesus was not promising the indwelling of the Spirit but the enduement of power from on High.

He had just told them about a man who went to his neighbor saying, ". . . lend me three loaves; For a friend of mine in his journey is come to me, and I have nothing to set before him." Here one wants three loaves, we suppose, and surely that must mean the power of the Father, Son and Holy Ghost, for all these have a part in the salvation of a soul. God gave His Son, and Jesus the Son died, and the Holy Spirit works the miracle of the new birth.

So that is a parable of a man begging bread for sinners. And in Luke 11:8 we are told, "I say unto you, Though he will not rise and give him, because he is his friend, yet because of his importunity. . . ."

So pleading, persistent prayer is the way to get the Bread from Heaven for sinners, another figure of speech for soul-winning power.

In this context Jesus tells how, if a son asked bread, the father would not give him a stone, etc. Then the blessed promise of verse 13—God gives the Holy Spirit "to them that ask him." It is only fair to say that the word "ask" is in the present tense, indicating continued action. So God gives the Holy Spirit to those who persistently ask.

Is not that implied also in that sweet promise of Isaiah 40:29-31?

"He giveth power to the faint; and to them that have no might he increaseth strength. Even the youths shall faint and be weary, and the young men shall utterly fall: But they that wait upon the Lord shall renew their strength; they shall mount up with wings as eagles; they shall run, and not be weary; and they shall walk, and not faint."

God gives power to those who wait upon the Lord. That is another way of saying He gives Holy Spirit enduement for soul winning to those who wait upon Him, those who persistently seek His power.

The same truth is implied in II Chronicles 7:14: "If my people, which are called by my name, shall humble themselves, and pray, and seek my face, and turn from their wicked ways; then will I hear from heaven, and will forgive their sin, and will heal their land." Those who "seek my face," says the Lord, may have the blessed reviving and power they need.

Retreating from the occasional excesses of the Pentecostal movement, some good people have thought that persistent, pleading prayer, tarrying, waiting on God for His power, might lead to rolling on the floor or to the tongues heresy or other sad things. No; will a father give his son who asks for bread a stone? Will he give a scorpion instead of an egg, or a serpent instead of fish? Then Jesus explains, "If ye then, being evil, know how to give good gifts unto your children: how much more shall your heavenly Father give the Holy Spirit to them that ask him?" Those who seek to talk in tongues may talk in tongues, some ecstatic jabber that is not like that at Pentecost, not the Bible gift of tongues—"in our tongue, wherein we were born." But God will not make a mockery of one honestly seeking the power of God. Those who wait upon the Lord shall renew their strength. God gives Holy Spirit power to those who persistently ask Him.

There are good people who say that if you just surrender to the Lord, then you have all the power that God has. But that is not what the Bible teaches. That is not what the disciples did before Pentecost. That is not what they did in Acts 4:31. Surrender is not enough. One should ask the Lord and ask persistently for Holy Spirit power.

2. The Holy Spirit Came on Jesus When He Prayed as Our Example

It is sweet and interesting that up to the time He was thirty years old, the dear Lord Jesus had never preached a sermon nor worked a miracle nor won a soul, but at His baptism He prayed and was filled with the Spirit, and the Holy Spirit came upon Him for His anointing for ministry.

Luke 3:21, 22 says, "Now when all the people were baptized, it came to pass, that Jesus also being baptized, and praying, the heaven was opened, And the Holy Ghost descended in a bodily shape like a dove upon him, and a voice came from heaven, which said, Thou art my beloved Son; in thee I am well pleased." So Jesus did all His ministry, all His preaching, in the power of the Holy Spirit, not simply in His position as Son of God. Jesus became a Man, was the pattern-Man, the Model Man, and thus He asked and had the same kind of Holy Spirit power that we may have to do His work. So in Acts 10:37, 38 is this inspired word:

"That word, I say, ye know, which was published throughout all Judaea, and began from Galilee, after the baptism which John preached; How God anointed Jesus of Nazareth with the Holy Ghost and with power: who went about doing good, and healing all that were oppressed of the devil; for God was with him."

And this anointing came in answer to earnest prayer as Jesus came from the waters of baptism.

Of course, for Jesus to be filled with the Spirit, it did not take the same long period of waiting on God as it did for the apostles in that Upper Room ten days before Pentecost. He had no sins to confess; He had no need to change direction or plan or opinion. Already all the adjusting to the plan of God, all the learning of God's will, all the avoidance of sin, was not necessary for Jesus, so Jesus simply asked for and had the power of the Holy Spirit. And we may be sure that in all His ministry, it is implied and to be expected that He claimed and had that wonderful, mighty, limitless power of the Holy Spirit.

In John 14:12 Jesus gave the apostles this promise: "Verily, verily, I say unto you, He that believeth on me, the works that I do shall he do also; and greater works than these shall he do; because I go unto my Father." The only way that we can do the very works that Jesus did in His ministry is to have the same Holy Spirit power He had. And that is promised to us who seek it.

The surrender of Jesus to the will of God, the seeking of His will, the renouncing of any personal desires or objectives outside the will of the Father was so perfect and complete that limit. So in John 3:34 we are told, "For he whom God hath Jesus Christ had all the power of the Holy Spirit without any sent speaketh the words of God: for God giveth not the Spirit by measure unto him." There is a perfection, a completeness, a miraculous absoluteness about the power of the Holy Spirit in the ministry of Jesus which we frail, sinful human beings never reach. But it is still true that Jesus is our Pattern. He was filled with the Spirit for service by asking for it. And we may be filled with the Spirit for witnessing also.

3. "Have Ye Received the Holy Ghost
Since Ye Believed?"

In conclusion, let me ask the pertinent question that Paul the apostle asked some converts at Ephesus. The Scripture calls them "certain disciples." We are told that they had "believed," so they were Christians. They were children of God, born again. But Paul said to them, "Have ye received the Holy Ghost since ye believed?" They did not understand, and they did not have Holy Spirit power, so Paul taught them that their baptism did not perfectly picture what it should picture if it did not mean they committed themselves wholly to live as resurrected Christians, in the will of God and with His power. So they were baptized again. Paul laid his hands upon them and the Holy Ghost came upon them and they witnessed.

How many, many Christians would have to say, as these did, that they do not even know about the Holy Spirit. Oh, in Jesus, name, Christians, seek and have your heritage! Have the mighty power of God upon you to witness for Jesus, to "prophesy," that is, to speak to others in the power of the Holy Spirit.

D. L. Moody tells us how when once he was in Wall Street, New York, asking help for the poor people of Chicago, that his heart became so burdened for Holy Spirit power, not in begging for money. As he walked on that narrow canyon-like street the power of the Holy Ghost which he had been seeking so earnestly came upon him mightily. And after that he was never the same. He launched into a worldwide ministry that is said to have won a million souls!

Do not be content without the power of God on you to do the one main thing the Lord Jesus has commanded us to do, that is, to win souls.